The Pastime
in Turbulence

The Pastime
in Turbulence

Interviews with
Baseball Players of the 1940s

by Brent Kelley

McFarland & Company, Inc., Publishers
Jefferson, North Carolina, and London

Library of Congress Cataloguing-in-Publication Data

Kelley, Brent P., 1941–
    The pastime in turbulence : interviews with baseball players
of the 1940s / by Brent Kelley.
        p.   cm.
    Includes bibliographical references (p.) and index.
    ISBN 0-7864-0975-4 (softcover : 50# alkaline paper) ∞
    1. Baseball players—United States—Interviews.   2. Baseball—
United States—History—20th century.   I. Title: Interviews
with baseball players of the 1940s.   II. Title.

GV865.A1 K436   2001
796.357'0973—dc21
                                                    2001031218

British Library cataloguing data are available

Manufactured in the United States of America

On the cover: Whitey Lockman of the New York Giants attempts to tag
Red Schoendienst of the Cardinals after taking a throw from catcher
Wes Westrum.

McFarland & Company, Inc., Publishers
    Box 611, Jefferson, North Carolina 28640
    www.mcfarlandpub.com

For Anna and Angela

Contents

Introduction

The interviews in the following pages are with several major league baseball players who have little in common other than the fact that they all played ball in the 1940s.

Some began in the '30s, some played until the '60s. Some were there for a long time, some so briefly that if you blinked you might have missed them. Some made it to the World Series as rookies, one never made it in 20 years. Some got to the majors because of the war, some left because of the war. Integration hurt one, the Mexican raid hurt some.

Some stayed in baseball all their lives, others walked away and never looked back. Some were long-time major league regulars, others never had a steady job in baseball.

One pitched a no-hitter, one hit a home run in his first major league at bat, one played in four decades, one was a league president, one was his team's MVP, one won the most important game of a season, one broke into the major leagues at 16, one was an All-American football player, one held the record for the longest hole-in-one in golf history, one went on to fame and fortune in Hollywood. There are college graduates here, and there are high school dropouts.

But why do we call the 1940s "baseball's most turbulent decade"? Because it was.

Chuck Hostetler was a 40-year-old rookie in 1944 with the Detroit Tigers. The next year he played in the World Series, then in 1946 he was gone from the major league scene.

Here's what happened, chronologically.

In 1939, Commissioner Kenesaw Mountain Landis was upset over the fact that some teams—principally the Cardinals and the Tigers—had such vast minor league systems that players were being buried and had no—or little—chance of advancement. There was no provision for minor league free agency after so many years as there is today. A player was trapped until either the parent club traded or released him, or he retired.

Landis's investigation of the situation led to his making free agents of dozens of minor league players, who then signed with other clubs (they could not re-sign with their original clubs for five years) and therefore were given new leases on life. These players hit the market in 1940.

Also in 1940, a team rebelled against its management. The Cleveland Indians players were unhappy with manager Ossie Vitt. This may have been the best team in the AL in 1940 and the dissension probably cost them the pennant, which they lost on the final weekend of the season when the most unlikely member of the Detroit Tigers' pitching staff beat Bob Feller, the best pitcher in baseball.

Then in December of 1941, Japan bombed Pearl Harbor and over the next few years major league baseball lost player after player to the war effort. Gone were DiMaggio, Feller, Williams, Greenberg, etc. It was a tough way to create parity, but one year the St. Louis Browns won a

Joe Nuxhall first pitched in the major leagues with the Cincinnati Reds at the age of 15 years, 10 months, in 1944. He did not reappear in the majors until 1952.

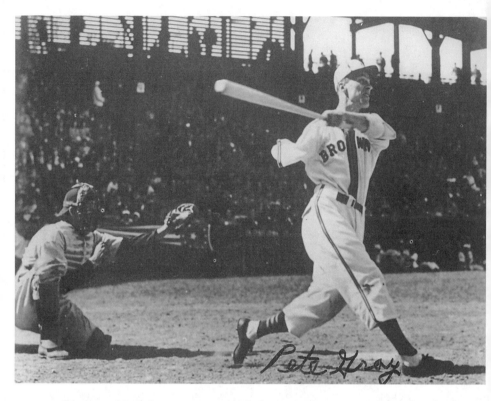

One-armed Pete Gray spent 1945 with the St. Louis Browns, batting .213. It was his only season in the majors.

pennant (the only one in franchise history) and even the Washington Senators had winning seasons.

To make up for the loss of manpower, many unlikely names appeared in box scores during the war. Players both below and above draft age were in major league lineups. Teenagers, one only 15, were signed, as were minor league veterans in their forties. A one-armed player made it to the major leagues, and a one-legged one played a short time later. Players who had been major leaguers earlier and found wanting for one reason or another were brought back.

And the war, while giving chances to some who otherwise may never have made it to the majors, ended or derailed the careers of others. Some never made it back to the big time, and others were never the same players again.

But the war finally ended and the stars returned, but with their return came the Pasquel brothers from Mexico. They wanted the Mexican League

Jackie Robinson made history in 1947.

Ebbets Field, home of the Brooklyn Dodgers.

to be equal to the major leagues so they offered big bucks to U.S. players to come south of the border to play. Several succumbed to the lure of large salaries; New York Giants' pitcher Ace Adams received $50,000 to go, while his salary in the NL was only $5,000. But new Commissioner A. B. "Happy" Chandler said come back or you're banned. One — Vern Stephens of the Browns—came back, but others did not ... until the Pasquels ran out of money. The returnees were banned for three years.

The first year after the war—1946—was noteworthy for other reasons as well. The NL had been playing baseball since 1876 — 70 years— and every season there had been a clear-cut pennant winner. Until '46. When the dust settled after 154 games, the St. Louis Cardinals and the Brooklyn Dodgers were tied for first with identical 96-58 records. What to do?

A best two-out-of-three playoff was decided upon, which St. Louis won in two but which may actually have cost the AL winning Boston Red Sox the World Series. The Red Sox played some exhibition games to stay

The Polo Grounds, home of the New York Giants.

sharp while the NL decided who was to face them and in one exhibition game Ted Williams was hit in the elbow by a pitch. He was sub par, therefore, in the only World Series in which he would ever play.

But that World Series contained what may have been the Fall Classic's most exciting moment, at least until Bill Mazeroski's home run in 1960. It was Enos Slaughter's "mad dash."

Of course, 1947 was the most important year in the history of the National Pastime, if not of the whole country. Integration. It was a brand new ballgame.

Then in 1948, the AL, not to be outdone by the NL, had a tie of its own. The Cleveland Indians and the Boston Red Sox, both 96-58, played a one-game, winner-take-all playoff. The subsequent World Series pitted a team that had not won a pennant in 28 years (Indians) against one that had not won a pennant in 34 years (Boston Braves).

Turbulent as the '40s were, however, there was also stability, although some teams (Browns, A's, Braves) were starving. Good players were dealt by these teams in exchange for cash so they could pay the not-as-good players they kept. But there were still eight teams in each league; franchise shifts and expansion were a few years in the future.

The teams remained in the ballparks they had called home since the 1920s and earlier. The "cookie-cutter" fad of new ballparks was more than a decade away. It was only after teams began moving and the leagues began to expand that the old ballparks started going by the wayside.

Gone early were Braves Field and beloved Ebbets Field, then one-by-one most of the others fell, too. The Polo Grounds, Forbes Field, Crosley Field, Connie Mack Stadium (Shibe Park), then the original Comiskey Park, and so on. Finally Tiger Stadium fell. At the beginning of the 2000 season, all that remained from the '40s were Fenway Park, Wrigley Field, and a remodeled Yankee Stadium.

The 1940s may be the last decade when baseball was pure baseball. The game withstood all the turbulence and came out on top. After that, even expansion and grillion-dollar salaries could not harm it.

GENE THOMPSON

A Missing Piece (1939–1947)

The 1938 Cincinnati Reds finished fourth in the National League, six games behind the pennant-winning Cubs. It was Bill McKechnie's first year at their helm and he took over a particularly inept 1937 team, which finished eighth (last), 40 games out.

The Reds' last previous first division finish had been in 1926 and in the intervening years they had been eighth five times and seventh twice, and only once had been above .500. In fact, as a rule they were below .400. It was the low point in the history of the franchise eventually known as "The Big Red Machine." Perhaps "Little Red Wagon" was a more fitting description of the Redlegs of the late '20s and most of the '30s.

McKechnie, however, cleaned house in '38. Of the eight regular position players from 1937's cellar-dwellers, only three kept their jobs under Deacon Bill: shortstop Billy Myers, right fielder Ival Goodman, and catcher Ernie Lombardi. The pitching staff was likewise rebuilt, with only Paul Derringer and Peaches Davis retaining their jobs.

The acquisitions, during the '38 season, of left fielder Wally Berger and pitcher Bucky Walters were especially important; the Reds were now solid at nearly every position.

And in 1939, with two more significant changes, it all came together.

9

Gene Thompson with Cincinnati, 1939 (courtesy Gene Thompson).

They set a franchise record with 97 wins and they won their first pennant since 1919 (and only the second in their history), finishing 4½ games ahead of the St. Louis Cardinals, another team undergoing a rebuilding (they would be heard from in a few years).

Those two significant changes were the addition of veteran third baseman Bill Werber, purchased from the Philadelphia Athletics during spring training, and the emergence of 22-year-old rookie right-hander Eugene "Junior" Thompson as the bullpen ace and spot starter.

Werber's attitude and hustle set the tempo for the club and Gene Thompson led the team in relief appearances (31) and tied Whitey Moore for most games (42). Thompson also tied Moore for third in victories (13) while losing only five. Out of the bullpen, he was a spectacular 8-1; those eight wins were tops in the league for a reliever and his ERA was a tough 2.54, second on the team only to Walters' 2.29.

Gene followed up his rookie year as the number three starter, behind Walters and Derringer, for the 1940 World Champions. He went 16-9 and completed 17 of his 31 starts as the Reds won 100 games for the first time in their history.

He has been a scout since 1951, mostly for the Giants, but more importantly he's been a part of baseball for more than 60 years. In that time he's seen a lot.

❖ ❖ ❖

You were called "Junior" when you first joined the Reds in 1939.

That's my right name. "Junior Eugene," but I usually went by Gene.

You started off great. Your first two years you won 13 and 16 games and then dropped off. What happened?

It was the weirdest thing in the world. I had pitched a game late in the season, not long before the World Series in '40, against the Cardinals in St. Louis, the first game of a doubleheader. I had pitched a two-hit shutout. Enos Slaughter got both hits. I shut 'em out, two-nothing.

Our home was fairly near St. Louis, about 125 miles. Since this game was on a Sunday, my wife had come down from Decatur. Mr. McKechnie, our manager, knew she was there, so after the first game, which I'd won — in those days it wasn't like it is today; just because you'd pitched nine innings didn't necessarily mean you were through for the day — he said to me, "I see Dorothy's here. Why don't you go on home with her and we'll see you in Cincinnati Tuesday." We were off Monday.

So we drove home and when I got up the next morning I could not lift my arm. I don't know to this day what happened. I couldn't wait 'til Tuesday night to get to Cincinnati to try to throw. My shoulder was hurting so badly. Doctors, everybody, said it was this and that, my teeth and so on. But no one knew. From then on I had problems.

You came back a few years later to have a darned good year in relief for the Giants.

Yes, I came back, but I was halfway under sedation with all the daily aspirin and such. And x-rays and everything else. I changed my style a lot; I couldn't throw as hard and I had to finesse. I was mainly used out of the bullpen from that point on. I could pitch for two or three innings and then rebound in a day or so, but if I pitched any more than that I was laid up for a week or ten days.

I tried to start the third game of the World Series against Detroit in 1940 and I didn't have anything — not enough to get by with.

What was your best pitch?

Sometimes I was considered a fastball pitcher, sometimes a curveball pitcher. I threw a lot of breaking stuff, cross-fired some, a little unorthodox at times.

What was your best game? Was it the one in which you were hurt?

Oh, I don't know if that was my best one. I was real close to a no-hitter one day in Brooklyn. I wound up with a one-hitter. Lew Riggs hit a

Gene Thompson, 1940 (courtesy Gene Thompson).

sort of flare off me for the one hit. I suppose the Cardinals game was one of my best, though.

Which team did you consistently do well against?

I guess everybody has these types of clubs. I think my best was against the Giants.

Which team was the toughest for you?

Oh, I don't know if I could single one out. On a given day I had trouble with everybody, but I suppose maybe Pittsburgh at the time.

Often over the years articles have appeared about the '39 and '40 Reds and how only manager Bill McKechnie was in the Hall of Fame. Now Ernie Lombardi is there, too. How about Derringer and Walters?

It was such a privilege and honor to be on the same staff with two men like Derringer and Walters. I looked up to those men in awe in their greatness and accomplishments. One year those guys won 52 games for us. Outstanding, simply outstanding.

You know, Paul's gone and now Bucky's gone, too. It makes me sick. They were outstanding people, outstanding performers, great competitors.

I looked up their records. Look at these boys now; one of 'em pitches a complete game and gets headlines. Those guys were pitching 20-25 complete games a year. Our club was a little short on publicity, but those guys belong in the Hall of Fame.

Our park [Crosley Field] was a little tough to play in, but our staff was molded for it; we had a lot of sinker ball pitchers. We had to keep the ball out of the air.

If we could keep it on the ground we were in the game. We had some of the greatest infielders I ever saw at turning the double play. Everybody talked about how great our pitching was, but those guys with the leather on made the difference.

What a combination we had, [Lonnie] Frey and [Billy] Myers at second and short, not to mention the guy at third, Werber, and, in my opinion, a guy who was most unheralded as a first baseman, Frank McCormick. In the opinion of a lot of people who played against him, he was outstanding.

Who do you feel was the best player you played against?

I would have to think the best player I played against wasn't in our league, but we played against him a number of times— spring training and the World Series in '39. [Joe] DiMaggio.

Who was the toughest batter for you?

Arky Vaughan. No problem in my mind in answering that. It took him a long time to get in the Hall of Fame.

Willard Hershberger, the Reds' backup catcher in '39 and '40, committed suicide during the 1940 season. Was there a way to foresee that?

I don't like to talk about this, but, yes, it was foreseen. Lombardi was hurt and out for a while and the whole load fell on Hershberger. He was a hypochondriac and couldn't take pressure. We were in a pennant drive. Bucky Walters was pitching in New York and a home run had beaten him — I don't remember who hit it; Ott, maybe — and Hershy felt it was his fault.

The club went on to Boston — I had been sent back to Cincinnati after getting hurt in a fight — and we had four doubleheaders in a row and Willard was gong to have to catch them all because our only other catcher was only mediocre. Bill Baker. He roomed with Hersh.

The first day at the ballpark, Hershy didn't show up. McKechnie asked Baker where he was and Baker said he had told him to go on, he'd be out later. Well, he was found in the room later.

McKechnie had a meeting with us later, back in Cincinnati. He said Willard had come to him and told him he was going to commit suicide and he had sat up with him half the night and was confident he had talked him out of it. Hershberger was worried about carrying the load. He was satisfied to be second, but couldn't stand the pressure of being number one. Hershberger was a good athlete, a good catcher and good hitter. I had played against him in the International League a few years before.

What kind of minor league record did you have?

I signed in 1934. In '35 I was only 17 and didn't do much. The next year I went down to the old Kitty League and won 20 games there. The next year I won 13 or 14 games at Peoria in the 3-I League by July and they sent me to the Western League for two or three days and then on to the International League, where I didn't play a whole lot. The next year — '38 — I went to the International League and still didn't pitch much and they sent me to the Sally League. I didn't get there 'til July tenth or something like that and I was 13-and-3 the rest of the way. And then I went to the big leagues in '39.

After I left the Giants in '48 I went to the [Pacific] Coast League. I played there in '48 and '49 and was sold to Sacramento in '50. In mid '50 I gave it up. I coached the rest of '50 for Joe Marty and then coached in

'51 for Joe Gordon. Then I went to South America to manage a club and then turned to scouting.

Who are the best players you signed?

That's a tricky question. For many years three of us scouts ran try-out camps in our spring training headquarters. The other scouts around the country weren't allowed to sign players; they sent them to us to look at first. Then we'd sign the best. The three of us never got credit for signing these people, but we'd sure have caught hell if we hadn't signed them and they turned up somewhere else. The scouts who sent them to us got the credit.

In one camp we signed six players, all Caribbeans. Three of them were [Orlando] Cepeda, [Jose] Pagan, and Julio Navarro. The next year [Willie] McCovey came from this camp. Over the years, though, I really haven't paid much attention to how many I've signed. A few that come to mind: with Chicago I signed [Craig] Lefferts and [Billy] Hatcher. And I signed [Tom] Haller for the Giants.

You've been in baseball in one capacity or another for more than 65 years. What are the main changes you've seen?

There's been a whole bunch of 'em! "What's happened to our game?" That's asked a whole lot by old-timers.

The biggest thing is the lack of respect today, for managers and for management. There's a lot of this. The other thing is the way pitching has been handled. Like I said, in my day just because you pitched nine innings in game one didn't mean you got the rest of the day off. Hell, if a guy pitches nine innings today he can go fishing the next five days. He won't even pitch batting practice.

They've made such a specialty game out of it and I'm not sure it's for the better. Owners today are not paying just one pitcher for each win; in most cases they're paying three or four pitchers for the same win. To elaborate on this, a starter only goes five or six innings, then there's the long man, the set-up man, and then the closer. Some guys today are pitching only 60-70 innings and making a million dollars! Like I said, Walters and those guys pitched 25-26 complete games a year. This is a tremendous change.

Do you think there are any changes that should be made?

I'm just about ready to get out of the game, so this is hard to go into.

I have never heard tell of or seen so many bad arms in my life. Disabled lists are flooded. I don't like to live in the past, and answering

Gene Thompson with New York Giants, 1946.

questions like this causes people to say, "Oh, hell, you old-timer, you're living in the past," so I usually won't talk about this.

But I think the ballclubs should go back to a four-man rotation. You can't hardly find four starters anymore; I don't know how they think they can find five.

Do you realize there's not a pitcher in the big leagues today who throws batting practice? They hire someone to do it or a coach does it. Even though we were on a four-man rotation, we threw batting practice between our starts. And we ran like hell all the time! We had to be in pretty good condition. And we pitched a hell of a lot more complete games than these people now.

We had people then who would throw more complete games than a whole staff does today. Today they're pitching less innings and taking more days' rest. Does that make sense? Three hundred innings-plus wasn't anything for the starters back then. Now they make a big deal out of someone who gets 200 innings.

In thinking back, I don't ever remember guys like Bucky or Paul ever being on the disabled list. Maybe they were, but I don't remember it.

A story along these lines I enjoy telling: Back in '39 or '40 I pitched a game against the Giants in Cincinnati. Hot! Damn, it was hot! I beat them in the first game of a doubleheader. Even though I'd pitched nine innings I didn't get dressed and head for the door. You didn't even ask the manager; he told you when to shower or get dressed or take off.

Well, I was sitting there between games and I looked up and McKechnie was standing there looking at me over the top of his glasses as he always did. "Go ahead and get dressed and go sit with your wife, but don't even drink a beer. I may need you." About the sixth inning I heard Bill's shrill whistle and he motioned me to come down and get my uniform on. [Lee] Grissom was pitching and getting in trouble and so I went in the seventh and finished it.

If you asked someone to do that now he'd call his agent. I'm not trying to blow my own horn; a lot of guys did the same thing. Back then, I guess a guy was afraid to get hurt because someone else would take his job. Today they have a guaranteed contract; why should they have to work?

Another difference today is the salaries. What did you receive?

I was making $350 a month when I went up. In June they raised me to $500. Today the minimum salary is $200,000, I think. That's a whole lot more than just inflation. These guys get more meal money today than we got in salary. My top salary was about $12,500. Back then if you got to the point where you were making ten [thousand] you were doing good.

Did you save souvenirs from your career?

Oh, yes, I have a few. I've picked up more here recently. I'm getting stuff now for my grandson. I've got about 30 baseballs signed and pictures and stuff. [Johnny] Vander Meer and I were close; I've got pictures of he and I and Walters and Derringer.

I gave away a lot of stuff, but I've got a bunch of programs and Series programs, New York and Detroit, and a bunch of World Series bats, the black ones. I've given a lot to my grandson.

A few years ago I sent some balls out to be signed; I'm trying to get a collection for my grandson. I sent some to Joe Amalfitano—we've been close ever since we signed him years ago—to get some Dodgers' autographs. I asked him to have one signed by Hershiser and one by Fernando and one by the team. Well, he got the two pitchers, but the team ball had very few names on it. Joe wrote an apologetic note saying a lot of the players wouldn't sign for anybody, even him.

It's ridiculous; some of these guys send pictures back asking for money to sign. I can understand if someone wants a dozen or so cards signed—they're selling them or something—but if someone just sends a picture or ball there's nothing wrong with signing it.

Do you receive a pension from baseball?

When the pension thing was started, I was one of the Giants, along with Buddy Blattner, who worked for it. We were left out of these raises and things and we were at least partially responsible for starting it.

The reason today's players give for not wanting to include us, and by us I mean the players of my day, is that it will reduce their pensions. The maximum was $90,000 a year and if they give some it would have reduced their $90,000 and they'd have to adjust their lifestyle. Isn't that something?

You mentioned your grandson. What do you think about kids' baseball today?

I get so darned upset when I'd go over to my daughter's to watch him play. It's not for the kids. The parents sit there and scream at the kids and scream at the umpires. What do you think these kids think when everybody's hollering at them?

This is another big difference over the years. When you were a kid or when I was a kid, we got three or four kids together and we'd go over to the park and play ball 'til night. Your mother would know where you were. No fancy equipment, old taped balls, old bats.

I don't believe they're helping as many kids as they think they are. Too many kids get soured. Instead of saying, "Did you have fun?" they ask, "Did you get a hit?" or "Did you win?" That's not right.

Sixty-five years in baseball. Would you do it again?

I wouldn't think about it twice! I think the most enjoyable part of my life was riding those minor league buses, eating crackers and cheese.

Would I do it again? In a minute, and for the same money. I've enjoyed all the 65 years I've been involved. Baseball's been good to me. I haven't made a lot of money, but I've made a living and I've enjoyed it.

The 1939 season was an excellent year for rookie pitchers. In addition to Gene Thompson, others of note that year were the Cardinals' pair of Bob Bowman (13-5, 2.61, league-leading nine saves), and Mort Cooper (12-6, 3.25), Hugh Casey of Brooklyn (15-10, 2.93), Kirby Higby (12-15, but stuck with the last-place Phillips), Atley Donald (13-3 for the Yankees), Dizzy Trout of the Tigers (9-10, 3.61), the Senators' Joe Haynes (8-12), and poor Bob Harris, only 4-13, but with the 111-game losing St. Louis Browns.

Eugene Earl "Junior" Thompson

Born June 7, 1917, Latham, IL
Ht. 6'1"   Wt. 185   Batted and Threw Right

Year	Team, Lg	G	IP	W	L	Pct	H	BB	SO	ERA
1939	Cinc., NL	42	152.1	13	5	.722	130	55	87	2.54
1940		33	225.1	16	9	.640	197	96	103	3.32
1941		27	109	6	6	.500	117	57	46	4.87
1942		29	101.2	4	7	.364	86	53	35	3.36
1943–45	Military service									
1946	NY, NL	39	62.2	4	6	.400	36	40	31	1.29
1947		15	35.2	4	2	.667	36	27	13	4.29
6 years		185	686.2	47	35	.573	602	328	315	3.26

World Series

Year	Team, Lg	G	IP	W	L	Pct	H	BB	SO	ERA
1939	Cinc., NL	1	4.2	0	1	.000	5	4	3	13.50
1940		1	3.1	0	1	.000	8	4	2	16.20
2 years		2	8	0	2	.000	13	8	5	14.63

JOHNNY BERARDINO

Aka Dr. Steve Hardy (1939–1952)

Johnny Berardino joined the perennially awful St. Louis Browns as a slick-fielding second baseman in 1939. The Browns at that time (at most times) were a unique blend of bad pitching and weak hitting, but the 22-year-old Berardino matured quickly and his play motivated the Brownies to trade veteran shortstop Red Kress. Don Heffner, 1938's second baseman, was moved to short and John became the regular second sacker, finishing the season with an average of six chances per game, second best in the league to future Hall of Famer Bobby Doerr's 6.2.

Shortstop proved a bit of a challenge for Heffner, however, so in 1940 the agile Berardino switched positions with him. It proved to be a stroke of genius by manager Fred Haney as both Don and John led the league in total chances per game at their positions.

(The Browns 1940 infield was an especially good one: first baseman George McQuinn led in assists, double plays, total chances, and average; second baseman Heffner in chances and average; shortstop Berardino in chances; and third baseman Harlond Clift in assists, double plays, and average.)

Even with the position change, John ignored the sophomore jinx and improved on his rookie performance at the plate. His 16 home runs and 85 RBI were the most by a Brownie shortstop since Kress's performance

10 years earlier and both figures ranked high for his position in a league that boasted future Hall of Fame shortstops Joe Cronin, Lou Boudreau, and Luke Appling.

In 1941 his average continued to improve. His RBI total rose to 89 and high batting average climbed to .271 and, still only 24, the future appeared to be bright. But as so many careers were ended or interrupted by World War II, so was John's. Uncle Sam took him early in '42 and he didn't return until '46. In '41 the Browns had finished a soundly beaten sixth and in '46 they were a more soundly beaten seventh, so it was as if he had never been away. The war, however, prevented him from being a part of the brightest period in St. Louis American League history; during his four-year ab-

Johnny Berardino with St. Louis Browns, 1940.

sence, the team had two thirds and its only pennant winner.

On his return in 1946, he moved back to his best position, second base, and was second only to Boston's Doerr offensively at the position.

Hampered by an injury in '47 and then 30 years old, he became expendable. The Browns were going nowhere with him and they couldn't be much worse without him, so in November of '47 he was traded to the Washington Senators for another second sacker, Gerry Priddy. Rather than go from one also-ran to another, John notified all concerned that he was through with baseball and would devote his energies to his second love, acting.

The trade was voided by Commissioner Happy Chandler and about two weeks later John was traded again, this time to Cleveland for Catfish

Metkovich and $50,000, a tremendous price for the time. Cleveland was a first division club, so John reconsidered and agreed to join the team. When Metkovich came up injured, he was returned to the Indians and St. Louis received an additional $15,000. In the meantime, the Browns purchased Priddy for $25,000, so John enabled them to acquire him after all.

His days as a regular were over at this point. He was the fifth infielder on the 1948 World Champion Indians, but then he began moving in a sort of round-robin between the Indians, Pirates, and Browns. His last season was 1952.

On leaving baseball, he turned to acting, something he had been doing in the off-seasons for several years, on a full-time basis. For umpteen years he gained more fame than baseball ever brought him as he portrayed Dr. Steve Hardy on television's daytime serial *General Hospital.* Lest you are confused, his acting name was spelled "Beradino."

You came to the Browns as a second baseman but you later became a short-stop. Which was your better position?

Either one was okay as far as I was concerned, but I really preferred second base. The reason I made the transition to shortstop was because they didn't have a good one then so I just moved over there. It was just a matter of fitting the ballclub together.

The service called when you were at your peak.

Oh, yeah. No question about that. Statistically my RBIs were increasing, my average was increasing; everything was going upward in my performance.

Your RBI totals were excellent for a middle infielder. Where did you bat in the order?

They moved me around quite a bit —fifth, sixth, seventh, second; any way to win a ballgame. I was never really what you might call a cleanup hitter because they always had somebody there.

But you had a little punch, too; you hit 16 homers in 1940.

Yeah, I had a little pop.

You have an unusual distinction: you went from the Browns to the Indians to the Pirates twice in your career.

Yeah, I made each ballclub twice. I don't know whether they got me back in the form of regret at having lost me or what. I ended up with three different ballclubs twice.

In December of 1947 the Indians paid a heck of a price for you. Cleveland seemingly had a solid infield. Why was the trade made?

Yeah, they had four good ones. I became the fifth one. As a matter of fact, they played virtually the whole season with only five infielders and they had eight outfielders. They were trying to bolster the infield; I played every position in the infield, so I was the fifth wheel. I ended up playing first base when Bob Lemon pitched his no-hitter. I'd never played first base in my life before.

Is it true that Bill Veeck insured your face for a million dollars?

That's true. That was one of his publicity stunts.

As a matter of fact, what happened was when I was with St. Louis I had been traded in the fall of '47 to the Washington Senators. I think they had finished either seventh or eighth and we were close to them at the bottom of the pits. I figured there was no point going from bad to worse and I was working in a movie so I just said to myself I might as well quit baseball and concentrate on movies.

That's when Bill Veeck entered the picture. When I made up my mind I wasn't going to go to the Washington Senators, the St. Louis Browns nixed the deal and then started dealing with Veeck, who became interested.

What kind of guy was Veeck to work for?

Beautiful! None better. No better owner at understanding a ballplayer than Bill Veeck. For the ballplayer all the way. I think if he were alive today he would be saying hurrah for everybody that's getting all the money they're getting.

What do you think of all the money that's being paid now?

I'm just sorry I'm not 20 years old. *[laughs]* I'm sure every ballplayer that I played with is saying, "I wish I was born 40 years later."

Many people say Veeck belongs in the Hall of Fame.

Yeah. I think he did a lot for baseball, I really do. I think he gave it a little lift that was really badly needed. Baseball was kind of dreary. [This interview was done in 1989. In 1991 Veeck was finally elected.]

I've always said baseball was show business. Ever since I was playing I called it show business. Nobody believed me, but that's what I thought

Johnny Berardino with Cleveland, 1948.

it was. The advent of television made it even more of a show business than ever. And I often wondered why these people hadn't joined a union because they were in show business.

I remember when I was a kid I had a 1952 baseball card of you and on the back it said you acted in the off-season. When did you start acting?

I was born and raised out here in L.A. and I started working as an extra in Our Gang comedies. My father and mother, or at least my mother, thought I had the makings of another child star. They invested a great deal of money at that time, which was $10,000, in 1927 or somewhere in there, in a movie in which I had a principal role as a child. The movie was never finished and they lost their money. That was the end of my acting career as a child and I never resumed it until I became an adult.

I never really lost the bug and in between [baseball] seasons I attended the Pasadena Playhouse. I was really looking forward to the day when I'd be through as a ballplayer and take up acting.

Who were the best ballplayers you saw?

I put Ted Williams and Joe DiMaggio at the top of the list of all-time greats. I really don't see players of that caliber anymore.

Who was the best pitcher?

Bob Feller, obviously, was one of them. Some of the great ones were on their way out when I came up, but I certainly had a lot of respect for them. There was Lefty Grove, Lefty Gomez, Dizzy Dean. It was awesome to bat against guys like that because growing up they were such great pitchers and I was in awe of them, of course.

But the outstanding pitcher I really had to face was Bob Feller.

You played for a while alongside Vern Stephens. Sometimes he's mentioned as a potential Hall of Famer. What do you think?

Vern had the good fortune of going to Boston. *[laughs]* Short porch. You know, if you look at his record I think his tops in St. Louis was maybe 20, 22 home runs, then when he got to Boston he had the stroke that was designed for that ballpark.

No, I don't think he's Hall of Fame. His stats were all in Boston, really. Once you start to analyze in the other seven — in those days there were only eight teams in each league — and you can say a man can hit home runs anywhere, then it's a different story. But his record was just Boston.

There have been a lot of changes since you entered the major leagues. Do you think they're for the better or the worse?

The only thing I think it's better for is the financial status of the ballplayer. I don't think I would enjoy playing ball today, having to fly from town to town as they do now. There was a lot of camaraderie when we were traveling by train that I don't think they get on the airplane, you know. We were on a train from city to city and there was a lot of fun involved. There was a better rapport between the players. I don't think that exists today; I think it's everybody for himself today.

The money aspect was really not a big issue at the time I was playing. Nobody was concerned about who else was making what, you know what I mean? Now it's made very public. Nobody envied Babe Ruth getting what he got, or Joe DiMaggio, because they deserved it, but, still in all, nobody was saying that if I can get as good as him I'm going to get that much. It wasn't that kind of a thing.

You know, going back in years, I think right after I got out of baseball I took three ballplayers to a Hollywood agent and tried to get them signed up with an agent and it never came to pass. They backed off at the last minute for some reason. It was Duke Snider and Bob Lemon and I can't remember the third guy now. They were all Californians. I took them up to this agent; I said it's about time baseball players got agents. They probably agreed at the time until they got up there talking to the agent and then they backed off. But this was back in '53, long before agents became very prominent.

You can't be a ballplayer without an agent today.

No way.

You had two careers that put you very highly in the public eye. I know which has been the most financially rewarding, but which one did you enjoy the most?

There's nothing can compare with being a major league ballplayer. I wouldn't even consider being a motion picture star equal to that. I've run into too many movie stars who wish they were major league ballplayers. *[laughs]* It's true. As kids growing up that's naturally their number one priority and when they don't make it they devote themselves to another profession, that's all.

You dropped the second "r" in your name when you started acting. Was it for ease of pronunciation?

Yeah, it was easier to pronounce. That was the only reason.

Did you collect souvenirs of your career during your playing days?

No, I never really got into that. I wish to heck I had. I think the only collection I made, and it was for the sake of my son, who's a pretty good ballplayer himself, was an autograph of Pete Rose in Tommy Lasorda's office one day when they were playing Cincinnati. That's the only real collection I've ever made.

Do you get much fan mail — baseball fan mail?

Actually I get a lot of fan mail — people wanting *baseball* autographs as well as autographs from the show. I get a lot of baseball cards to autograph. I think I may be one of the few guys who doesn't mind signing a baseball card without having to say, "You've got to pay for it." I don't understand those card shows at all. I wouldn't think of charging any kid any money to sign a baseball card. It

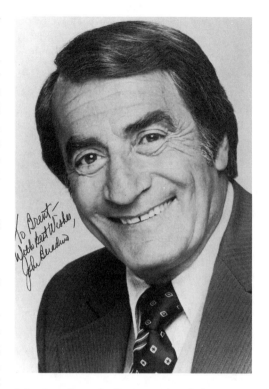

John Beradino, aka "Dr. Steve Hardy," 1990 (courtesy John Berardino).

just doesn't suit my personality. It's a business. Obviously up front these guys are getting money and it means a lot to them.

I thought somebody had a good idea once. All this money that they're making for signing these baseball cards should go to the Baseball Players' Association fund or a charity of some sort.

I don't understand it at all. It's not a money thing; these guys make good money playing.

My daughter was a big fan of General Hospital. Whenever she was out of school she watched it. She told me at one point that Dr. Hardy was being phased out. Was he?

No, but it's like everything else in show business, you know. The inclination is to show younger people. I guess you can say it's a form of phase-out because of age, but it's got nothing to do with acting. It's just that they feel that there's an audience out there that prefers to watch younger people, so they write primarily for the younger people. It has nothing to do with one's ability as an actor.

Conversely, at nighttime they don't mind you showing older people, but the daytime audience they figure is a different audience altogether. They cater to a group, they say, between 18 and 49, and that's it; that's their main basic viewing audience, they feel. That's what they go for.

And God forbid someone over 50 should be in a bedroom scene! *[laughs]* Not that that doesn't really happen in life; it's not something you want to show on the screen. They want to see young bodies.

If you were to go back to your youth, would you play baseball again?

Oh, yeah, that would be my number one priority. No question about that.

No regrets from playing?

No regrets, no. I had more fun and laughs; even with the four years of military service, I enjoyed it tremendously. It gives me something I won't forget. Ever.

JOHN BERARDINO

Born May 1, 1917, Los Angeles, CA
Died May 19, 1996, Los Angeles, CA
Ht. 5'11½"   Wt. 175   Batted and Threw Right

Year	Team, Lg	G	AB	R	H	2B	3B	HR	RBI	BA
1939	St. L., AL	126	468	42	120	24	5	5	58	.256
1940		142	523	71	135	31	4	16	85	.258
1941		128	469	48	127	30	4	5	89	.271
1942		29	74	11	21	6	0	1	10	.284
1943-45	Military service									
1946	St. L., AL	144	582	70	154	29	5	5	68	.265
1947		90	306	29	80	22	1	1	20	.261
1948	Cle., AL	66	147	19	28	5	1	2	10	.190
157.		50	116	11	23	6	1	0	13	.198
1950	Cl., AL; Pit., NL	44	136	13	29	3	1	1	15	.213
1951	St. L., AL	39	119	13	27	7	1	0	13	.227
1952	Cl., AL; Pit., NL	54	88	7	11	4	0	0	6	.125
11 years		912	3028	334	755	167	23	36	387	.249

JOHNNY WELAJ

Cobb Said He Could Fly (1939–1943)

Welaj excelled as a baserunner, getting a bigger jump
and sliding more elusively than speedier teammate
George Case, the AL's top stealer.
— *Norman L. Macht,*
in The Ballplayers

John Welaj (Well-eye) played four seasons in the major leagues, three with the Washington Senators at a time when that franchise was struggling. (The franchise, of course, had more periods of struggle than otherwise.)

The struggle was not due to the Senators' outfielders, however. For John's three years (1939-41) in our nation's capital, the team boasted one of the best groups of outfielders in the game. There were only two constants out there for the three years, Welaj and George Case, but the rest of the outfield was manned by some of the best players of the era. Regulars in this period included Taft Wright, Sam Rice, Buddy Lewis, Gee Walker, and Doc Cramer.

John was the fourth outfielder to a starting three as good as any in baseball. Being the fourth man dictated fewer opportunities, but the only man in the major leagues in those three years who made more of his opportunities to steal was Case.

After leaving Washington, John played one more major league season — 1943 with the Athletics — and he led the team in steals despite playing only about half the time. He entered the military service after that season and when the War was over spent several more years in Triple-A.

There were four Welaj brothers who played professional baseball. In addition to John, there were Lou, Tony, and Walt. Only John made it to the big time, but Lou played as high as Triple-A.

The Welaj brothers are from New Jersey and John's first appearance in Yankee Stadium was on Lou Gehrig Day (July 4, 1939). About 1,500 people from Manville, New Jersey, the Welaj's hometown, attended the doubleheader that day. John didn't let them down; he had four hits, including a double and a home run, in the twin bill.

When he left the playing ranks, John rejoined the Senators in the front office after managing in the minors. When the original club moved to Minnesota, John joined the new Senators and when that franchise moved to Texas he went with it. At the time of his retirement, he was the Texas Rangers' Spring Training Director.

Actually, I played only three years in the minors. I had played one year when I came up in 1936; I was sold to a major league club at the time, the Washington Senators. That happened after our season. What happened, I got a bonus and [Joe] Cambria didn't want to pay me any money but after all I got it coming and I said, "I'm going home."

I hit .338 my first year out of Albany. I was with a bunch of old men, see, back there in 1936. I was just 21 years old at the time. In those days you couldn't sign a contract; you had to be 21 years of age or your father had to sign. The bonus was [$]1100. My father kept a thousand and gave me a hundred. I hit .339 and they farmed me out to Trenton. First of all, we had fellows that must have been 30 to 35 up there in that Triple-A ballclub — Shanty Hogan and guys like that — and I was just a kid out of home in New Jersey.

It turns out that they shipped me to Chattanooga. Well, as fate would have it, I got stuck in Cincinnati. They just built a new railroad station in Cincinnati, not too far from the ballpark — Crosley Field — and we had to sleep two days in the Pullman because we couldn't get out of town because of the flood.

Anyway, I got to Chattanooga and the ballclub had just left for

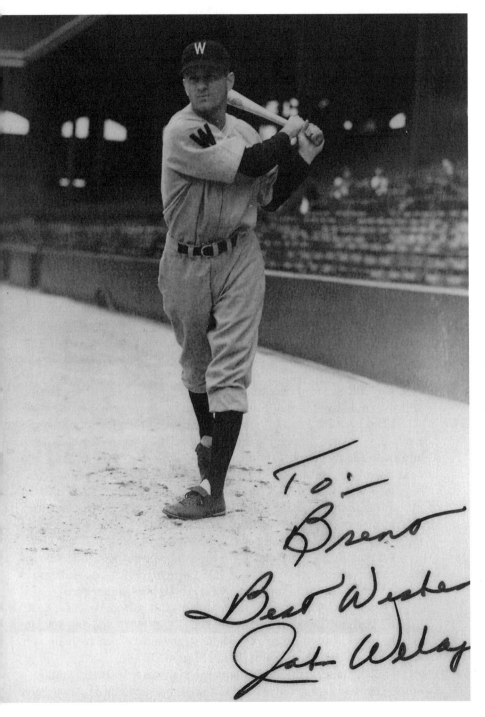

Johnny Welaj as a rookie with Washington, 1939 (courtesy John Welaj).

Nashville. Joe Engel was the owner at the time and he said, "We're gonna keep you down here to work out with several other ballplayers that are here." And it turns out I stayed there for a week and the first day they said you gotta eat at the hotel. "We'll give you food." And I saw collard greens and beets! I said, "We used to feed the pigs with that!"

So I stayed there for a week. Clyde Milan was managing and the ballclub came back. They said, "You sign a contract for [$]75 down here and let the Triple-A club give the other money."

I said, "No. I signed for $150 here. I wasn't born yesterday." So it turns out they wouldn't do that so I said, "I'm gonna go back to Harrisburg, Pennsylvania," where all the kids that I knew — my age–were playing.

They had a flood there, too, and it turns out the ballpark was washed down the river, so we went to York and from York we went to Trenton. At the end of the year I went to Washington and Mr. [Clark] Griffith said, "Sign a contract for 1937 for 200, take $100 cut, and you can finish the season up here."

I said, "I'm going back home where I can make anywhere from 4- to $500 playing semipro ball," and I did. It was the Depression and I could go down to South Carolina, North Carolina, and work in a mill and their company will give my father a house and put him to work and all that stuff and you could live there all your life. I didn't have to work, just play ball.

Then I put in '36, '37, '38 in the minors and then Joe Cambria sold me to the Yankees. I was going out of the gate and I was sold to the Giants and that didn't work out, and then I was gonna go to Connie Mack and next thing Joe Cambria said, "We're sending you back to Washington."

Joe Cambria owned me because major league ballclubs didn't own minor league clubs. They could do what they wanted between the minors and the majors. They could just rip up the contracts. Baseball was different then; they'd tell you you gotta sign for this or sign for that.

I'm making $500 playing ball in the minors, from 300, and then I go back to the same ballclub and I got $125 raise. After three years they said they'd have to sell me to somebody. "Everybody's asking for you."

Then I go back to Washington and they send me a contract for $500. I didn't sign it. They didn't draw anybody. They were drawing 200,000 and the ticket prices were only two dollars. The most expensive ballplayer when I joined that ballclub was Buddy Myer — $7500.

I finally went to spring training. Joe Stripp was from Perth-Amboy — not too far — so I went and worked out in his baseball school down there, didn't tell anybody I was in there.

I waited until about a week before spring training to report to Orlando and it turns out I got into the hotel instead of with the other rookies. They bring 'em in early and see who they're gonna keep and send the rest to the minors. I came in a week before they started and I was in St. Augustine down there and they had Cubans come in to work out there. Joe Cambria brought in some Cubans and they were smoking the marijuana weed; they're running like little jackrabbits.

I come into camp and nobody could pronounce my name. They give me number 24 and about a week later we start playing Detroit exhibition ballgames. There was a guy in the minors by the name of Harry Eisenstat — he played for Detroit — went up there a year ahead of me. Left-handed pitcher. Hell, I could hit him blindfolded.

In the seventh inning I get called in but they couldn't pronounce my name. There was another guy, Grilli, that almost sounded like Welaj and he was running and they said, "No, no. We want 24." So there were a couple on base and I got a basehit to tie up the ballgame, 3-to-3, in the bottom of the seventh. They said, "Okay, go play right field." I replaced Sam West.

It comes in the bottom of the ninth, a guy triples, they walk two guys, and then I get a basehit to win the ballgame.

That night we go back to the hotel and it's [Walt] Masterson, [Jim] Bloodworth, Jake Early, and Joe Haynes, who married Thelma [Griffith] later on, and we're all sitting at the table hungry as hell because we had to walk to the ballpark, 'bout a mile-and-a-half from the hotel.

For lunch, they gave you two pieces of white bread with one slice of cheese and a little thing of milk and I wouldn't eat either one of 'em. I said, "Hell, no! I don't wanna clutter up my eyes!" I was going to take a grapefruit and eat that thing, skin and all.

So, anyway, that night Milan came up to the dining room and came to our table and said, "How do you pronounce your name?" Before he left, he said, "Good game. You're making the trip with the big club tomorrow to Lakeland to play Detroit."

When he left, all those guys said, "Boy, you're gonna make this ballclub!"

Well, they had Bobo Newsom pitching out there and I started in left field and it turns out, when I go to bat — they had me leading off — Bucky Harris and Sam West and some of the others said, "He's gonna throw you a change-of-pace on the first pitch. He thinks you're a greenhorn."

They knew I hit two balls to left field. They shifted [Hank] Greenberg about 15 feet away from first base and I hit a ground ball down the right field line for a triple. I wound up 3-for-5 and had a hell of a day, so we go back to the hotel and Thelma, the adopted daughter — she was a

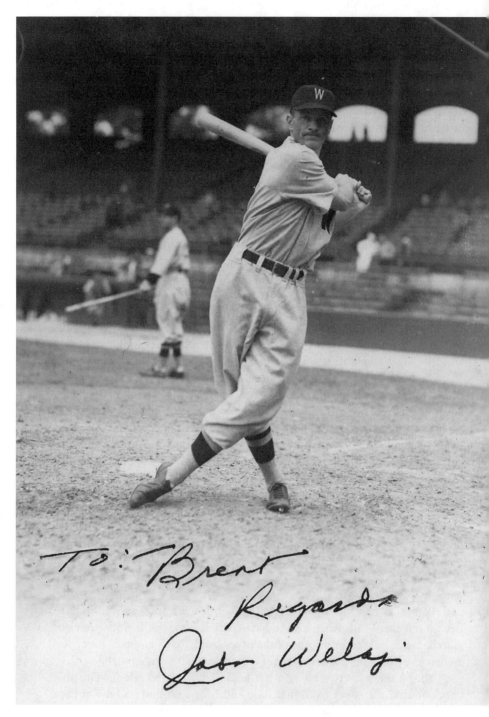

Johnny Welaj, 1940 (courtesy John Welaj).

niece officially; he adopted her, Calvin, and Bruce, but Brucie died young—came over to me. She was a doll, too, when you came right down to it and she gave you that drawl talk and she said, "Unc would like to see ya."

So I went up and took the elevator up to that suite up there where they were sitting and he said, "You have your contract with you?"

I said, "Yes, down in my room."

He said, "Go get it."

I went and got the contract and give it to him. He ripped the damned thing up. I thought, "Well, I guess I better pack my bag and go home."

Then he drew another one out and put $600 a month.

I was in Washington three years. [Joe] Cronin was with Boston and he wanted me so he got me. [Ken] Chase and I were traded for [Jack] Wilson and. oh, the lefthanded outfielder who became a good hitter [Stan Spence]. I go up there and I have a good spring and everything else and I'm supposed to play against lefthanded pitching and [Lou] Finney is supposed to hit against righthanders.

It turns out that they put somebody else to play in there. He didn't put Finney in there; he put somebody else that was on the ballclub at the time. The guy struck out four times and we were playing the Yankees so we lost.

Everybody in the clubhouse—[Ted] Williams, Dom DiMaggio, Finney, the pitchers—they were complaining; they were saying, "If we had you in the lineup we would have won the ballgame." A couple days before that, against the Boston Bees and [Casey] Stengel, I had 3-for-5, hit a home run, and drove in all the runs.

I was married and my wife said, "We could've stayed in Washington instead of you sitting on the bench here like this." I told her the situation and the money was all right because, what the hell, we got $5,000 to sign with Boston. I got a raise.

Cronin hears everybody moaning. I'm keeping quiet; I didn't say much because I was timid in a lot of ways. Then Cronin came up and said something to me and I just turned around and jumped on him. I said, "Look, I don't wanna play ball for you!"

He says, "Go see Eddie Collins [the general manager]."

Collins says, "What's the problem?" I told him the story and Collins says, "You think you can make a deal for yourself?" And the season started!

I looked at him; I said. "May I use your phone?" I must have shocked him.

I called Joe McCarthy and told him to call Mr. [George] Weiss. And about 15 minutes later, I'm a Yankee.

Mr. Weiss told me, "Eric Tipton broke his ankle as Kansas City. Will you go down there and play and we're gonna get another outfielder to come down there. We're gonna hide you. [Tommy] Henrich's gonna go in the service and then we'll bring you up here."

I get down there. I play one game and I don't play for three more weeks. One guy in Buffalo saw me play ball in Washington and I got 4-for-6, drove in six runs against the Philadelphia A's, won a ballgame.

The Yankees sold Buffalo three ballplayers and they were inducted into the service. So now, that [Buffalo general manager John] Stiglmeier – may he rest in peace — he told Weiss, "Look, these guys were inducted. How about giving us that Polack that you're hiding down there in Kansas City?" You know, Buffalo — Tonawanda — is nothing but about a couple hundred thousand Polacks.

It worked out very good for me. I went up there, I finished third in the league in hitting, second in stolen bases and I think I got there in May sometime. [John batted .309 with 11 HR, 57 RBI, and 30 SB.] Bill Terry wanted to pay $50,000 for me. I said, "No, Bill. I gotta be going in the service."

I was drafted. I was hoping it wasn't the St. Louis Browns or the Phillies or the Athletics, but Connie Mack had first call so they grabbed me. After the [1943] season was over the Army got me.

My daughter was born on the 12th of October. The nest day I got the damned notice in Cedar Rapids, Iowa: report for induction. I got an extension and got 27 days to see my daughter.

Actually, I spent 28 months overseas. We had a good baseball year and in the fall of '45 I came home. I went to play ball in Louisville in '46. I was making $7500 now and the GI's were guaranteed their salaries. They tell me they'll take me back to Boston and I start to thinking, "All these ballplayers come out of the service — Williams, DiMaggio, and Doerr and others — hell, I'm better off at Triple-A."

It turns out we played in the Little World Series against Jackie Robinson [Montreal] — I'm in his book — and it turns out that I had a hell of a year. I went back there in '47 and next thing I know my wife took a job in Washington, D.C., working for the Veterans Administration.

While I was in Louisville, the Red Sox sold me to Toronto. They sold me for two ballplayers—[Matt] Batts and Cot Deal — and $50,000! So I got myself $5,000 bonus to go to Toronto. I played there two years at $8,000 a year, then they traded me to Montreal. I stayed there two years.

They traded me for three ballplayers so then I got $2500 from [Branch] Rickey to go to Montreal. That year we finished second and the next year we won the pennant—1951—and we got beat by Milwaukee. That's the best year I had in baseball, as far as money's concerned.

The only club [in the Dodger's system] that didn't win the pennant that year was the big club. They got beat by the Giants with [Bobby] Thomson's home run. Everybody else in the Dodgers' minor league organization got a ring—cost $70; that's worth 5,000 today.

When I finished [playing], Mr. Griffith asked me if I'd scout the [American] league for him. He said he'd give me $500 to do it. I said, "No. I'm doing it out of my generosity that you gave me a chance to play ball. I live here, you invite me to your parties."

Johnny Welaj, 1989 (courtesy John Welaj).

Before I quit playing baseball, I was gonna manage for the Dodgers because [Walter] Alston was going up. I went up to New York to the Commodore Hotel and talked to [Buzzie] Bavasi and I was gonna manage Pueblo in Colorado. [Frank] Shaughnessy of the International League saw me. Havana was coming into the league, so he said, "You know the league. Why don't you help Bobby Maduro?"

I was going to make $6,000 to go manage the ballclub so I told Buzzie, "You know what I'm gonna tell 'em? I want $12,000; send a check today for 2,000 to my wife and I'll take the 10,000 as the pay." And they did it.

At the end of the year, Mr. Griffith said, "How 'bout you coming to manage the club at Hagerstown?" That's where I had Bobby Allison and a couple other good ballplayers.

Then I went to Europe on a baseball clinic for the Air Force. Mickey Cochrane, Ed Hurley, Joe Haynes, and some others went along. Then I managed Erie and Midland and then they brought me back and put me in the front office [in 1957] and I've been in the front office ever since.

I'm retired [now]. After the retirement party, they said, "You're the Spring Training Director."

In your playing days with Washington, the outfield was fantastic.

Oh, hell, we could run! We had a good outfield. We could carry our gloves with anybody, anyplace, but I think the Yankees were best with [Joe] DiMaggio and [George] Selkirk that first year [1936] and the left fielder, I think it was Myril Hoag. [Red] Rolfe was the third baseman and [Lou] Gehrig was at first and [Tony] Lazzeri and [Frank] Crosetti at second and short and Bill Dickey was the catcher. Joe Gallagher was there for a while; I played against him in the minors.

The pitchers were [Red] Ruffing, [Lefty] Gomez, [Johnny] Murphy, [Spud] Chandler. Atley Donald came the following year; I played against Atley in the minors. [Marv] Breuer — I played against him in the minors, too.

Your reputation was as a good, smart baserunner.

You hit it on the head. We got a guy — Craig Wright — who's a sabermetrician and here about five-six years ago he said, percent-wise, I'm seventh or eighth.

[Mike] Shatzkin's book [*The Ballplayers*] says I was "elusive." Rick Ferrell might have come up with that because a few years ago in Port Charlotte I walked away to answer a telephone call and there were two kids that worked in the ticket office and one was the assistant general manager. While they were there a couple scouts asked Rick Ferrell, "What kind of ballplayer was John?"

He said, "Let me tell you something. He was the fastest guy in the majors and the best base stealer, better than George Case. And he could go get a ball!"

When I came up in 1939, up there in Detroit I got walked four or five times leading off and Ty Cobb came into our clubhouse, uninvited, and came straight to my locker. He said, "Son, are you from Georgia?" because I had sort of a Southern accent — Polish accent mixed in with some people that came from the South.

I said, "No, sir." I didn't even know it was Ty Cobb.

He said, "Let me tell you, son. I haven't seen anybody play center field as you have today. You could fly! You have a motor in your fanny!"

I'm thinking, "Who the hell's this guy?" When he left, Bucky Harris, Myer, West, and Pete Appleton, who was from New Jersey, said, "Did you know who that guy was?"

"No. Who is he?"

"Ty Cobb."

But the best one happened in Chicago. Jimmy Dykes is managing [the White Sox]. We have to come through that dugout at third base — we all dressed in the same place in that area — and I walked in and Jimmy Dykes said, "Hey. bush, come over here and autograph this program for this man."

He's sitting on an ice cake where they've got ice underneath getting water cooled off. I just autographed it and I see this guy — I don't know who the hell he is — over on the right side of the dugout with his hat drawn over his eyes. The man calls me, "Hey, son, come over here." I come over there and say, "Yes, sir."

He said, "Do you know that man? What did he want you to do?"

"Oh, just write an autograph for him."

He said, "You know who that man is?"

"No."

"Okay, fine. Thank you. Go back to the dugout."

I go back there and the guys jump at me and say, "Hey, what did the commissioner want?" It was Judge Landis.

"The commissioner? He asked me did I know that guy. I said, 'Hell, no.' Who is he?"

"That's Al Capone."

Do you still receive autograph requests?

Yes, I do. Plenty. I'd rather sign for nothing. Nolan Ryan — he gave 'em out for nothing. Hell, there's a line out here. They know he worked out from nine to 10:30 and there's gotta be a hundred people out there and he stops and autographs. He's one down-to-earth guy.

Only three men stole at a rate greater than ten percent when John Welaj was playing. By subtracting the total home runs and triples from the number of times a man reached base, we arrive at the hypothetical number of opportunities a man has to steal. Of course, sometimes someone will be occupying the next base but we are assuming these would somewhat negate themselves between players over a period of time. What we have is the number of times a man reached first or second base and by dividing that into the number of steals, we arrive at the percentage of steals from opportunities.

Here are the Top Three in the major leagues for the period 1939–1941.

George Case	18.1%
John Welaj	14.8%
Mike Kreevich	10.6%

JOHN LUDWIG WELAJ

Born May 27, 1914, Moss Creek, PA
Ht. 6'   Wt. 164   Batted and Threw Right

Year	Team, Lg	G	AB	R	H	2B	3B	HR	RBI	BA
1939	Wash., AL	63	201	23	55	11	2	1	33	.274
1940		88	215	31	55	9	0	3	21	.256
1941		49	96	16	20	4	0	0	5	.208
1943	Phi., AL	93	281	45	68	16	1	0	15	.242
4 Years		293	793	115	198	40	3	4	74	.250

FLOYD GIEBELL

King for a Day (1939–1941)

In 1940, the Cleveland Indians had the best team they'd had since at least 1925, when they finished second, only three games behind the Yankees. In the 13 seasons since 1925, the Tribe had been extremely mediocre. A soundly beaten third or fourth was their usual finish, and they averaged more than 23 games back each year.

The 1940 New York Yankees, on the other hand, entered the season with the same team, nearly to a man, that had destroyed the rest of the American League in 1939 (17 games ahead of second-place Boston) and swept the Reds in the World Series. That had been their fourth consecutive World Championship.

The Detroit Tigers of 1940 appeared to be a fading team. Back-to-back AL pennants in '34 and '35, and a World Championship the latter year, had been followed by two seconds, then a fourth and a fifth (in 1939). Preseason predictions placed them anywhere from fourth to seventh.

But on Friday morning, September 27, 1940, with only the weekend to go, this is how these three stood:

	W	L	GB	To Play
Detroit	89	62	—	3
Cleveland	87	64	2	3
New York	86	64	2½	4

Floyd Giebell (courtesy Floyd Giebell).

The Tigers were in Cleveland to close out the season there, while the Yankees would play the eighth-place Athletics in Philadelphia that day and then finish out the season with three games (a doubleheader on Saturday) in Washington versus the seventh-place Senators.

For Cleveland to win the pennant, the Indians would have to sweep the Tigers. But if the Yankees won their remaining four, they could tie for the title with either Detroit or Cleveland, depending on the division of the series in Cleveland.

One win by the Tigers would eliminate Cleveland. One more Tiger win and one Yankee loss would also eliminate New York, but these were still the four-straight World Champs playing the two worst teams, by far, in the league.

There had been a great deal of dissension in Cleveland that summer. The players had petitioned to have manager Ossie Vitt fired, but the front office kept him. It was not a team of happy ballplayers and the revolt earned them the tag "Cry Babies." It's not possible to say how many games this discord cost the Indians, but if it was only one it was one too many.

On Cleveland's last trip into Detroit a short time earlier, baby bottles attached to strings were lowered from the upper deck and dangled in front of the Indians' dugout. There was not a feeling of friendliness toward the Tigers, therefore, when Detroit came to Cleveland for that last weekend of the season.

Going into that series, the Tigers, of course, were in the driver's eat, but their pitching was wearing thin. Bobo Newsom had won 21 games and was at the peak of his career, but Tommy Bridges was aging and had won only 12 games, while Schoolboy Rowe went 16-3 but was coming off years of arm problems and could not be the workhorse he once was. Beyond them were rookies Hal Newhouser and Johnny Gorsica and second-year men Dizzy Trout and Fred Hutchinson, both of whom spent a good part of the season with Buffalo. None of the four had been very effective in the latter part of the season.

Meanwhile, the Cincinnati Reds had long since wrapped up the National League title and were coasting to an eventual 12 game bulge over the second-place Brooklyn Dodgers. Manager Bill McKechnie had a well-rested, excellent pitching staff to throw at whomever the AL ended up presenting to them.

For the Friday game in Cleveland, the morning papers listed Bob Feller, 27-10 with a 2.62 ERA (against a league ERA of 4.38), as the Indians' starter, and Rowe (16-3, 3.46) for the Tigers. Feller led the league in wins, starts, complete games, innings, strikeouts, and ERA; in fact, the only major pitching category he *didn't* lead in was W-L Percentage, and Rowe was the leader there.

But as game time approached, Rowe was not warming up in the Tigers' bullpen. Instead, 30-year-old rookie righthander Floyd Giebell was loosening up. (The papers at the time gave his age as 24.)

Giebell had been up briefly in '39. In nine games (15.1 innings) in relief that year, he had gone 1-1, 2.93, but was with Buffalo at the beginning of the 1940 season, where he had a 15-17 record. Called up about ten days earlier, he had been given a start against the last-place Athletics, and he was the winner in a 13-2 laugher.

But this was different. Manager Del Baker was pitting a rookie with 24 major league innings against the best pitcher in baseball. Evidently he was conceding game one of the series to Cleveland in order to come back with a better-rested Rowe, or even Newsom, in the second game.

The Cleveland fans were upset with the treatment their team had received earlier in Detroit, and now this— this ridiculous mismatch — had the Ladies' Day crowd of 45,553 nearly riotous.

Trouble started early. Hank Greenberg, playing left field for the Tigers, was pelted with overripe fruit and vegetables as he warmed up before the game. Later, as he made a catch in the game, more fruit and vegetables came at him.

And in the bullpen, catcher Birdie Tebbetts was bombarded with a half bushel of green tomatoes dropped from the upper deck about 60 feet up, knocking him to the ground and stunning him. Rowe was believed to be the target, as he was sitting next to Tebbetts at the time.

The perpetrator of this, one Carmen Guerra, was arrested and as he was being escorted from the park, was met by the angry Tebbetts, who punched him several times as the police watched.

Plate umpire Bill Summers threatened to forfeit the game to the Tigers if this didn't cease, and Indians' manager Vitt made an appeal to the fans to let the better team win on merit.

In the actual playing of the game, Feller was his usual brilliant self, holding the Tigers to only three hits. One of those hits, however, was a fourth inning home run by Rudy York with Charlie Gehringer, who had walked, on base. That was all Giebell needed, and all he got, as he allowed Cleveland only six hits and won the game — and the pennant — two to nothing.

Ben Chapman, Cleveland's left fielder, had a particularly rough afternoon. York's home run just cleared the fence in left at the 320-feet mark, and actually flicked off the tip on Chapman's glove as he leaped for it. But more importantly, Chapman was the victim of three of Giebell's six strikeouts. And each time he left men in scoring position. After leading off the game with a walk, he came up in the third inning with men on first and third, in the fifth with men on first and second, and in the seventh with men on second and third, and each time he was no match for Giebell. The magnitude of this feat increases when you realize that Chapman only fanned 42 other times all season and was a career .302 hitter. For his long and distinguished career he was one of the most difficult men in the game to whiff, striking out only once every 13.1 plate appearances.

In the ninth, the game, and Cleveland's pennant hopes, ended when pinch-hitter Jeff Heath hit a blistering grounder toward York, much-maligned as a glove man, who made a fine stop and stepped on first base for the final out.

Meanwhile, in Philadelphia, the Yankees were also eliminated as the A's downed them, 6-to-2. Johnny Babich was the winning pitcher, and that may sum up the Yankees' 1940 season; Babich beat them *five* times that year.

Floyd Giebell was not eligible for the World Series, but his effort allowed the Tigers to go in with a well-rested staff. And, although the Reds won the Series in seven games, Detroit out-pitched them.

Giebell began the 1941 season with Detroit, but was used sparingly. He never won another major league game and ended the season back with Buffalo. He finally retired from the game in 1948.

❖ ❖ ❖

You were a famous man for one ballgame.

Maybe some sportswriters think so, but that's not quite true.

Of course, your career amounted to much more than that, but that one game was an extremely big game. It clinched the pennant and enabled the Tigers' starting pitchers to have a much-needed rest. You out-pitched the best pitcher in baseball that day.

Yes, at that time. That's right.

You struck out more batters than he did and you walked fewer. What are your recollections of the game?

There's a lot of different write-ups about that ballgame over a period of many years. I knew the night before that I was going to work, although the sportswriters didn't. They thought that Schoolboy Rowe was going to pitch, or maybe Newhouser. At that time he wasn't getting too many people out. It probably would have been Rowe.

The next day at the ballpark, when it was time for the pitchers to warm up — Feller and myself — they thought that maybe it was a farce or something, but it didn't turn out that way.

At the start of the day, the Indians were two games out and the Yankees were only two-and-a-half back.

If the Tigers would have lost the three game series, they'd have been out of it. If Feller had won against me, that would have put them only one back. They could have won it by sweeping us. The Yankees lost to the Athletics that day.

How about the vegetable incidents?

The first one happened about the second or third inning when they hit Greenberg. There were pictures of him hauling off a wheelbarrow of vegetables from left field. Summers was the umpire behind the plate and he, of course, called time out.

The second time it happened — dropping a basket of stuff on Tebbetts' head in the bullpen — that was about the fifth inning, I think. Summers told the fans then — they were pretty rowdy — that if things didn't settle down the Indians would have to forfeit the game. At that time, they decided they better settle down because no doubt they thought that they would win.

The game was really over by that time. York had hit his home run and you were in total command. That was the closest the Indians had been in years.

Yeah. A little later, towards the middle of Feller's career, they won it a couple of times in the late '40s and early '50s.

You struck out Ben Chapman three times that day and he only struck out 45 times all season. What were you doing to him?

He was a .300 hitter. I was a control pitcher, more or less, and I could throw around 91-92 miles an hour. I came inside on Chapman just to show him a fastball, then I struck him out two of the three times on a slider on the outside half of the plate. I think there was a man on second and third once and if he had put the ball in play to the second baseman or short-stop, probably the run would have scored.

They made two errors behind me that day. [Dick] Bartell made one and Gehringer made one, which got me in trouble in one of the innings. They made a double play for me [York unassisted] and I was keeping the ball away a good bit from the righthanded hitters. [Hal] Trosky, a big left-handed hitter — he was one of the people I was really trying to be careful with 'cause he could hurt you pretty badly. He was a power hitter, a big boy.

As far as I'm concerned, I think the Cleveland team overall was the best team in the league. With their all-around ability and their pitching staff, they could have won it very easily. That was the year of Vitt's Cry Babies; that hurt them.

You won a game a short time before that.

It was about a week before. I beat the Athletics, 13-to-2, in Detroit.

Where had you been that season?

I came up from Buffalo. Steve O'Neill managed me there. That was the year I lost 13 ballgames by one run. I was pitching for a 15-win bonus and I just made it: 15-and-17. Every time I walked out there I'm trying to win 1-to-nothing, 2-to-1.

When we came north from spring training, my first three games were on the road: Newark, Jersey City, and Syracuse. I lost all three of 'em, 2-to-1. When the third game was over, I was hot! I picked up a fungo bat and all through the passageway from the dugout to the clubhouse I knocked out every damn light in there. O'Neill didn't say a word 'cause he felt the same way I did.

How many years did you pitch?

I wrote the commissioner and voluntarily retired after nine years. I was making pretty good money with Buffalo and I ended up down in Dallas, but I made up my mind a long time before that I wasn't gonna drag my family around like I've seen some people do — taking your children in and out of school and so on.

I'd been to college and had experience against the Homestead Grays and good ballclubs in the industrial league in West Virginia. We won the league there and went that fall — the last of September — to Dayton, Ohio, where 52 teams from all over the eastern part of the United States met. We won that and that's where Bill Doyle, the scout for Detroit, signed me. I was Detroit property all but my last two years.

Were you in the service during World War II?

Yeah, I was in there over two years. I played ball my first summer in the service. I came out at the end of '45 and I played '46, '7, and '8, and I wrote the commissioner and

Floyd Giebell being carried off the field after winning the 1940 pennant-clincher for Detroit over Cleveland. At right is manager Del Baker (courtesy Floyd Giebell).

voluntarily retired in '48. I had a good job in Greenville, South Carolina, and I went there from Dallas.

Who was the best player you saw?

[Joe] DiMaggio. The best hitter I've ever seen was [Ted] Williams. The first time I faced DiMaggio in Yankee Stadium I struck him out on a slider. *[laughs]* He didn't strike out very often. Probably he's one of the premier outfielders, all-around, of all time. You can't get away from that.

There were some excellent ballplayers around; there's some excellent ballplayers around today, but I don't think a lot of them today are hungry enough.

Pitchers are looking toward the bullpen after the fourth inning. In our day we never thought about going out of the ballgame. Of course, we did every once in a while 'cause we didn't have our best stuff every day we walked out there, but I never went out there unless I thought I was gonna go nine.

Who was the best pitcher you saw?

I have to go along with Feller for one, 'cause he proved that he was one of the best of the day. Buck Newsom, on our team, was a good pitcher, and Rowe was, in his prime. Bridges was a pretty good pitcher in his prime. Newhouser came on a little bit later, after I had left. When I was there he was doing quite a little bit of bullpen work and they were bringing him on.

Dizzy Trout was around. He was a wild man. Talk about ornery — man, he was ornery! Nothing fazed him. I watched [Mel] Harder pitch and he was a good pitcher. That's more than 50 years ago; it's kind of hard to remember.

I think the best team of all time were the '27-'28 Yankees and the '30-'31 Athletics.

What about the '34-'35 Tigers?

I don't think that they were as good through the lineup as the Athletics and Yankees were. The Athletics not only had hitting, with all their power and everything, but when you take [Lefty] Grove and [George] Earnshaw and [Rube] Walberg and pitchers of their caliber, you know they must have had a tremendous team. [Mickey] Cochrane, [Jimmie] Foxx, [Al] Simmons, Bing Miller — goodness, what a ballclub they had!

What's the biggest change today from when you played?

Personally, I think they've got too many teams to stock 'em with good ballplayers. You've got teams in both leagues that are just showing up; they just don't have the ballplayers to compete.

Another thing, when I went up, there was over 230 minor leagues in the country, from Class D up. Now there's only a handful. Newhouser came from a Class D league. He was in the Evangeline League down in Louisiana. He told me some stories about the natives down there. *[laughs]* If the umpires made a bad call or two against the home team, they were escorted back to the hotel and led out of town. That's how bad it was. *[laughs]*

I saw ballplayers who should have had a shot who never got it. Look at the Cardinals and even Detroit. Remember, [Commissioner Kenesaw M.] Landis turned over a million-and-a-half dollars worth of ballplayers from Detroit, and the Cardinals had so many ballplayers pigeon-holed you were lucky to even get a shot.

I broke in in the Three-I League in Evansville and we won the pennant there. Bob Coleman, the old catcher, was the manager there and Detroit sent me there for tutoring 'cause he was a good baseball man. I think some of the teams in that Class D league could beat a lot of your A clubs today. Some ballplayers went from our club into A or Double-A, which was unusual in those days. I was lucky enough that Detroit took me to spring training the following year. I won 21 and lost 5 and had an earned run average of one-point-nine-eight or something like that.

You said you went to college. Where?

Salem College in West Virginia. I was born and raised in West Virginia, in the mountain country in the middle part of the state.

Did you save souvenirs from your baseball career?

I have one of the bats York used in the 1940 World Series. I have the autographs of the whole team.

The fans of Detroit gave each of the ballplayers a sterling silver tray with a picture of ol' man [Walter] Briggs, the owner, in the middle of it and the authentic autographs of all the ballplayers and coaches right in the face of the tray. This tray is about 34 inches long and 18 inches wide and it's got latticework all around with nice handles and everything. It's a beautiful thing and I kept it in a safety deposit compartment for many years.

Would you be a ballplayer again?

Yeah.

Any regrets?

I had one. After the season in '40, I didn't get a start until the sixteenth day of July in '41. I was in the bullpen and some days I pitched a hell of a lot more than the guy out on the mound did, trying to stay warm. I went to Baker and I went to Jack Zeller, the general manager, and asked 'em to trade me and they wouldn't do it. By the sixteenth day of July I didn't give a damn whether I pitched or not. I was in shape physically, but mentally I didn't give a damn. You know, I was a happy boy to get back to Buffalo and to be able to work and live somewhat of a normal life. It's hard to believe, isn't it?

❖ ❖ ❖

Floyd George Giebell

Born December 10, 1909, Pennsboro, WV
Ht. 6'2½"   Wt. 172   Batted Left, Threw Right

Year	Team, Lg	G	IP	W	L	Pct	H	BB	SO	ERA
1939	Detroit, AL	9	15.1	1	1	.500	19	12	9	2.93
1940		2	18	2	0	1.000	14	4	11	1.00
1941		17	34.1	0	0	—	45	26	10	6.03
3 years		28	67.2	3	1	.750	78	42	30	3.99

ELMER VALO

Hustle (1940–1961)

A fairly regular occurrence among baseball fans is the naming of "All-something" all-star teams: All-Caribbean, All-Canadian, All-Irish descent, All-Ohio born, etc. On the All-European team, one of the outfielders has to be Elmer Valo.

Elmer was born in Ribnik, Czechoslovakia, in 1921. A few years earlier or a few years later and he may have spent his entire life there, but emigration was not too difficult in the late 1920s so the Valos, with their six-year-old son, came to America in 1927 and settled in Pennsylvania.

Elmer learned a great deal in his new country. First he learned the language and the next most important thing he learned was the game of baseball. It was so important that it supported him for his entire adult life.

As good as the game was to him, he was equally good to it. None other than Ty Cobb said Elmer "has the right attitude" and Valo was widely considered to be among the top hustlers of his day or any day.

His .282 career average included five seasons above .300 and from 1946, when he returned for the service, through 1951, he compiled a .295 batting average and a .429 on base average. His career OBA was an exceptional .399, due to his excellent batting eye and great ability to make contact. Twice he walked more than 100 times in a season and the highest strike out total he ever had was 32 in nearly 700 plate appearances in 1949.

Probably his most amazing totals occurred in 1952; he walked 101 times and fanned only 16!

In 20 seasons, he K'd only 284 times (that's two years for many of today's players) and his career walk to strike ratio was 3.3:1.

In the mid 1950s, when Elmer was in his mid thirties, he turned to pinch-hitting and became one of the best of all time. Today, nearly 40 years after he last came off the bench, he still holds a couple of pinch-hitting records: most bases on balls, season, 18 (1960); and most games PH, AL, 81 (1960). And that was still in the old 154-game schedule. At one time he also held the record for most career bases on balls by a pinch-hitter with 91.

At the time of his retirement, his 90 pinch hits were the third best ever and his .452 average (14-for-31) in 1955 was also the third best single-season pinch-hitting performance. Both figures are still high on the lists.

Now we're going to ease off onto a side track for a few minutes. Let's say you have a great big jar of pennies. You're going to put them in stacks of ten. You start counting: 1, 2, 3, 4, 5, 6, 7, 8, 9, 10. Number 10 belongs in that first stack. Stack number 2 begins with penny number 11, then 12, 13, and so on, up to number 20. Number 20 doesn't start the third pile; it ends the second one. Eventually you get up to ten stacks of 10 — 100 pennies — and number 100 is the last penny in the tenth stack, not the first penny in the next 100.

So it is with decades and centuries. The first year of the 21st century was 2001. The first year of the decade known as the 1990s was 1991.

Okay, let's go back to our subject, Elmer Valo. The following story may or may not be totally true; Elmer neither confirmed nor denied it. At the end of the 1939 season, the 18-year-old Valo had been summoned to Philadelphia after a banner first year in the minors by Connie Mack to see what life was like in the major leagues. There was no intention of playing the kid so there was no formality of a signed contract, but, on the final day of the season, Mack sent Elmer to the plate to pinch-hit. He walked, but Red Smith, the official scorekeeper that day, pointed out the lack of a contract to Mr. Mack. So, to avoid a fine, Valo's name was not entered into the scorebook. In the *Baseball Encyclopedia,* Elmer's first line is 1940.

Several people through the years have wanted this supposed 1939 appearance to be included so Elmer can be a "four-decade man." This brings us back to our derailment of a couple of paragraphs ago.

Opposite: **Elmer Valo early in his career with Philadelphia Athletics (courtesy Elmer Valo).**

There is a bunch of four-decade men. But are they really?

Let's look at a couple of prominent examples. Ted Williams and Mickey Vernon played in the '30s, '40s, '50s, and *1960*. Tim McCarver played in the '50s, '60s, '70s, and *1980*. By the definition of a decade, these guys played in only three. However, if you want a classification entitled "Players Who Played in Years in Which the Second-from-Last Number Is Different Four Times" (a cumbersome heading for a short column in a record book) then they qualify.

But, if you really want four-decade men, scratch them from the list and add Elmer Valo. He played in 1940, the last year of the decade of the 1930s, and he played in 1961, the first year of the decade of the 1960s.

Elmer has a couple of other distinctions that rudimentary research seems to indicate are singular to him. He is the only man to ever accompany three teams on franchise shifts: 1955, Philadelphia to Kansas City; 1958, Brooklyn to Los Angeles; and 1961, Washington to Minnesota. And he is the only player ever to play on two teams which endured 20-game losing streaks: 1943 A's, 20; and 1961, Phillies, 23. And in the same city!

But Elmer Valo has other distinctions: He always gave it all he had and he always appreciated his fans.

❖ ❖ ❖

How old were you when you came to the United States?

I was six in March and we came in April. My parents came here out of financial need. They had a small farm over there but they figured they could improve their lot by coming here.

How many children were there?

Only one — me. A spoiled brat. *[laughs]*

What did your father do when he got here?

He worked at the New Jersey Zinc Company at the time.

Did you, indeed, improve your lot by coming here?

To a degree, yes. I certainly did, but my parents worked very, very hard. So did my wife's parents. Everybody worked hard here to get ahead, to save a couple of bucks, to buy a home and stuff like that.

You started playing ball with other kids here.

Yes, just in the back lots. At least we had lots in those days *[laughs]*; now they've got to walk three miles or have a ride to go to a little park.

Connie Mack signed you at 18.

Yes. When I was 17, actually.

Were you still in high school?

Yes. I graduated and went to Federalsburg, Maryland, in the Eastern Shore League.

And hit the daylights out of the ball.

Well, I was pretty fortunate. I had a good year. [43-for-115, .374]

Over the years you had a reputation for being one of the top hustlers in the game and several times you hustled right into brick walls.

That was out of necessity, when you're trying to win a ballgame and help the team. I only did it when there was a close ballgame, where it could mean the ballgame.

How many times did you hit the wall? I remember hearing about it frequently when I was a kid.

I don't know. I hit a few — maybe twice a year. You know, you hit 'em and nothing happens. But I got hurt about four or five times.

Several announcers in the '40s and '50s called you the top hustler in the game.

I don't know what they considered me, but I always tried the best I could. I tried to win every ballgame any possible way that I could, but sometimes I screwed up, too.

You had an outstanding batting eye. Was this something you developed or did it come naturally?

I was taught by the old-timers to get a strike zone. When I found my strike zone, which was early in my career, that helped. You've *got* to know your strike zone. Sometimes a walk is just as important as a basehit. You're getting on base.

You also had some speed on the bases. You stole in double figures ten times, but you played in a time when stealing was not emphasized.

You stole when you were behind, when you needed 'em.

If you had been asked to steal as they are today, what do you think you would have done?

I really don't know. It all depends. We played the percentages. Kids today are running; they're fast and they study the pitchers more intensely than I used to. I studied the pitchers, but not like they do today.

You were with the A's during a time when they didn't have too many good teams. Mr. Mack kind of lost the knack there at the end.

They wouldn't give him any help — the other clubs. We needed left-handed pitching. We got 'em a little too late — in '49 and '50. [Bobby] Shantz and [Alex] Kellner, and [Lou] Brissie, too. If we had those three in '46, '47, and '48 I think we could have won.

Late in your career you became an outstanding pinch-hitter. This takes a different attitude entirely from playing every day. If you start and make an out in the first inning you know you're going to see the guy again in the third or fourth. Was this something that came easy to you or did you have to adjust your outlook?

Oh, yes, you have to adjust. You have to prepare yourself. You see the situation in a ballgame and how the pitcher's going and if there's men on base. Or maybe they just want you to just get on, like the tying run or something. Or maybe they want a home run, but if they pitch around you a little bit you can't hit a pitch you can't handle for a home run but you might get a single or take a walk.

You sure did. At one time you held the record for most career walks as a pinch-hitter. You still hold the American League season record.

You know more about me than I know about myself. *[laughs]*

I know it [pinch-hitting] kept me in the game a little bit longer. *[laughs]*

You played 20 years in the major leagues. Who was the one best player or hitter you saw in that time?

You can go for hitting only, you know, and he wasn't too bad a fielder, and it was [Ted] Williams. And then you have [Joe] DiMaggio, you have Willie Mays, you have Stan Musial. You could name a lot of good hitters, consistent hitters.

Generally speaking, I would consider the best in my day — like [Mickey] Mantle — to be so good, they were extraordinary people. I admired the extraordinary ones and even the ones that weren't extraordinary that put out all the time.

You had the advantage of seeing the best in both leagues. Which league did you prefer?

It didn't matter as long as I was playing in the majors. *[laughs]*

You've got to study the pitchers. If you don't, you don't know how to react to 'em when you get up to the plate. You watch 'em on the side. The first time you see a pitcher, you see him warming up on the side. When I used to lead off I'd watch 'em throw. Don't let them get ahead of you. Then they play with you.

Who was the best pitcher you saw in your 20 years?

You can mention several dozen, I guess, but you've got [Bob] Feller and [Hal] Newhouser and Spud Chandler. There's so many; Cleveland had four of 'em. Each team had three or four pitchers that were troublesome and you were happy if you got 1-for-3 or 1-for-4 or 1-for-5 out of the situation — you know, a walk and maybe one hit.

Elmer Valo with Cleveland in 1959.

Who was the toughest pitcher on you?

Of, Feller, I guess, would be the most difficult.

Did you see much of Sandy Koufax?

Oh, he was wild when I faced him. But [Don] Drysdale was tough. He was another one, but he was just a young kid, too, when I was with the Phillies.

I played with Koufax when he started to win. That was something. Not only that, but [he had] a great personality. Drysdale, too.

You scouted for a while. Did you sign anyone we'd know?

Not in the major leagues. They came into Triple-A.

See, when I started to scout, they started this draft business. That kills your potential to get a number one draft choice a lot of times. You don't get the choice you used to get. You scout and just make recommendations and they have follow-up scouts, what they call cross-checkers. The thing is, if they see him on a bad day they won't evaluate him like I did. I can watch a boy 50 times in two years, and the cross-checker can see him on an off day. But it [the draft] does help the lower clubs get better picks.

Did you save souvenirs from your career?

No, I never did. My wife and some friends saved some things. I get some from people now that I'm saving, but I never did save anything during the time I played except a couple of bats that I gave my kids to play with.

How many kids do you have?

I have four children, two boys and two girls.

Did either of the boys have baseball inclinations?

Oh, yeah. They were pretty good college players. One would have been given the chance to play [professionally] but he was given a college scholarship and the scholarship was more at that time than what they offered him to play. I said to him, "It's up to you, but I would rather you go to school." All that reading in school, or something, caused his eyes to change a little bit.

I'm happy they all went to college. They're doing pretty decent for themselves.

Grandkids?

Six. Five girls and one boy. *[laughs]*

What's the most significant change you've seen in the game?

Oh, boy.

The artificial turf. And the ballparks are completely different. The artificial turf — they can't slow the ball down like they used to on the regular turf. They can't let the grass grow and then wet it down so a ground ball can't get through the infield. The players can play deeper now, but the ball gets on 'em quicker. Your reflexes have to be *real* quick.

If you went back to high school, would you do this all again?

Oh, absolutely! Hey, baseball gave me a wonderful living and I've been in it for over 50 years. I really enjoy it and I got my kids through school with it and I'm still making a living out of it with the pension. I enjoyed every minute of it, to be truthful, except when I went 0-for-24 or 0-for-25. *[laughs]* Or when you lose too many ballgames.

ELMER WILLIAM VALO

Born March 5, 1921, Ribnik, Czechoslovakia
Died July 19, 1998, Palmerton, PA
Ht. 5'11"   Wt. 190   Batted Left, Threw Right

Year	Team, Lg	G	AB	R	H	2B	3B	HR	RBI	BA
1939	Phi., AL	Joined team at end of season but not put on roster.								
1940		6	23	6	8	0	0	0	0	.348
1941		15	50	13	21	0	1	2	6	.420
1942		133	459	64	115	13	10	2	40	.251
1943		77	249	31	55	6	2	3	18	.221
1944–45	Military service									
1946		108	348	59	107	21	6	1	31	.307
1947		112	370	60	111	12	6	5	36	.300
1948		113	383	72	117	17	4	3	46	.305
1949		150	547	86	155	27	12	5	85	.283
1950		129	446	62	125	16	5	10	46	.280
1951		123	444	75	134	27	8	7	55	.302
1952		129	388	69	109	26	4	5	47	.281
1953		50	85	15	19	3	0	0	9	.224
1954		95	224	28	48	11	6	1	33	.214
1955	KC, AL	112	283	50	103	17	4	3	37	.364
1956	KCAL, PhNL	107	300	41	86	13	3	5	39	.287
1957	Brk., NL	81	161	14	44	10	1	4	26	.273
1958	L.A., NL	65	101	9	25	2	1	1	14	.248
1959	Clev., AL	34	24	3	7	0	0	0	5	.292
1960	NY-Was. AL	84	69	7	18	3	0	0	16	.261
1961	MinAL-PhNL	83	75	4	13	4	0	1	12	.173
20 years		1806	5029	768	1420	228	73	58	601	.282

PAUL CAMPBELL

Name It and He Did It (1941–1950)

Paul Campbell entered baseball in 1938 and didn't leave it until the mid 1990s. In all that time, the only job he didn't hold was that of umpire.

He was a player, a coach, a manager, a business manager, a general manager, a traveling secretary, a team president, a scout, and a consultant. You'll have to dig deep to find someone else with such wide and varied experience in the game.

His stay in the majors as a player was only moderate — six seasons — and when that ended in 1950 he became a playing coach in the minors. After two years, he became a playing manager, still in the minors.

Then he spent two-and-a-half years as a business manager before becoming the general manager of the Louisville Colonels in 1957. The next year he was that team's president. Next, he joined the scouting department of the Cincinnati Reds for six years and was with the team continuously from 1959 until he retired.

In 1965, he became the Reds' traveling secretary, if not baseball's toughest job certainly its most time-consuming. He remained in that position through 1977, when he became a consulting scout.

In Campbell's stay in the majors as a player, he only had one season in which he was close to being a regular. That was 1949 with the Detroit Tigers, when he shared the first base duties with Don Kolloway and George

Vico, but appeared in more games than either of the other two.

❖ ❖ ❖

Were you signed originally by the Red Sox?

Yes. Billy Lavelle was the baseball coach at Presbyterian College in South Carolina and he worked also as a scout for the Red Sox and he signed me.

I played in the Red Sox organization through '40 and then I was loaned to Montreal, which was a Brooklyn farm club, in '41. We were in the Little World Series. In '41, the only time I was with the Red Sox was at the start of the season. I stayed up there about a week before they sent me to Montreal. I was in one game [for Boston] as a

Paul Campbell, 1946 (courtesy Paul Campbell).

pinch-hitter in '41. I was with the Red Sox all of '42 and '46 and then the service [Air Force] in between.

Did you play ball in the service?

Oh, yeah. I was in England for 31 months and we toured all the air bases and played there. And then they had one game over there at Wembley Stadium in London between the Air Force professional players and the ground force professional players and we beat 'em, one-to-nothing. A lot of these ballplayers weren't major league ballplayers; they played pro ball, but it might have been A ball or Double-A ball. Most of 'em were in the minor leagues.

Monte Weaver, who was a righthanded pitcher for the Red Sox and

Washington, was one of our coaches. As far as players were concerned, I don't believe we had any bona fide major league ballplayers. A lot of 'em [major leaguers] were in the Navy.

After the War, the Red Sox played in the 1946 World Series. Did you play?

Yes. I came in in the top of the ninth inning in Game 7. Rudy York got on base and I pinch ran for him. That was the extent of my playing.

You played in Louisville in 1947 and then in Detroit in 1948. How did the Tigers acquire you?

Billy Evans, he was the farm director of the Red Sox when I played with 'em and he became general manager of the Tigers. The Red Sox out-righted me to Louisville and they couldn't get me back until I would go through the draft, so Evans bought me from Louisville. I spent '48, '49, and the first month of '50 in Detroit.

In '49, we didn't have a real regular first baseman. I played probably as much as anybody. We had me and George Vico and Don Kolloway that year. I had a good enough year to stay the next year, but for some reason they weren't gonna keep me so we worked out a deal where I went to Toledo as a player-coach, eventually going into managing for 'em, which I did.

On July 17, 1949, you had a great day. You hit a grand slam in the first game off Carl Scheib. Who did you get the game-winning hit off in the second game?

I think it was Bobby Shantz. Actually, that was my best day in professional baseball, including the minor leagues.

After several years of being a playing-coach and a playing manager, you turned to the administrative end of game.

In the middle of the season, 1954, I was with a Washington farm club — Hagerstown — and they had a chance to get some players. One of the leagues folded up and the Yankees had a farm club in that league and Zeke Bonura was the manager. They had a chance to get several ballplayers *if* they took Bonura as the manager, so they made me assistant business manager that year and Bonura managed the rest of the year.

Then I stayed in the business end of baseball for several years. I eventually went to Louisville and stayed there two years. I was general manager the first year and president the second year. Then I went to the big leagues as a scout with the Reds in 1959 and I've been with 'em ever since.

Who were some of the players you scouted?

Tommy Helms was the first player I signed and then I was in on the deal with Tom Browning, who went to school at Tennessee Wesleyan at Athens. I scouted him and told our area supervisor about him. I don't sign any ballplayers now; I'm a consulting scout for eastern Tennessee. I just look at ballplayers and tell 'em who I think are good enough to sign.

You were the Reds' traveling secretary for years.

Fourteen years. I enjoyed it, but I wouldn't want to go through it again. Rough on the home life; I'd go to the ballpark at 8:30 in the morning and be there 'til

Paul Campbell, 1949 (courtesy Paul Campbell).

midnight if we had a ballgame. Then when the team left to go on the road I'd go with it. I was the only executive in the front office that didn't get to stay home when the club went on the road. My wife didn't like that 'cause I was always gone. The only time we had any normal life was in wintertime.

In your playing days, who was the best player or best hitter you saw?

The best player was Joe DiMaggio and the best hitter was Ted Williams. It's hard to compare them. DiMaggio I think probably worked harder as an all-around ballplayer. Ted worked as a hitter. Ted could run and Ted could throw and Ted was a great fielder, but he didn't run every ball out. DiMaggio played everything to the hilt.

Ted and I are good friends. He went to the Red Sox in '38 and I went to the Red Sox in '39 and we used to date together and run around together. He's still a good friend of mine.

We had an old-timers game in '86, 40 year reunion of the old '46 team. I told Ted at that time, "If you had hit a few bad balls and hit to the opposite field and beat out a bunt now and then, you'd have hit .400 every year." He said, "Hell, if I could run like you, I'd have hit .400 every year anyway."

But Ted *could* run. We used to come north on the train and stop in little towns and play exhibition games. We used to come north with Cincinnati. We'd get out there and do our running in the outfield and I would be running as fast as I could and Ted'd be right along 'side me. And I could fly. I stole a lot of bases and if I hadn't been able to run I couldn't have played big league ball. I was the fastest guy on the team probably and Ted was running as fast as I was so he *could* do it, but he just didn't. He was all hitting.

He was five or six inches taller than you were. That must have helped him cover ground.

I was 5-10 and he was 6-4 or -5.

You know, Ted spent those two times in the service. Think what kind of records he would have put up if he hadn't.

Ted was a perfectionist. He was a Marine flyer and when he was in Florida at the training base he set a record for shooting with the airplane. He was a perfectionist at everything he did. He's a professional fisherman. He used to work for Sears and Roebuck as their fishing expert.

Who was the best pitcher you saw?

There were a lot of good pitchers. Hal Newhouser was a good pitcher. Bob Feller was probably the best when he was in his prime.

But there was a lot of guys who threw between 95 and a hundred miles per hour when I first went to the American League: Virgil Trucks and two or three guys on the Yankees. There were more fastball pitchers then than there are now.

You were involved in professional baseball for more than 50 years. What do you think is the biggest change in the game?

RP: I think attitude of the ballplayers. When I first started playing, guys were getting 85-90-100 dollars a month and they played four-and-a-half months. Players played because they loved to play baseball and they weren't worried about the money. Good money in the big leagues in those days was 12-14-16 thousand dollars. Now everything is a bonus for signing and agents and everything. The attitude of the players toward their playing careers and the money is the biggest change.

I signed a contract in 1935 and my first year [playing] was 1936. At that time, the farm system was *just* starting. I think the Dodgers and the Cardinals had farm systems and then the Red Sox were just starting theirs. My life and my playing career ran from the time the farm clubs first started up to now, when guys are making four, five million dollars a year.

Did you collect souvenirs along the way?

Yes. I have autographed balls and some autographed bats and pictures and scrapbooks—most everything. I've got a 1934 American Legion ball autographed by the players on my team and I think I've got a ball from every team I played with. As traveling secretary, I've got autographed bats from World Series and All-Stars and playoffs and everything.

If you went back, would you be a ballplayer again?

Oh, yes! I grew up in a baseball family. My father was the manager of a semi-pro team in my hometown, Charlotte, North Carolina. He played second base. I had a uniform on by the time I was two years old. On my mother's side I had an uncle who was a catcher and on my father's side I had another uncle who was a catcher and one who was an outfielder, so I grew up in baseball.

Any regrets from your career?

No. I used to say I wished that I had been in the National League instead of the American League 'cause I could have played as a regular in the National League 'cause there wasn't as many home run hitters, but after looking back I don't.

I'm making more money now than I ever made playing. I've got several pensions. I was with the Reds more than 30 years and I've got the Reds' pension, the baseball pension, baseball profit sharing, and my job that I do with the Reds, and social security.

July 17, 1949, was mentioned up there. The Tigers played the Philadelphia Athletics a doubleheader in Detroit. In the first game, against Carl Scheib, Campbell hit a grand slam to start the scoring. The final score was 8-0, Detroit.

Then in the nightcap, the teams entered the eleventh inning tied at four apiece. Catcher Aaron Robinson led off the Tigers' half of the inning with a double and Art Houtteman went in to run for him. Shortstop Johnny Lipon was walked intentionally and then pinch-hitter Eddie Lake beat out an infield single to load the bases for Campbell. Paul singled to right off Bobby Shantz to score Houtteman and give Detroit the win, 5-4.

For the day, Campbell had six hits (three in each game), including the home run in game one and two doubles in game two. It was a pretty good day.

PAUL MCLAUGHLIN CAMPBELL

Born September 1, 1917, Paw Creek, NC   Deceased
Ht. 5'10"   Wt. 185   Batted and Threw Left

Year	Team, Lg	G	AB	R	H	2B	3B	HR	RBI	BA
1941	Boston, AL	1	0	0	0	0	0	0	0	—
1942		26	15	4	1	0	0	0	0	.067
1943-1945	Military service									
1946		28	26	3	3	1	0	0	0	.115
1948	Detroit, AL	59	83	15	22	1	1	1	11	.265
1949		87	255	38	71	15	4	3	30	.278
1950		3	1	1	0	0	0	0	0	.000
6 years		204	380	61	97	17	5	4	41	.255

World Series

Year	Team, Lg	G	AB	R	H	2B	3B	HR	RBI	BA
1946	Boston, AL	1	0	0	0	0	0	0	0	—

BILLY HITCHCOCK

Mr. President (1942–1953)

They're called "role players" today, the guys who fill in at various positions when a starter needs a rest or is injured. That's a new term, however; years ago they were "utility players" and as far as most old-timers are concerned, they still are.

There have been some good utility players in recent years: Tony Phillips, Mariano Duncan, Rex Hudler, Tom Brookens. Back in the '50s, though, there were some *great* utility men: Billy Goodman, Rocky Bridges, Sibby Sisti, Jim Gilliam, and so on. Nearly every team had one man who could do a good job at three or four positions.

Perhaps the quintessential utility infielder of the late 1940s and early 1950s was Billy Hitchcock. Billy could do a major league job at any infield position; in fact, he could do the jobs so well that, at one time or another, he was a regular shortstop (1942, Tigers), second baseman (1950, A's), and third baseman 1952, A's). And in 1949, he was the number two first baseman for the Red Sox, a team that lost the pennant by only one game.

Versatility on the field was just the beginning of Billy's talents. His versatility continued long after his playing days ended; he was never an umpire or a hot dog vender, but he did everything else. He was a coach for many years, he scouted for many years, and he was a highly successful major league manager (.512 winning percentage). His greatest contribution, though, probably came as an executive; for ten years (1971–1980) he was the president of the Southern League. This was a decade that saw great growth in the popularity of baseball throughout the South and the Southern League turning from a borderline circuit to one of health and prosperity.

Billy retired in 1980 and says he owes a lot to baseball. Maybe so, but baseball also owes a lot to him.

❖ ❖ ❖

You were a top college football player.

Yes, I played football at Auburn in 1935, '36, and '7.

Was there any consideration of professional football?

Well, I had a conversation with Mr. Bell with the Philadelphia Eagles at that time, but that's all it was — just conversation — because I had made up my mind that I was gonna play professional baseball and scouts had contacted me. Soon as I finished Auburn I signed with the Yankees.

Your brother was an All-American football player.

Jimmy was Auburn's first All-American in 1932, and of course, he had an opportunity to play pro football, but he also turned it down because he was involved in baseball and he'd also signed with the Yankees in 1933 when he finished Auburn.

He eventually played for the Boston Braves.

Yeah, he was in the Yankee organization, let's see, from 1933 and in 1936 and 1937 he played at Oakland in the [Pacific] Coast League, still in the Yankee organization, and then at Chattanooga in 1938 and '39. At the end of the '38 season the old Boston club called him up for a look. He played just a very few games and they turned him back to Chattanooga and he played there again in '39.

He played in 1940 at Columbus [Ohio] in the American Association and I was at Kansas City, so we played against each other that year. As you know, he would come back during the off-season and was backfield coach at Auburn. He was my backfield coach. And he was made baseball coach and also football coach at Auburn 'til he went in the Navy.

Was he rougher on you than he was on the other football players?

I think he was probably a little more demandin', yes.

When the Yankees signed you, you started at the top of the chain.

Well, I was very fortunate. I went to spring training with Kansas City. That was Double-A, which was tops at that time; now it's Triple-A, of course. We had a bunch of young fellas down there: Phil Rizzuto and Gerry Priddy. Of course, I was a first-year man. They had played two or three years in the lower minors. I was just fortunate enough to have a good spring and fit in.

Jack Saltzgaver, the old Yankee infielder, was the third baseman. 'Course, Jack had a few years on him and he couldn't play every day. Johnny Sturm was the first baseman. Johnny'd been around a little bit. Billy Meyer, the manager, said, "I'll just take you along as my fifth infielder." I had an opportunity to play third base some that year and a couple of games at

Billy Hitchcock, 1947.

shortstop when Rizzuto was out. Things worked out for me real well that first year and I stayed there three years.

You were in the lineup 75 percent of the time that first year.

Yeah, I was. I had an opportunity to play and got off to a good start, had a good spring training, and things went well for me. I was very fortunate.

You played everywhere in the infield over the years. What was your best position?

Yeah, all four infield positions. I would say third base was probably my best position defensively.

First base was really the easiest position to play. 'Course, I had never played any first base until late in my career but I enjoyed playing first base. It was a lot of fun over there; you were in on everything, you know, and I really enjoyed it.

How did the Tigers acquire you?

They bought me from the Yankees at the end of the 1941 season. At that time, the Yankees had two Triple-A clubs; they had Newark and Kansas City and had a lot of fine young ballplayers. Prior to that, the Yankees would have a young player and they would control him for five or six years with the option rule. Couldn't do it these days, but they did then. Finally they began to sort of break that club up and sell some of their young players. They sold me at the end of the '41 season to the Tigers.

You were essentially the Tigers' regular shortstop in '42.

I played 85 games at shortstop in 1942 and then I left in August, about August the 13th, to go into service.

Draft or enlist?

I had a commission from Auburn, ROTC commission in field artillery. I had had a physical in 1941, before Pearl Harbor. I had some knee trouble and had a knee operation and I had a little trouble with it playing ball, so they put me on the inactive list at that time.

Then after Pearl Harbor, of course, things were different. In August of 1942 I didn't get a telegram to go have a physical taken; I got a telegram to report for duty. The Air Corps at this time was a new branch of service and what they did, they transferred a lot of officers— reserve officers— from one branch of the service or another to the Air Corps. So I was transferred from the field artillery.

You were decorated in the war.

[laughs] I was in a place where no action was goin' on. I was a Special Service officer and at that time they gave some honors for doin' the job and so forth. I was Special Service officer for the Air Force overseas, in the Pacific Ocean area, which was a big outfit, you know, and I was fortunate enough to be honored with that.

Did you play ball in the service?

Yeah. This was it. We had a situation in Honolulu where we had three

Air Force teams over there. And a lot of fellas had been transferred over-
seas to Honolulu. We moved 'em around from Hickham Field to Bellows
Field to Wheeler Field and had three teams, mostly major league players.
We had about 42 players and 38 of 'em were major league players.

The Navy had a wonderful team over there, and they tore the Air
Force up in 1943, so the general over there said, "We need some of these
boys from the Air Force over here on our team." The idea was to provide
entertainment for the service personnel. The islands were just full of service people, you know. We played on the base and played down at Honolulu Stadium. That was a great entertainment for the service personnel.
All the fellas were big baseball fans.

We got a telegram one day from Guam, the commanding general
down there saying that the 42 ballplayers should proceed to the forward
areas to provide entertainment for those fellas down there that are making these flights over Japan and doin' the real fightin'.

So that's exactly what happened. I loaded up 42 ballplayers on a boat
one day and a third of 'em went to Saipan and two-thirds of 'em went to
Tinian. The engineers got busy and ballplayers helped build two diamonds
on Tinian and one diamond on Saipan and we played baseball.

Opening day at Tinian, they made the stands out of bomb crates.
They put one bomb crate for the first row and then stacked 'em right up
and built bleachers. I have pictures that show the opening day crowd there
at Tinian. They'd just bring in the Army trucks and jeeps and so forth and
park 'em around the outfield grass beyond the little fence they built. The
soldiers would pack all on those trucks and then the heavy equipment they
had to use — cranes and so forth — I have pictures of fellas on those cranes,
five or six of 'em just all the way up in the air watchin' the ballgame. It
was 12,000 there for that opening, just scattered everywhere, all over the
field. Didn't have much foul line because they were sittin' there in foul ter-
ritory.

It was just a great event. It gave them some relief from their hard
work, you know. There were a lot of flights over Japan — bombing — and
they'd come back and need a little entertainment.

I'll never forget Enos Slaughter. You know, Slaughter had the reputation of being a hustling ballplayer; well, listen, he played just that way on
those islands and those *hard* coral infields he'd slide in and come up with
strawberries. He played hard and the kids, they appreciated that. They
enjoyed it.

'Course, things were pretty much over at Iwo Jima but the Seabees
cut a field in the side of a hill up there, it looked like, and built stands. We
went up there and played a week. The last day we played an American

League-National League All-Star game. When we played in the afternoon they counted the number of troops there — about 12,000, at least. And that night, Bob Hope was there for a USO show and he had 15,000 people, so that's the kind of entertainment that went on.

Some of my buddies are always teasin' me about that war that I fought, you know — playin' baseball. *[laughs]* But I realize that this was somethin' that was necessary for these troops and, as you know, the USO did such a great job. Out of our office, we had a Special Service officer and they had all sorts of entertainment. We had tennis players — Don Budge and Bobby Riggs and several others — and we put on tennis exhibitions. The kids, they'd miss it. They had seen these things back at home and they missed it and it gave 'em somethin' to do on those islands. It was tough.

Morale is every bit as important as fighting, maybe more so.

Well, it surely is. You've got to have that fella in a proper mental condition to fight a war if he's gonna do a job for you. That goes for anything, you know; your mental condition is so important in anything you might do.

You eventually got out of the service, came back to Detroit and then played for several teams. It seems the older you got, the better hitter you were.

[laughs] I like to think that. I guess I matured a little bit. At one time I *worried* so much about it. It seemed like if I didn't get a hit every time I worried. Well, that meant there was a lot of worryin' 'cause I didn't get a hit every time.

I had the good fortune of playin' with some fine, mature ballplayers — experienced ballplayers — and I guess if I had to pick one — a lot of 'em helped me, they did — but I favor Wally Moses. Wally's the old Chicago outfielder from down in South Georgia, a fine fella and a real great ballplayer, a good hitter and a good runner. And he had a great idea about hittin'. He used to talk to me and he said, "Listen, you're not gonna get a hit every time you walk up there. Just try to adopt a philosophy of when you go to that plate, you're gonna give it your best shot." And he said, "If that pitcher gets you out that time, well I'll be back again. I'll get him next time." And that was sort of a philosophical approach to hittin', you know.

Then, of course, I weighed 180 pounds but I wasn't a big, strong guy and I had a right field stroke and Wally used to tell me, "Don't try to pull the ball. Try to hit the ball right back through the box and get the bat on the ball." So, when I became a right field hitter I think I became a little better hitter. He helped me a great deal.

Of course, I had those two years with Ted Williams, watchin' him and listenin' to him, and he was a great teacher, not only a great hitter. He *made* himself a great hitter but he was a good teacher, too. He had great theories about hittin'. He could carry out those theories; not many people could do it like he could.

He was the best hitter I've ever seen. I want to say this: I spent all my time in the American League so I didn't see, day-in and day-out, fellas like Stan Musial. As far as a player, all-around player, I think I'd have to say Joe DiMaggio.

But Williams was a great hitter. He worked at it. I was not playin' regular [with Boston] and I had a pretty good arm and could throw good battin' practice, so if Ted went a couple-three days without really hittin' the ball good he'd get at that ballpark early — nine or ten o'clock in the morning — and I'd go out and throw battin' practice to him. He'd hit and hit and hit to get his stroke and his timin' back. And the wonderful thing about him, he'd hit for 30 or 40 minutes and when he got through, he'd say, "Get your bat." He'd wanna throw to the fella that pitched battin' practice to him, too. He was just a nice fella.

I interviewed someone who told me when he came to Boston he'd be bored and go to the ballpark maybe four or five hours before a game and Williams would be out there taking batting practice then.

The clubhouse boy, Vince Orlando, used to throw battin' practice to Williams. And Mr. Yawkey, in his younger days, would come out and work out with Ted some. But Vince Orlando was Ted's number one battin' practice pitcher. And the fellas who weren't playin' would come out there and a lot of times with him and throw to him.

Who was the best pitcher?

Well, there was a *lot* of good ones in those times. I'd have to say Feller was the best pitcher. I didn't see Bob Feller before the service and all the fellas that *did* hit against him before the War said he lost a *little* bit off his fastball after he came back. Thank goodness. He had such a good curveball and he developed a slider there in '46 when he struck out, what?, 348-350 hitters. He had a good slider and you just couldn't sit on Feller's fastball. 'Course, he was just wild enough to be effective and he had that big, high kick that hid the ball from you, so I'd say Feller had to be the best pitcher.

But I saw fellas like Allie Reynolds, Hal Newhouser, Vic Raschi — fellas like that were good pitchers, too. Like Eddie Lopat — we worked together at Montreal — he was a good pitcher because he had control of all his pitches, you know, and he was sneaky fast and he'd throw you a lot of sloppy stuff— slow curves, turn the ball over — and then — zip!— he'd throw the fastball by you. He was a tough pitcher.

Bob Lemon — awful tough. Early Wynn — he was a mean rascal on that mound. He'd knock you down if you dug in on him, but Early was a good pitcher. He was a high ball pitcher. He'd get away with high sliders but he was tough, won over 300 games. Bob Lemon — sinker, curve — good pitcher. 'Course, they had a good pitching staff over there [in Cleveland]; Lemon and Feller and Garcia and later on Hal Newhouser came in from Detroit and joined 'em.

Those were some of the pitchers that were tough, but I say all of 'em were tough for me. I tell you a fella who was tough on me was Sid Hudson. Sid was a big, tall, slender righthander, sort of a three-quarter guy, had a good sinkin' fastball and he'd just take the bat right out of my hands. *[laughs]* He was a fine pitcher. Good hitter, too. Good fielder. And a fine fella, too.

Is there one game that stands out?

This game was late in my career. In fact, the most thrilling moment I've seen in baseball, I think, was the first night that I became manager of the Atlanta Braves. We were in Atlanta playin' the Dodgers and I was named manager that morning. 'Course, who do we face that night but Sandy Koufax. Denver Lemaster was our pitcher that night, so these two lefthanders hooked up in a real deal.

Just a little background on this thing. Felipe Alou was our first baseman; he'd been playin' some center field but he was our first baseman and had been hittin' third, fourth, and fifth. Felipe *liked* to lead off. He was a strong hitter and a home run hitter; he'd hit 25-30 home runs [a year].

And I'm goin' back a little bit now, just sort of history. Hank Bauer was one of my coaches at Baltimore in 1963 and I asked him, "Hank, why in the world did Casey Stengel lead you off? Here you are, a home run hitter hittin' 20-25 home runs, and he's got you leadin' off."

He said, "The old man used to make me so mad 'cause I didn't like to lead off. I liked to bat down there where I could knock some runs in." He said Stengel would tell him, "Listen, Bauer, you're the first man hittin'. In the bottom of the first innin' we might be ahead 1-to-nothin'." And Hank said, "You know, it's a strange thing. I hit a lot of home runs leadin' off."

So in talkin' to Felipe that night, I said, "Felipe, you're gonna be the leadoff man." And I told him that little story.

The other thing I did, Eddie Mathews was sort of over-the-hill, so to speak, but he had a lot of good baseball left in him. I'd go out early and pitch to the pitchers and Eddie would hit and I felt like Eddie would still play. He'd been in and out of the lineup so I told him, "Eddie, you're the third baseman now the rest of the season, against lefthanders and against righthanders. If you get a little tired, we'll get you out of there for a couple-three days, but you're gonna play third base." And he looked at me like I was crazy and said, "You know who's pitchin' tonight, don't you?"

Well, to make a long story short, there were 52,000 in the stands that night. It was a rainy night. We had two or three rain delays; the game finally ended about 1:00 in the morning. Felipe Alou leads off the ballgame with a home run, so it's 1-to-nothin'. And it's 1-to-nothin' up through the eighth innin' and Jim Lefebvre hit a home run off of Lemaster to tie it up, 1-to-1.

So we go in the bottom of the ninth, two men out, and Eddie Mathews is the hitter. He told me this story later: "I was walkin' to the plate lookin' over my shoulder, thinkin' you're gonna use a hitter for me." On the second pitch he got a *long* drive down the right field line; it was about four or five feet foul and we thought the ballgame was over. The whole dugout rushed out to see whether it was fair or foul. And 'bout two pitches later he hit another drive into right field but this one was fair. It was a home run and we won the ballgame, 2-to-1.

I don't think any of the 52,000 that were there that night had left. They all stayed. It was a pitchers' battle — just great pitching by Koufax *and* Lemaster and all the runs were scored on home runs. Well, the dugout erupted and met Eddie at home plate and just picked him up and took him to the dugout. Just real excitement! And in the clubhouse, it was just bedlam!

Eddie said, "I've been in World Series and winnin' World Series games, but I've never had this much excitement in all my life!"

Well, to me, it was just one of those nights. When people ask me about one game, this one always comes to mind. It was one of the greatest ballgames I've ever seen and to have it end like it did. Lemaster went all the way and won it, 2-to-1.

Mathews was winding down then, but he was still a solid player.

He was a great player. Hank [Aaron] was a great hitter; he was really behind Mathews. Eddie was captain, you know, and that's the way it should have been. He was a great leader on that field; he played *hard* all the time.

He didn't get a good shot as a manager.

I don't think so. I think probably his personal habits got him in a little trouble there and he didn't gee-haw very much with [Paul] Richards. Richards finally got rid of [Joe] Torre, too.

And Eddie went on to Houston and played a little bit out there and then ended up in Detroit and did some designated hittin'. He was a good player. I always felt strongly that Eddie Mathews should have finished out his career in a Braves' uniform. I was very much opposed to the trade to Houston. We got Bob Bruce, a big righthanded pitcher, for him. Richards wanted to trade him. I told Paul, I said, "Paul, he can play some first base and pinch hit." We had [Clete] Boyer at third base. He said, "Listen, he'll be in that dugout. He'll drive you crazy." I said, "I'll take a chance on it." But Richards was the boss and he traded him.

Richards did a lot of good, but there were some iffy things along the way.

I always felt that he was good at takin' old pitchers—you know, retreads—and teachin' 'em that slip pitch and makin' 'em good pitchers for a couple-three years. Bad on the arm — a lot of bad arms.

He got a lot out of some of the young guys, too — guys like Chuck Estrada — but they didn't seem to last.

Estrada ended up with a bad arm and [Steve] Barber always had a bad arm, bur he was a good pitcher. Jack Fisher, it didn't bother him, and, 'course, [Milt] Pappas never did it. He had a good slider and consequently he stayed strong.

You were a very successful manager. When you took over the Braves in 1966, no one could beat you.

[*laughs*] We finished up the season real good. We had a good ballclub — clutch hittin' and our pitchin' was pretty good and the fellas had a new lease on life, relaxin' a little bit, and they played good at the end of the season.

You talk about that streak—19 out of 21, I think; that came in 1966 at the end of the season. I think we were 33-and-18 or somethin' like that in the last 50 games, so we ended up the season real good. Things didn't work out in '67 as we hoped it would.

What about your time managing in Baltimore?

That was a tempestuous time there and I inherited some good young pitchers, but most of 'em had some sort of arm trouble.

[Ron] Hansen had been an outstanding shortstop but he was spending some time in the service so we didn't have full time from him. We had Jerry Adair, who was normally a second baseman, at shortstop and, of course, Steve Barber spent a lot of time in the service. We'd get him on the weekends and he wasn't in shape. Estrada came up with a bad arm. I'm not makin' excuses; I'm just tellin' you the way it was.

But we had a good ballclub. [Jim] Gentile had had a great year the year before [46 HR, 141 RBI] and Jim had an off year. Things just didn't work out like we thought they would.

One of the men who played for you said you were too nice a guy to be the manager.

[laughs] Well, I don't know 'bout that. I tried to treat ballplayers like I wanted to be treated. You know, [Leo] Durocher always said, "Nice guys finish last," and I certainly don't believe in that. I think a fella just has to be himself. I guess I could have been a little more of a disciplinarian than I was, but I just felt like a ballplayer was a professional, that he knew what he was supposed to do and I expected him to do it.

You were president of the Southern League for ten years.

This was a very, very enjoyable job. I enjoyed goin' to the ballgames and watchin' these young fellas. You know, they were young, a lot of 'em right out of college, played one or two years of pro ball. They were in the developmental stage and I liked to watch 'em improve. I'd see a young fella at the beginnin' of the season — he was really strugglin', havin' a tough time — and see him two or three months later and he's hittin' the ball good and doin' everythin' — just really maturin'. I really enjoyed it. My office was right here in Opelika so I could work out of here and I was close to Montgomery and to Columbus so I could visit those places and see everybody — the umpires, the managers, and the players.

How did you get the position?

Sam Smith had been president of the Southern League for quite a few years. I had known Sam and he was livin' in Knoxville at this time. 'Course, I had been with Montreal in 1970 and then I decided to come home. I was workin' here with a company.

I had some friends around the league, particularly in Montgomery, and after Sam died his wife took over the league for the rest of the year and they asked me if I would be interested and I said I sure would. I had a trip planned, the wife and I, to Scandinavia and I told them I couldn't do anything 'til after that trip. They had the meeting while I was on this trip and elected me president, so I took over the league later in 1971.

It was ten years and I really enjoyed it. It was great fun, we had a good league, we picked up in attendance; we drew around a million, 800,000 there one year. Always had an All-Star game with the Braves, which turned out real well for us. Sent a lot of young players to the major leagues and I

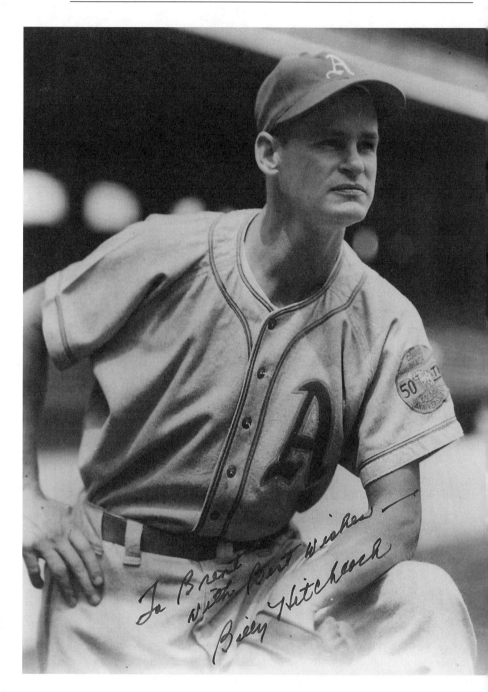

Billy Hitchcock, 1951.

checked those box scores every day to see if a kid that came through the Southern League was still there.

It was a good job and I thoroughly enjoyed it.

It has been said that the league wouldn't have lasted without you.

Well, I'm sure it would have, but Nashville and Memphis comin' into the league *really* helped us 'cause those were two good baseball towns. They drew well. 'Course, Nashville built a new ballpark. Larry Schmittou did a great job up there. Memphis had the old ballpark, but they did a good job in promotin'.

Birmingham was still in the league, but they were not drawin' anybody and finally I moved that franchise to Chattanooga and in Chattanooga they just went in that old Ames Stadium and really cleaned it out. It was a mess. I remember goin' in there and it was in just such terrible, terrible shape and they must have hauled a hundred truckloads of garbage and stuff out of that stadium. They repainted it and fixed the field and just did a *great* job on it.

All around the league they refurbished the ballparks and had some good young general managers that really got out and hustled. We tried to make it *family* baseball, you know; encouraged the families to come to the game and I think it went real well. It was fun.

We'll have a South Atlantic League team here in Lexington starting in 2001. I'm really looking forward to it but this is first a basketball area and football is second. For baseball to be a success it will have to be done correctly. The closest baseball is Cincinnati and Louisville, but one and a half or two hours each way takes a little edge off the enjoyment.

It does. We had that situation with Columbus, Georgia. It's so close to Atlanta.

At Columbus they had a young fella named John Dietrich that's been in baseball for many years. He worked for Bobby Bragan when Bobby was president of the Texas League. John Dietrich just brought Columbus alive, doin' all sorts of promotin'. A lot of people from Opelika go to Columbus to see the Redstixx play. One reason is it's tough to get Brave tickets 'cause they're sold out.

They were the Mudcats and the Mudcats moved to North Carolina. Now they're called the Redstixx. It came in all this controversy about the chop, you know, and Redstixx was an Indian through this part of the country.

On our radio, they give the Columbus Redstixx score every morning, so this is the kind of thing you have to do to promote. And he really works on family baseball — somethin' goin' on all the time, somethin' for the family.

When you weren't playing, coaching, managing, or presiding, you were scouting. You did a little bit of everything.

Yeah, I think I've done everythin'. In fact, at Vancouver in 1961 I used to help 'em get the field in shape. *[laughs]* I worked on the ground crew, too.

Baseball has been real good to me. I thoroughly enjoyed it. I spent 41 years in professional baseball and it was good to me and I like to think that I put somethin' back in the game. I used to be active with the Dixie Youth and Little Leagues around here, but I'm sorta past that stage now. They look at me and someone says, "This is Billy Hitchcock," and they say, "Billy who?" *[laughs]*

But I really enjoyed it. It was good to me; it's a wonderful game.

Do you still receive fan mail?

Oh, gosh. The only thing that hurts my feelin's, though, I used to get letters from kids that say, "My *father* used to see you play ball"; now I'm gettin' 'em and they say, "My *grand*father used to see you play ball." That hurts my feelins. *[laughs]*

The next step may not be too far away.

I don't know if I'll make that one or not.

What do you think of the salaries today?

We can't be envious of the guys that are makin' the good salary just because we didn't make the good salary. I wish 'em luck. I really think it's a little bit out of proportion, but still I don't blame the ballplayer if he can get it. More power to him.

If a man hands you several million dollars, you have to take it.

That's exactly right.

How do you feel about autograph requests?

I really feel strongly on this. In fact, I think they put out a little questionnaire on this thing about chargin' five dollars for an autograph and I'm *very, very* much opposed to it. It's unfortunate.

This is a game and in these autograph sessions sometimes the fellas don't do a good job. I was at Columbus a few years ago and [a current star] was over there and they had a couple of us old-timers there. Shotgun

Shuba and I were there. We sat up front and a kid would come by and they'd look at us like "Who are you?" They'd want an autograph and have a picture taken. We had a good time; we just carried on with 'em.

Then the kid would go on back and [the current star] was back there. They'd come back and tell us, particularly the parents, "This guy's terrible!" He's sittin' back there with a radio on goin' full blast, has his kinfolks sittin' there and visitin' with him. The kids would come up, he wouldn't shake hands with 'em, he'd just sign an autograph and never look up at 'em, never smile, wouldn't have a picture taken with 'em. He was there about two hours and I guess they had to pay him about $5,000. Now this, to me, is lousy. It's bad for baseball. It really just shouldn't be.

Do you have any regrets from 41 years in baseball?

I just would have liked to have performed better, that's all I can say, I think. I enjoyed it and I don't know that I'd make too many changes. As I say, I wish I could have performed better than I did, but I'm thankful for the time I had there and for my experiences and particularly for the people that I met in baseball.

In fact, one summer Boo Ferriss of the Red Sox and his wife and my wife took a trip out to Yellowstone Park, Mount Rushmore, and Jackson Hole, and just had a great trip. This was the third trip we've taken with the Ferrisses. We went to Guam several years ago and then we went to Alaska and now this trip. What I'm sayin', the friendships that you create in baseball are so great.

Those are the good things that come out of baseball and it's certainly been good to me. I appreciate it.

Would you go back and do it all again?

Ooh, yeah, 'cause look at the money I'd make! *[laughs]*

Goodness, yes. What would a .300-hitting infielder be worth today?

Good night alive! That one year I hit .306, I'd have demanded two million the next year. *[laughs]*

Oh, yeah, I'd go through it again and it's a different ballgame now, I'll tell you. It's a *different* ballgame than it was when we came along. But it's still exciting. You still have to run and still have to catch the ball and throw the ball and hit the ball and pitch the ball. Basically, you know, you do the same thing—the old bunt play is there, the old hit-and-run, hittin' the cutoff man. The basics are still there.

There are fewer boys who know how to execute the basics now.

I think our major leagues are so diluted. We've got so many teams now. There's just not that many ballplayers. When you had 16 teams, 25 men — that's 400 players. Now you have 30 teams, 25 men — that's 750 players. When you stretch 400 into 750, you're *bound* to lose a little performance there, aren't you?

It has to be.

It's diluted, but I'm glad to see fellas have an opportunity to play. Watchin' the Cardinals — you know, Rex Hudler bounced around for a long time, but he's from the old school. He played hard, he hustled, and he did everything he could to help a team. There's a fella that had an opportunity to play major league baseball that, it we didn't have expansion, he wouldn't be there.

Our college baseball has become so much better and the reason for that, we're gettin' a lot of ex-professionals coaching in college now. They're supposed to know the basics anyway.

We spoke of Billy batting .306 one year. In 1951 with the Philadelphia Athletics, he divided his time between third and second and had his best season offensively. His .306 average was second on the team to Ferris Fain's league-leading .344 and — pay attention, this is impressive — *eighth* best in the major leagues among *all* infielders who had more than 200 plate appearances. There were *80* — count 'em: 80 — major league infielders that season who had 200 or more trips to the plate. Here are the Top 10 in batting average.

Ferris Fain, A's	.344
Jackie Robinson, Dodgers	.338
*Minnie Minoso, Indians/White Sox	.326
George Kell, Tigers	.319
Nellie Fox, White Sox	.3129
Johnny Pesky, Red Sox	.3125
Phil Cavaretta, Cubs	.311
Billy Hitchcock, A's	.3063
Gil McDougald, Yankees	.3060
Bobby Avila, Indians	.304

*Minoso, normally an outfielder, played more than half of his games in the infield in 1951.

Lest you think there were a bunch of dogs manning the infields around the country in 1951, here are some of the men Billy out-hit that year: Johnny Mize, Lou Boudreau, Luke Easter, Al Rosen, Ray Boone, Bobby Doerr, Vern Stephens, Billy Goodman, Mickey Vernon, Pete Runnels, Bob Dillinger, Bobby Thomson (see the note on Minoso), Gil Hodges, Red Schoendienst, Bob Elliott, Granny Hamner, Ted Kluszewski, and Al Dark. It was a good year.

WILLIAM CLYDE HITCHCOCK

Born July 31, 1916, Inverness, AL
Ht. 6'1½"   Wt. 185   Batted and Threw Right

Year	Team, Lg	G	AB	R	H	2B	3B	HR	RBI	BA
1942	Detroit, AL	85	280	27	59	8	1	0	29	.211
1943–45	Military service									
1946	Det-Was. AL	101	357	27	75	8	3	0	25	.210
1947	St. L., AL	80	275	25	61	2	2	1	28	.222
1948	Boston, AL	49	124	15	37	3	2	1	20	.298
1949		55	147	22	30	6	1	0	9	.204
1950	Phi., AL	115	399	35	109	22	5	1	54	.273
1951		77	222	27	68	10	4	1	36	.306
1952		119	407	45	100	8	4	1	56	.246
1953	Detroit, AL	22	38	8	8	0	0	0	0	.211
9 years		703	2249	231	547	67	22	5	257	.243

JOHNNY LIPON

Builder of Ballplayers (1942–1954)

(The following interview with the late Johnny Lipon was done in 1992. Some of the information may appear to be dated today.)

We see it several times every year: a manager is fired because his team is not winning. It' s a precarious job, yet some men make it last.

Sparky Anderson and Tom LaSorda managed what seemed like forever. The all-time long-term managerial record, however, belongs to Connie Mack; he lasted 53 years as the leader of the Philadelphia Athletics, aided immeasurably by the fact he owned the ballclub.

But the dean of today's baseball managers, although no threat to Mack's record, is Johnny Lipon, now in his 31st year as a skipper. And all but one have been as a minor league manager.

He's doing his job now for the Lakeland Tigers of the Florida State League and he must be doing it pretty well. He's doing it where winning is not stressed. Winning is nice, of course, and John's teams have done it over the years. In his 29 minor league seasons through 1991, his record was 2,106–1,909 (.525).

But winning is not what it's all about in the minor leagues. The bottom line there is Player Development. That means teaching the young players to play the game, helping them to refine their skills, building their confidence, listening to their problems, encouraging them — doing all the things that go into making a ballplayer who can win at the major league level so the manager of the big club can try to keep *his* job.

And evidently Johnny Lipon is doing that. He wouldn't be in his 30th year as a minor league manager if he weren't.

Your 2,106 wins as a minor league manager are way up on the list.

To me, in a sense, that's not important. Records were set to be broken but I have no chance to break Stan Wasiak's record; he's got almost 2500 and that would take me another five years and I don't plan on managing that long. This, conceivably, could my last season. I'll be 70, although I'd like to manage as long as I feel able to and right now I'm still in pretty good condition. My weight is similar to my playing weight and I jog 30 minutes a day, play golf, and do a little walking, but when you get to this age you never know. I'm losing some friends that are younger than me.

Who are some of the boys you've managed?

There's been a lot of 'em. Right now there's two active managers. I had Sparky Anderson in '61; Chuck Tanner was also on that ballclub in Toronto. And I had Lou Piniella from three years in the minors.

I had Bobby Bonilla at Alexandria, Virginia, when I was with Pittsburgh. Bobby was a special kind of kid. He had the good natural talent but he always had a smile on his face and just *loved* to play. He worked hard at it. I never thought he was gonna be the highest-paid player in baseball, but he made it. He's a good player.

You had a long major league career, then went down. How long did you play in the minors after you left the majors?

In '54, right about cut-down time, I was traded to Cincinnati [by the Chicago White Sox, who had acquired him from the St. Louis Browns after the 1953 season]. They had a good ballclub over there. They had Johnny Temple at second, [Roy] McMillan was at shortstop, and they had Rocky Bridges as the spare infielder and when I came over there, there just wasn't any room, and I'd had some back trouble that had slowed me down.

I was still comparatively young. I had a chance to get my free agency from Cincinnati, but the late Bobby Madera and Gabe Paul had talked me into going to Havana, Cuba, to finish the season and sign a two-year contract. They would get me a job managing in winter ball, which is what I really wanted to do. I wanted to get started on my managing career.

And it worked out okay. I played the year-and-a-half in Havana, managed a year in Mexico and enjoyed it and was successful. After I got through with my minor league [playing] career, which was '58, I went into managing on a full-time basis.

In 1959 I went to Selma, Alabama, in the Cleveland organization and I've managed ever since, with the exception of four years when I went to the major leagues under Alvin Dark at Cleveland, where I was a coach. With the exception of that, I've managed every year, which is 30 years now.

I had a short time as [major league] manager in 1971, when we had a lot of problems in Cleveland — Alvin Dark was the manager and also the acting general manager — and the year was a disaster. They let him go about July 30 and I finished the season.

I probably had the worst record managing in baseball because all I did when I took over was say, "Let's go out and have some fun, fellas!" on the baseball field, 'cause it was not a situation where you could completely turn it around. We had a bunch of injuries and other things.

That was 20 years ago and Cleveland still hasn't turned it around.

They've had some good players come through there, too. I don't know what it's gonna take, but they're gonna win one of these years. They won back in '46, '47, '48; '48 was when they won it all. And then in '54 they had that big year. They had the great pitching staff and that's what it takes in baseball.

You began your playing career in 1941 with Muskegon of the Michigan State League and had a phenomenal year [*35 HR, *115 RBI, .359 BA, *.645 SA, *126 runs] [Hereafter, asterisks will be used within interviews to denote league-leading totals.]

I was 18 years old. I had good stats there and I was very confident.

One thing that happens when a player enters pro ball and has a big year like that, his confidence builds. You'll find that happens with other players; as soon as a player has a big year, I don't care whether it's Class D, he gets so much confidence knowing that he can hit. In fact, I wrote the Detroit Tigers that I thought I could help right then. *[laughs]*

You get that ego thing and that's just so important in a baseball player's career because every sport has a tendency to try to break you down. We get high school stars, college stars and the first year they might have trouble because they're playing against other high school stars and college stars. If you don't have the right temperament and are not successful the first year, oftentimes you are not able to bounce back for some reason.

The mental part of our business is so important.

You were with the Tigers by the end of the next season.

I had a good year at Beaumont [in 1942]. The Texas League was a tough league. At that time they used to send more players to the big leagues than the Triple-A clubs did. The Triple-A clubs were all privately owned.

The Texas League and the Southern Association had working agreements with the major league clubs so they used to send all their young players to these leagues. For instance, we had Dick Wakefield on our club, Hoot Evers; those fellows and the guys that went through there, like Hank Greenberg, never went to Triple-A. Pat Mullin, Bar-

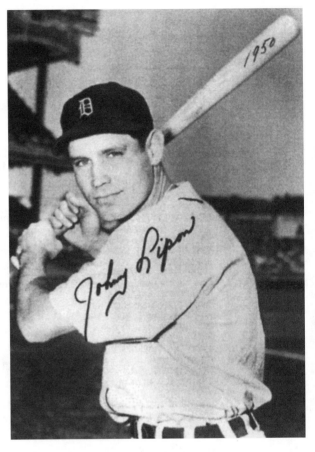

Johnny Lipon (courtesy John Lipon).

ney McCosky—those guys all went right from Beaumont to the major leagues. That was their top farm club.

Triple-A was good baseball but they had older players playing. They'd been in the minor leagues maybe ten years, maybe couldn't run fast or do something where they had an opportunity to make a major league team. Some of 'em, of course, had been in the majors for a few years. Triple-A was tough, but the Double-A clubs were the ones with the better young prospects in those days.

You entered the Navy in 1942.

I enlisted. I would've been drafted. I was 19 years old. Pearl Harbor was in December of '41 and I got through with '42 and I enlisted shortly after the season was over. I tried to get in the Air Force as a pilot but there were so many candidates ahead of me that were college graduates. Later I ended up in the Air Force as a flight engineer.

I played very little baseball [in the service] and that's where I came up with problems. When I came out I had a sore arm and sore back. I never really was as good a player when I came back out.

Your back kept you from playing full seasons.

I had a couple of years when I had legitimate injuries, like in 1950. I had 17 stitches in a spike wound and a couple of other times I dove for baseballs and got injuries. But you're right; there was a period there when I got these nagging injuries probably caused by back problems.

I didn't have as much power when I came back out [of the service]. I was a contact hitter; I struck out very seldom. [John's most strikeouts in a major league season was 27; in nearly 700 plate appearances in 1950 he fanned only 26 times.] Most of my time in the big leagues I was a leadoff hitter, so I used to take two strikes unless somebody was in scoring position. They used to tell us years ago a base on balls was just as good as a basehit and that's so true.

In 1950, you teamed with Gerry Priddy to set a new record for double plays.

We had a good infield then. George Kell was a fine player at third base; of course, he's a Hall of Famer and he was a good aggressive player and a good contact hitter.

When I first went into the big leagues we had Charlie Gehringer [at second]; he was my hero. That was before I went in the service and I didn't play with him that much.

When Priddy came over in 1950, here's a guy that went through his minor league career with Phil Rizzuto. He was a fine defensive player, knew how to play his position, and helped me a lot. When you gave Gerry Priddy the ball, he got rid of it very quickly. One thing he'd tell me, "As soon as you catch the ball, just get it to me." A lot of guys, even today, wait 'til the player gets to the bag and it just takes time. As soon as you get him the ball, he's gonna be able to get rid of it that much quicker, even though he may be five-six steps away from second base. It takes an awful lot of practice. We were helped by the fact that he was an experienced player and I was, too, at that time.

In 1952, the Tigers traded you to the Boston Red Sox as part of a big trade.

We [Detroit] finished strong in '50. We probably should have won the pennant. We had one major injury: Virgil Trucks was out for a long time because he injured his arm in a train accident — stuck his elbow through the window.

Then in '51, we had a fairly strong year but kind of a disappointing season for us because we thought we were gonna win it in '50 and in '51 we didn't. Then in '52 we got off to a slow start and they traded away their ballclub, in my opinion, 'cause they traded George Kell for one and Hoot Evers and Dizzy Trout. They got some favorites of Boston, like Johnny Pesky, but Pesky was an older player and he wasn't gonna play much anymore, and Fred Hatfield, who was a pretty good major league player. And they got Walt Dropo, which was the big guy they wanted. There were two other players: Bill Wight and Don Lenhardt. George Kell was such a productive player that Boston might have got the best of that deal.

You were never the same player after that. Is this when your back really started acting up?

Yes. I ended up with back trouble in Boston. The weather in Boston is conducive to back problems. If you'll notice, some of those players come up with back problems in the Boston area. Wade Boggs is a super talent, so was [Carl] Yastrzemski, but he had some years there where he had sub-par starts because it's so cold in Boston in April and May and oftentimes you get some nagging injuries. I really admire the guys that played a long time on the Boston ballclub and never got hurt because, to me, it's a very tough place to play.

Who was the best hitter you saw?

Oh, Ted Williams, in my opinion. He's the *best* hitter I ever saw.

I saw some great players, including Willie Mays. [Joe] DiMaggio was a super talent. A guy I really liked was [Roberto] Clemente 'cause I saw him when I managed in Puerto Rico. He's one of the superstars of all time. I'll take Mays, Clemente, Williams, DiMaggio — they were so super. Those are the four guys I really felt were something special.

Who was the best pitcher?

Bob Feller threw nothing but aspirin tablets up there. *[laughs]* He was the best arm, the best velocity. Hal Newhouser had that good curve-ball and he had a better than average fastball. He came up with an excellent change.

The guy I was impressed with was the guy from the Dodgers: [Sandy] Koufax. He just threw that fastball and it used to jump. Just super stuff — for a couple years there he was unhittable. [Juan] Marichal was another;

they were special people. And we've got 'em today. You've got your [Roger] Clemens and several others.

That's the greatest thing about *every* sport, not only baseball. You're always coming up with these superstars that draw the fans, whether it's Bo Jackson or whoever.

Is there a game that stands out?

There's been so many. In '42, my first day in the big leagues, just the fact that I was playing alongside of Charlie Gehringer, who was my boyhood hero, and the fact that I got three hits that day, was a big day. But then I had seven hits in a doubleheader in New York, one a grand slam home run.

We all have certain things we remember. We're all egotists in a way, so some of best days I had were the most hits I had. You've got to be an egotist; you've got to like yourself and know that you can play.

Did you save souvenirs along the way?

Very few. I had a St. Louis Browns uniform, but when you move around somehow things get misplaced. I used to have a couple of gloves and I gave 'em away, so I have very few souvenirs. I used to have a Babe Ruth signature on a baseball I got when I was about 12 years old, but I put that in a ballgame a couple weeks later. *[laughs]*

Do you receive much fan mail?

Oh, yes. A lot from older fans. They get back in to the baseball picture, which I think is a great thing for us to have an opportunity to keep in touch with the old baseball fans. And, of course, the young people — young boys and girls— are very active in receiving the cards, so we in baseball have to, in our own little way, help the young fans.

Sometimes they'll ask questions. Normally, unless it's a special case or something, I don't usually go into detail. Every once in a while a fan asks for my most exciting moment and oftentimes I don't answer those, but I'll always autograph their photos or baseballs or whatever they send. I get a lot of those '53 reprint cards now to sign.

I'm gone from home all summer and I don't have my mail forwarded, but when I get home after the season I catch up. I sign everything and send it back.

I received a questionnaire to fill out, whether to charge or not [for autographs]. Of course, I didn't particularly care to charge because I think it's gonna hurt the future fans to charge 'em for somebody's autograph, but everybody has their own opinion.

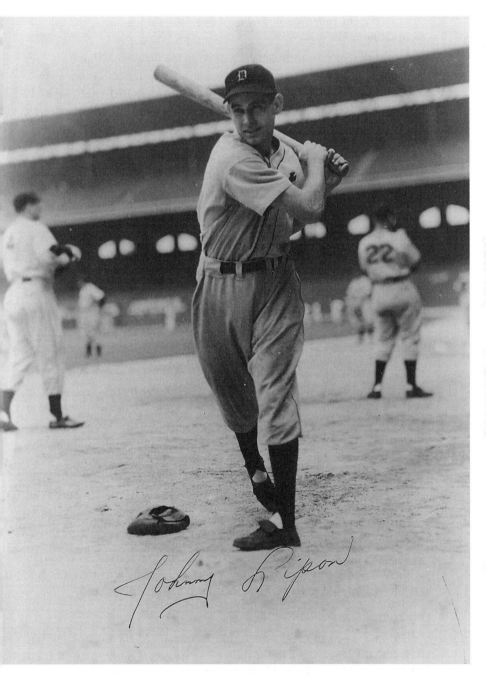

Johnny Lipon.

Some of the old-timers may need the money they can get from charging for their autographs.

I think that's up to Baseball, especially for the people that have very little major league experience. In my opinion, even the minor league guys deserve part of the pension. The minor league guys that have played 15 years and never got an opportunity to play in the major leagues and for some reason are destitute now, I think Baseball, with all their money available, should find some kind of way to help these guys out.

I was in the minor leagues after I got through with my major league career and I think in '56, '7, or '8 that the Triple-A International League wanted to start a union for minor league baseball players. Anybody that had been in the minor leagues for ten years they thought deserved some kind of a pension, but, of course, the general managers and owners of the Triple-A clubs laughed at us. *[laughs]* Tom LaSorda was one of the leaders. I can remember them laughing at us because they said, "You guys go ahead and go on strike. We'll get Double-A players up here quick." That was true; they could do that years ago.

Of course, the major league union is so strong they can't do much.

Recently the benefits to players from the '40s and '50s have been increased with money frozen in the pension fund. It seems some of this could have gone toward helping minor leaguers.

I agree. I know they helped guys in my era. I've had two raises. I feel there's gotta be some way they can help the minor leaguer that's played at least ten years. I would think five years, but if a guy's played ten years he certainly deserves some kind of pension money because of the years he put in Baseball. I don't have the answer.

I've collected my pension since I was 52 years old. That's almost 18 years ago. I'm gonna be 70 this November. At the time, I started out with about $900 a month pension; it's about $2,000 now. With the Social Security, if I wanted to take it, it would be an amount you could live on. My living standards have never been as high as some people's.

I enjoy jogging and I enjoy my baseball and take an occasional trip to Mexico and see my family, I like to play golf and fish occasionally, but outside of that, life is very simple. Just keep breathing.

Any regrets?

At one time I thought I might like to manage in the big leagues, but the fact that I've managed in the minor leagues for so many years—I don't know if I would have been able to do that if I was a major league manager. Managing in the major leagues is a stressful job and if you're not successful you get fired pretty quick. All-in-all, I think the fact that I've managed this long in the minor leagues is great. I have no regrets really.

You've been a good manager. You can't judge a minor league manager's success by winning percentage, although yours is outstanding, but you would not have had a job for this length of time had you not been a good manager.

Let me put it this way, I have no idea what kind of manager I'd have made in the big leagues but I did manage against some successful managers when I started out, like Earl Weaver. We managed against each other a couple of years in the minor leagues, and there were others. I think I'd have done all right, but I have no regrets.

Would you do it all again?

Oh, yes! Definitely! I had this planned even when I was playing. I used to admire the guys I played for: Del Baker, who was my first manager in the big leagues, and then Steve O'Neill, who I played for in Beaumont, Texas, and Detroit, and then Red Rolfe came over [to Detroit] and then Lou Boudreau [in Boston].

I was a great admirer of Casey Stengel. I think Casey had the knack of handling the press and he handled his players so well. Of course, he had the good talent but you have to have good talent to win in the major leagues. You're not gonna win because of your good managing; you have to have the talent.

❖ ❖ ❖

In 1950, the Tigers' pitching staff must have kept the ball down. Second baseman Gerry Priddy set the all-time major league record for double plays for his position with 150 (since surpassed by Bill Mazeroski's 161 in a 162-game schedule in 1966). Johnny Lipon took part in 126, at that time the second highest total by a major league shortstop (the record at the time was 128).

Priddy and Lipon's total of 276 established a major league record that stood until Mazeroski and Gene Alley combined for 289 in a 162-game schedule in 1966. Here are the Top Five one-season double play combos.

Player, Pos.	Team/Year	G	DP	DP/G
Bill Mazeroslki, 2B	Pit/1966	162	161	
Gene Alley, SS			128	
			289	1.78

Player, Pos.	Team/Year	G	DP	DP/G
Gerry Priddy, 2B	Det/1950	157	150	
Johnny Lipon, SS			<u>126</u>	
			276	1.76
Bill Mazeroski, 2B	Pit/1962	161	138	
Dick Groat, SS			<u>126</u>	
			264	1.64
Bobby Doerr, 2B	BosA/1949	155	134	
Vern Stephens, SS			<u>128</u>	
			262	1.690
Bill Mazeroski, 2B	Pit/1961	154	144	
Dick Groat, SS			<u>117</u>	
			261	1.695

JOHN JOSEPH "SKIDS" LIPON

Born November 10, 1922, Martin's Ferry, OH
Died August 17, 1998, Houston, TX
Ht. 6'   Wt. 175   Batted and Threw Right

Year	Team., Lg	G	AB	R	H	2B	3B	HR	RBI	BA
1942	Detroit, AL	34	131	5	25	2	0	0	9	.191
1943–45	Military service									
1946	Detroit, AL	14	20	4	6	0	0	0	1	.300
1948		121	458	65	133	18	8	5	52	.290
1949		127	439	57	110	14	6	3	59	.251
1950		147	601	104	176	27	6	2	63	.293
1951		129	487	56	129	15	1	0	38	.265
1952	Det-Bos, AL	118	370	42	78	12	3	0	30	.211
1953	Bos-StL, AL	67	154	18	33	7	0	0	14	.214
1954	Cinc., NL	1	1	0	0	0	0	0	0	.000
9 years		758	2661	351	690	95	24	10	266	.259

PETE CENTER

Everything Is Relative (1942–1946)

Pete Center was in the major leagues in 1942, '43, '45, and '46. It might have been longer but he was 30 when he got there and World War II claimed him in 1944, then he hurt his arm in '46, but four years is a lot longer than many guys who got there a lot younger than Pete did.

He spent the entire time with the Indians. His busiest season was 1945, when he went 6-3 in 31 games and 85⅔ innings. Although primarily a long man out of the bullpen, he made eight starts, compiling a 3-1 record with two complete games.

As the season got underway, though, manager Lou Boudreau seemed to forget Pete. He didn't make his first appearance until May 11, 24 days after the April 17 opener. He finished up an 8-4 loss to Boston. It was 19 more days before he pitched again and it was again against the Red Sox. He appeared in both ends of a Memorial Day doubleheader, winning the first game in relief and stopping a six-run Bosox eighth-inning rally in the second, won by Boston, 7-6.

Still, he wasn't overly used. From Memorial Day through the end of June, he pitched only five more times and then only in Cleveland losses. At mid-season, then, he had pitched in only eight games (19 innings) with a 1-0 record.

In the second half, Boudreau evidently realized Pete could pitch a

95

little. His first start came on July 1 versus Washington in Cleveland. He ran out of gas in the ninth, however, and his roommate, Allie Reynolds, relieved, picking up the win as the Tribe rallied for two in the bottom of the ninth.

From then on, Pete was used both ways: staring and relieving. Two landmark games for him occurred later in July. On the eighth was the game he talks about in the following interview, in which Boudreau started him in Reynolds' place. Pete won and Allie got the save.

Then, on the twelfth, the Yankees were starting a long home stand. The Tigers were on top, the Senators were in second, and New York was in third, tied with Boston. Detroit had not been sharp for a few games and this was an ideal time for the Yankees to make a move; indeed, the Tigers lost more than they won over the next two weeks, but New York actually lost ground during that period.

That day, July 12, Reynolds started for Cleveland but couldn't find home plate. By the fourth inning, he was down, 4-2, and had walked the ballpark. When he couldn't retire the side, Pete was brought in and began the slide that doomed the Yankees for the season. He held them scoreless through the sixth, then was taken out for a pinch hitter in a Cleveland three-run rally in the seventh. Al Smith finished the game for his only save of the year. New York went 4-and-8 over the next two weeks and it was all over for Yankee hopes. New York finished fourth a half-game out of third; it was the only time between 1925 and 1964 that they weren't one, two, or three.

Pete was an important part of the Indians' staff from then through the end of the season. The Tribe had gotten off to a horrible start and was still under .500 at mid-season, the time during which Pete pitched sparingly, but a second-half surge, during which Pete was used on a regular basis, brought them home with a winning record for the season (73-72).

Arm trouble in 1946 pretty much ended Pete's career, although he held on in the high minors a while longer. Finally he retired and returned home to the mountains of eastern Kentucky.

Your name is Marvin Earl Center. Where did you get the nickname "Pete"?

They called my dad Pete back when I was a little boy. They called us Old Pete and Young Pete and that's stayed with me ever since.

As a kid, where did you start playing baseball?

Hazel Green Academy, ten miles east of here. That's a church institution. It's sponsored by the United Christian Disciples of Christ out of

Indianapolis. When I started school over there I was just six years old and I graduated in 1931. I went to school the whole time there.

When did you decide you wanted to play professional baseball?

I went over to Morehead to college. I was over there for three semesters. I had a brother-in-law [that] lived in Seco, Kentucky, out in the coal fields, and he wanted me to come up there when school was out. I went up there and they had a baseball team and they needed a pitcher and I pitched for 'em. We won that game on the Fourth of July and then I pitched another game for 'em.

While I was there, the superintendent of Consolidated Coal Com-

Pete Center (courtesy Pete Center).

pany, down in Jenkins [Kentucky] was at the game and he came down after the game and he said, "How would you like to come up here and play for me next year at Jenkins? We've got a little league up there." I said, "That'd be fine." He said, "I'll make you a foreman in the mines." I said, "Well, I don't know anything about mining," and he said, "You don't have to go in the mines," and we didn't.

Harry Walker was up there — Harry the Hat — and I roomed with him. One day [the superintendent] said, "Get your glove and your shoes and we'll go down to Knoxville" — that's the Knoxville Smokies in the Southern Association — "and you can work out with them down there." We went down there and they gave me a uniform and I put that on and they gave me a catcher — Ray Mueller — and after the game I threw out there about 15 minutes, I guess, and they asked me if I wanted to sign a contract. I did, and that's the way I got started. I was 23 then.

I stayed with Knoxville the rest of that year and went back with 'em to spring training and they sent me down to Americus, Georgia. I was down there for a year and then after that I went to Jackson, Mississippi, in the Southeastern League, and from there I went to New Orleans, back in the Southern Association, and Cleveland bought my contract in 1939 from New Orleans. I hadn't pitched very many games for New Orleans; I was there about the last month of that year.

In '39, Cleveland farmed me out to the Eastern League with Wilkes-Barre, Pennsylvania, and each year I'd go to spring training but I never could make the club until 1942. I went to Baltimore from the Eastern League; that's when Baltimore was in the International League, along with Toronto and Montreal. I stayed there in 1942 and spent '43 with Cleveland.

At the end of '43, I went in the service and stayed there the rest of '43 and all of '44, up until spring training of '45. I was discharged then. I stayed in Cleveland in '45 and '46 and I hurt my arm in '46. In '47, Cleveland sold me to Baltimore and I stayed there in '47 and '48. I quit in '48 about the middle of the season. The arm was bad and I was getting pretty old, too; I was about 36, 37 years old.

Do you recall any of your minor league stats?

When I went to Wilkes-Barre, I think I had a 13-and-12 and had the same thing at Baltimore. When I went to Cleveland, I finished up there at 7-and-7.

When you entered the service, did you enlist or were you drafted?

I was drafted. First they were taking the boys that weren't married. Most of 'em were enlisting because they knew they were gonna be drafted. And then they took the ones that were married and didn't have any children and then the ones that did have a family, a lot of 'em didn't have to go. Like Allie Reynolds—I roomed with Allie—he had about four children and he didn't have to go. I don't think he went at all.

Did you play ball in the service?

Yeah. We had a pretty good ballclub. We had about five that had played professional ball. We were at Daniel Field in Augusta, Georgia, then from there I went to Wright Field. I didn't play any there.

You had two hits in the major leagues.

Two hits, and I think they were bunts. I bunted over the third baseman's head on one, I remember that. I didn't go to bat very many times.

In 1945 you made eight starts and won three and lost one with two complete games. Your record as a starter was better than it was as a reliever — lower ERA, etc.

Well, as a reliever [if] you go in for one inning and they score four runs on you, your earned run average goes up awfully high.

I don't know what year it was, but I won one and lost one in the same day. It was a doubleheader. I lost the first game in relief and won the second game against Washington, back when they were in the league. [The year was 1943.]

Do you remember your complete games?

I remember Boston was one of 'em. [Pete was 3-0 versus the Red Sox in 1945.] The score was 8-to-2. I remember I lost a game against the Browns — St. Louis Browns; I started it and they got to me pretty quick. That was my only loss as a starter.

Does one game or day stand out?

That day at Washington when I won one and lost one in one day stands out more than anything. I had a good day that day. The first game I lost by not fielding a bunt properly and that's when the run scored. In the second game, I pitched seven innings and gave up one hit and I got credit for that one.

One game I remember, Ted Williams hit a home run up in old League Park [Cleveland]. There was a high wall in right field, a screen up there, then the highway, and then there was a brick building. I remember that one. He hit Feller just about as well as he hit anybody. He was a good hitter — best lefthanded hitter I ever saw. I *never* got him out. Yeah, one time I did. He hit a hard line drive and it was caught.

We were in Boston and we had an off day and they had scheduled an exhibition game out there in some little town and the proceeds were going to charity. It rained and we all came into this big field house — all the Boston Red Sox players and all the Cleveland players – and Ted Williams was talking and we all gathered around him. Feller was there and he told Feller, "I can see the spin on your ball 20 feet before it gets to me." I heard that and I thought that was pretty unusual — you pick up a spin 20 feet in front of you; that's fractions of a second.

You know, [Lou] Boudreau, our manager, he was the one that pulled that shifting [of] his fielders all to the right side of the diamond. He did that in Boston and Williams hit a home run and the headline in the paper said, "Boudreau should have put a fielder in the seats."

Was Williams the best hitter you saw?

He was the best lefthanded and Joe DiMaggio was the best right-handed hitter. I had better luck with DiMaggio than I ever had with Williams. I was righthanded.

Who was the best overall player you saw?

Overall player? I'd say DiMaggio.

How was Boudreau as a manager?

He was all right. He was a good ballplayer and he knew the game real well. He had so many ballplayers *older* than him and they'd been around longer than him, like Mel Harder and Al Smith and Clint Brown, Willis Hudlin, and all those fellas. They were older, much older. The fact is, most of his ballplayers were older.

Who was the best pitcher you saw?

Feller had the best stuff of any of 'em. [Hal] Newhouser was a good pitcher — lefthander. Those are the two that stand out. Feller was faster'n any of 'em and he came up with a good curveball, too.

Allie Reynolds was a good pitcher with Cleveland, but he became a great pitcher with the Yankees.

He wasn't happy at Cleveland. He had a family and he wasn't making much money and I think he went over Boudreau's head and went to the front office asking for more money and he didn't get along there too well with Boudreau. He had a meeting — Boudreau did — about that, had all the pitchers in there. He made his speech and he asked me how long it took me to get hot and I said, "I'm already hot." And he said, "Well, get ready. You're starting." In that game I went five innings and shut then out and in the sixth inning I got the first two men on base and he brought Reynolds in as a relief pitcher. He did that just to show him who was boss. So Reynolds had a few things that he didn't like and Boudreau knew it, so they traded him to the Yankees for Joe Gordon, the second baseman.

When Reynolds got up there they had a bullpen catcher — Ralph Houk — and he got him so where he could get the ball over the plate. He had a good fastball, a good live fastball.

I roomed with him. We got robbed up in New York. We were asleep and somebody, I guess the maid, had a key to the room and came in and took all of our money. Didn't take our watches or anything like that.

Does Reynolds belong in the Hall of Fame?

I don't know what all they take into consideration in the Hall of Fame. He had the ability.

It's hard to figure what they consider sometimes. Rick Ferrell was a good catcher but I can't see him as a Hall of Famer, can you?

No, I can't. I can't see how they keep Pete Rose out, either. I think the Hall of Fame is a place for the best players, don't you? Best records, anyway.

Mel Harder. There may not be a nicer man in the world, but he was an awfully good pitcher, too.

I didn't see Mel when he was younger. While I was there, he was pretty much in his last years. Like you said, he's an awful nice fella. I don't know if his record would be good enough for the Hall of Fame or not.

Did he help out as pitching coach?

Not while I was there. We didn't have any pitching coach. We had a bullpen catcher, George Susce [Sr.], and Oscar Melillo was first base coach, Burt Shotten was third base coach. That's all we had; we didn't have any tutors or we didn't have anyone to work with you. George Susce would work with you while you were warming up in the bullpen — tell you to keep your ball down — but nothing more than that. Back in those days, the good pitchers weren't gonna help a rookie because if he made it, why, he might lose a job.

So the general thinking was, if you were good enough to be there you didn't need help?

Real close. I know we had a meeting of all the rookies when I first went up there — that's when Oscar Vitt was the manager — and he said, "Now you're in the big league; I want you to dress like one and act like one!" That was about all that was said.

You played 13 years, major and minor. Did you save souvenirs?

No. I had a glove and a few signed baseballs and an old uniform and I've got a boy who wanted to play ball and I don't know what he did with 'em. We never can find 'em. I haven't got a thing left. I get letters — I've got one in there now. Wants to buy anything you've got from back in the days that you played.

One thing happened that I wish I had've known it was gonna be like this. We were playing the White Sox in Cleveland a doubleheader and Tris Speaker, Babe Ruth, and another old-timer were sitting back of our dugout and they talked Babe Ruth to coming in the 20-minute intermission between games to take some batting practice. He agreed to do it and he came down to our clubhouse to get dressed. They gave him a uniform and he was needing a pair of shoes and I had the only pair of shoes he'd wear. He wore those shoes and I wish I'd kept those shoes and had him autograph 'em.

They may be the last baseball shoes he wore.

Yeah, I wouldn't be surprised. They were new shoes; I hadn't worn 'em much. I remember what he said when he put 'em on, "You call these things shoes?"

I'll tell you what they did have back then. They had these round plastic coasters that had the autographs of everyone on the ballclub and they gave us a bunch of 'em. I had a whole bunch in a trunk but after a few years they crumpled up — just disintegrated.

But I never dreamed — and nobody else ever dreamed — that this [baseball] card system would be what it is. Feller had a card show down here in Lexington a few years ago. My son, he kinda likes baseball, and my granddaughter, she's crazy about it, and I said, "Well, let's go down to Lexington to the show." So we did.

I had a cap — BAT cap — and my son was wearing it and he was asked, "Who'd you play with?" and he said, "I didn't play with anybody. My dad here played with Cleveland with Feller." They got the word to Feller and Feller said to come on back and we had a picture made and they had us on television and I enjoyed it. That's the first time I'd seen him since I left Cleveland. He's an awful nice fella.

I know my boy — he's in his fifties now — but back when he was a teenager he was gonna be a catcher. He's as big as I am. And I called Jim Hegan — he was catcher when I was there — and I told him to have his company send us a Jim Hegan model [glove]. He kept it for years. I don't know what went with that.

I used to go to Cincinnati when they had the old-timer games — they invited me up there — and one year they gave us cocktail glasses with the Cincinnati Reds insignia on 'em. I think I've got three or four of 'em around here somewhere.

You say your son is as big as you. You were a big man in those days: 6'4".

When I was playing professional ball I weighed about 195 pounds. Yeah, I was one of the taller ones.

Was there ever a better handler of pitchers than Jim Hegan?

No. He was the best I ever saw, best I ever pitched to. And one of the nicest guys I ever knew.

How much fan mail do you receive?

There's not a lot. I guess I probably get a couple a week. They send some crazy things. I get a few requests that they say, "When you played ball it was really baseball." I think that's one reason I get from the older fans.

It's become a different game over the past 50 or 60 years.

There's quite a bit of difference. The biggest difference is the black ballplayer. When I played, the blacks weren't there. They've added a lot to it; you know, speed and the way they play. They're pretty colorful.

The baseball uniforms are much different. The ones we had were flannel and they were big and they were hot, bulky. And, of course, the way they decorate their shoes and wearing [batting] gloves and all the broken bats. Back then you hardly ever had a broken bat. I mean, they're broken! One piece'll go one way and they'll have the other in their hands. Some of 'em go up in the seats. You never saw that. On the wooden bats, you know where the trademark is? Well, we were taught to hold that up. I notice now they don't pay any attention to it.

And the gloves are better. They've got bigger gloves now. The pocket's bigger and the glove is bigger. A pitcher now can hide his pitches better. 'Course, they've got that forkball now — that split-finger fastball, we called it a forkball — and they can hide the whole thing. Back then, you didn't have that big glove.

And they get more stolen bases now. There's more ballplayers running now than there were then.

I don't know whether the pitching was better then than it is now or not. I believe the real *good* ones were better than they are now, like Feller and [Sandy] Koufax and Dizzy Dean and Paul Dean and Lon Warneke over with the Cardinals, and Mel Harder with Cleveland. That's back when [Lefty] Gomez and [Red] Ruffing were with the Yankees, you know. I think they were better pitchers than they have now; they had better stuff.

Back then, you only had eight clubs in each league and 25 men to the club, so that was 400 men. That's all there were in major league baseball. If you took out 400 men now you'd have an awful lot of fellas going back to the minors. If you consider that, you can see the strength of the game as compared to now. There weren't so many and what you did have were the best.

Pete Center (courtesy Pete Center).

So you feel expansion has weakened the game?

In some phases, I think it has. You don't have any Ted Williams hitters now, or Joe DiMaggios. You don't have any center fielders like Joe DiMaggio. And you don't have any pitchers like Dizzy Dean, like Bob Feller. You could just go back and name a lot of 'em from each league.

But you've still got some good ballplayers now. You've got some good baserunners. Like I said, the black man, he likes to run and they *can* run. Just like in basketball; they can jump out of the gym and they're good athletes, but I don't think they're as good a hitters as the fellows I mentioned.

Would you go back 60 years and be a baseball player again?

Yeah, I'm sure I would. The way the salaries are now, I believe I'd work a little harder at it, too. *[laughs]*

What was your top salary?

I think 7500. That wasn't bad. My first contract I had was 3500. At Baltimore in the minors, I got 5,000. I had a pretty good year in Baltimore. I was a pretty good minor league ballplayer but I wasn't nothing special.

You wouldn't have stayed in the majors if you weren't an outstanding ballplayer.

I guess you had something or they wouldn't have had you up there.

Any regrets?

Nothing more than I hurt my arm. I wish I could have gone on a little longer. I wish I could've started earlier, but up here in the mountains we didn't have anybody to teach us anything. What we learned we learned listening to the radio.

We had one man here — Hope Hutchins — that if we'da had any money, he'da had us some better equipment and everything, but we played with a twine ball with tape on it. *[laughs]* When I got out of here and in professional ball, I didn't know how to stand on the rubber. I had to go from scratch, and I *mean* scratch, too. Down in Lexington or maybe Paris or Louisville or bigger cities, they probably had somebody that could help 'em, but we didn't have any of that up here. We had that one man — Hope Hutchins — but we didn't have any money to buy equipment with and we traveled in an old truck with a flatbed with sideboards on it.

Today, with the scouting bureau and regional scouts for each team, it's hard for a boy not to be seen, but back then, here where you are, it had to be an accident if you were seen.

Yeah. Hope got a man down here from Cincinnati. He came on a Monday and I pitched on Sunday. We were up in the river swimming and he came up and got us and we talked to him and he said, "Well, you will hear from me later," but I never did.

What did you do after baseball?

I saved enough money to go into the automotive parts business. I stayed here 13 years in that and I got up to retirement age and I just retired. My wife, she was a child welfare worker; she had a good job. We only had the one kid and when we came here, why, we built this home. I had a good business, too. Nothing you could get rich at, but you could live comfortably.

And I like it up here 'cause I like to hunt and I like to fish and we had pretty good quail hunting up here then, and grouse hunting. And Cave Run Lake's over here — it wasn't built then — and lakes like Cumberland and Herrington Lake and the Kentucky River on this side and the Licking River on that side and the Red River through the middle — good fishing.

And I'd go to Wisconsin grouse hunting and I'd go to Nebraska quail and pheasant hunting and I had a bunch of good dogs and I've lived the life that I like to live. That's one thing I'll always cherish. Now that I'm retired I'm all crippled up with arthritis I still try to hunt.

But we're still hanging on. I raise a garden and try to keep the lawn mowed. That's about it. I like to be outside. I don't like to stay inside. If I ever did anything that I had to stay inside, I'd probably give up, I believe.

As far as baseball, I never did anything that's outstanding. That's, I guess, what they look for. I took this magazine, *The Diamond,* and all you read about is Hall of Famers. And I thought I wish they'd put some of the fellas like me in there. If it hadn't been for us, they wouldn't be in the Hall of Fame. We threw that home run ball up there that put 'em in the Hall of Fame, a lot of 'em, so if the scrubbinies like me weren't there, they wouldn't be in the Hall of Fame.

I enjoy reading about and interviewing the lesser-known players. If you want to read about Williams or Feller or players such as them, there are a lot of places to go.

You see them so many times, you can tell about them from memory. I don't see too much about Bob Lemon and you know he was a good one. I played minor league ball with him in Wilkes-Barre and Baltimore. He was a third baseman. On that Baltimore ballclub we had quite a few (who) went to the majors. We had Eddie Robinson and George Staller; Bob

Lemon and I went to Cleveland. Joe Becker was catcher; he'd been in the majors. I guess that was it: four or five of us.

Pete Center is right, of course. How would we know how great Ted Williams or Sandy Koufax were if everyone had that level of talent? Everything is relative.

Marvin Earl "Pete" Center

Born April 22, 1912, Hazel Green, KY
Ht. 6'4"   Wt. 190   Batted and Threw Right

Year	Team, Lg.	G	IP	W	L	Pct	H	BB	SO	ERA
1942	Cle., AL	1	3.1	0	0	—	7	4	0	16.20
1943		24	42.1	1	2	.333	29	18	19	2.76
1945		31	85.2	6	3	.667	89	28	24	3.99
1946		21	29	0	2	.000	29	20	6	4.97
4 years		77	160.1	7	7	.500	154	70	50	4.10

Damon "Dee" Phillips

Double or Nothing (1942–1946)

Doubles and double plays. Damon Phillips had an affinity for both.

He was a line-drive hitting shortstop who, for a variety of reasons, had a limited major league career.

First, he was trapped in the massive minor league system of the Detroit Tigers in the late 1930s. The Tigers and the St. Louis Cardinals had extensive farm systems in those days and players were unable to advance (Johnny Sain spent *three years* in Class D because of this) and finally Commissioner Kenesaw Mountain Landis stepped in and made free agents of these players.

Damon advanced quickly after that and in 1942 he was a backup infielder with the Cincinnati Reds. Back in the minors in '43, the Boston Braves obtained him after that season and in '44 he was an everyday player for Boston's sixth-place club. Of all Braves that year, only Tommy Holmes had more at bats than Damon.

But most of the time — 90 games out of the 140 in which he played — he was the third baseman. Whitey Wietelmann was the shortstop because he really couldn't play anywhere else, but when Whitey's bat went into remission, which it often did (.232 lifetime), Damon would get to play his natural position of shortstop. Also, he would switch over to short late in games when Wietelmann was taken out for a pinch hitter.

Phillips was a good third baseman even though it wasn't the position at which he was most comfortable. In those 90 games at third, many of which were only partial because of a late-inning move to short, he led the National League third sackers in double plays.

On August 29 of that year, Damon really had a chance to show off his glove. He became the first third baseman in the 20th century to have 11 assists in a nine-inning game.

After 1944, a second reason limited his major league time: Uncle Sam called. He spent all of 1945 and essentially all of '46 in the Army. When he returned, he found a third reason blocking him: the Braves had taken a new approach. Bob Elliott had been acquired from Pittsburgh to play third and shortstop was shared by a rare three-man platoon (Dick Culler, Nanny Fernandez, and Sibby Sisti), and manager Billy Southworth used the two who weren't playing that day as his reserve infielders.

Damon's major league days were over at this point, but he eventually became a scout and today, more than 50 years after his only season as a major league regular, he's still influencing the game. He originally signed two of baseball's top managers: Don Baylor and Davey Johnson.

❖ ❖ ❖

How were you signed originally?

I was never scouted by a scout as a free agent for professional ball. I was signed by the Detroit Tigers, that I worked for. I was a scout for the Detroit Tigers.

I grew up on a farm in west Texas and I grew up in a little farming community called Veribest; it's about 12 miles from a town of about 25-30,000 population at that time called San Angelo. It's about 80,000 or so now, I guess. I never played high school baseball; I played semipro baseball when I was 14, 15, 16 years old or so with older people.

We were playing a doubleheader in San Angelo and when the games were over some fella came down and introduced himself and wanted to know if I wanted to play professional baseball. I said, "Well, yes." He said, "I'm not a scout," but he says, "My name is Galloway and I played first base a few years in professional ball and I have some friends in the Detroit organization. Their Texas League farm team is at Beaumont and they told me if I saw any young players that I thought might play that I should contact them." He said they would watch me play down at Beaumont. I said, "I can't do that now. I'm only 17 years old. I have another year in high school." So we stayed in touch and when I got out of high school I went to Beaumont and that's how I got into professional baseball. I never met a scout before I got into professional baseball. I signed in 1938.

You were a shortstop then.

Yeah. I played shortstop and I played second base. They wanted me to be a shortstop. I always played the infield.

A lot of good ballplayers went through Beaumont.

I didn't stay with that team that year. They sent me to a smaller team, but they had some people like Barney McCosky, an outfielder, later played in the big leagues a while; Pat Mullin, played in the big leagues a while. I don't remember too much about the pitching they had. They had a big first baseman named [Les] Fleming and he was later traded to Cleveland, maybe got up there for a little while. He played a lot of Triple-A ball.

He was the regular first baseman for Cleveland for a while but he sealed his own fate when they brought Larry Doby in and he didn't want to play with blacks and he made it known.

I thought the blacks should have played long before they got into it, really. I played winter ball in later years over in Cuba with people like Minnie Minoso and [Ray] Dandridge, the third baseman. We played on a club over there about five years together. Lord, there were some good ballplayers—the black kids—back in those days. Some were so good and didn't get to play before they did, when their careers were almost over.

Where did the Tigers send you from Beaumont?

I played a lot of places. I played in Lake Charles in the Evangeline League when they sent me out from Beaumont.

How did you come to leave the Tigers' organization?

I was in a group at the end of the '39 season that Commissioner Landis made free agents. I'd had two good years in the low minors and I was supposed to go to Beaumont the next year as the regular shortstop. They made me a free agent and I didn't wanna leave but I had no choice and I signed with the Cincinnati Reds. I couldn't re-sign with the Tigers for five years and I couldn't be a part of the organization for five years; I was barred from that. There was somewhere about 95-96 players released and I know in my situation I couldn't be a part of the Detroit organization for five years, so I signed for the '40 season with the Cincinnati organization.

I played in Columbia, South Carolina, and I played a little while in Pensacola and a little while in Riverside, California, in the California State

Damon Phillips, 1944.

League and I played some in Dayton in the Mid-Atlantic League. Then I went back to Columbia a couple years later, was having a good year, and they needed an extra infielder and they called me to Cincinnati in '42, just shortly after the season started. I spent the rest of the year there in Cincinnati. I believe I was called up in June.

Do you remember your first game in the major leagues?

Yeah. I can't remember the club I played against; I want to say it was the Giants but I'm not sure. It was a very hot day in Cincinnati and what got me in the lineup at that time was there were several players that had a problem with the heat and had to be taken out of the game. That's when I got to play my first game and the heat didn't bother me, I guess, because I grew up on a farm out in west Texas and worked in the cotton fields and the feed fields and all that sorta thing when I was growing up, so it didn't get to me that much. I played the doubleheader that day. [It was July 19, 1942.]

I always thought in my mind, if I ever got to the major leagues, I'd like to get a hit the first time I went to bat. We had a runner on second base and I came up and got a single to center field and scored the run. I can remember that but I don't remember too much about the total thing; I just know I played all the games that day because I was the one that was left to play.

After that I got to play quite a few games that year, and the next year I went to spring training and I didn't stay with the club. They sent me to Syracuse in the International League and that's where the Boston Braves bought me.

Then I went with Boston the next spring training and I played 140 games there that year. They moved me to third base because they had another fella there they left at shortstop. Sometimes they'd take him out for a pinch hitter and I'd go to shortstop and finish up and they had an outfielder [Chuck Workman] there they'd bring into third. Sometimes I played some short there, too; started the game and played for a few games.

Right after that I went in the service and stayed about two years. I missed all of '45 and '46 both. I came back to join the club, I think, about two weeks before the season finished [in '46] but I only got in to pinch-hit a couple of times. I never did get in a regular game to play, start a game or anything.

They made a lot of changes. Billy Southworth had been brought over from the Cardinals [to manage] and there was two big contractors—the Perini brothers—and they had a lot of money and bought a lot of players and they had a lot of players there that had been in the big leagues several years. I just didn't get much chance to play there and Milwaukee was their Triple-A club and I went down there and had a good year. I hit over .300 in Triple-A and they moved me to third base, which I didn't really want to play because actually I was a shortstop and I thought I hit well for a shortstop but I didn't have that much power for a third baseman.

I had a good year but there was no one interested in me enough to give me a chance to get back to the major leagues, so I started playing winter ball over in Cuba.

I played 'til, oh, about '56; that was my last regular year. I was in my late thirties then; I was playing ball in Cuba and I ended up playing with Baltimore in the International League and that's when the St. Louis Browns' franchise was moved over. They thought they was possibly gonna need another infielder so they bought my contract and left me on the Baltimore club and I went to spring training with them in Yuma, Arizona. There was deals made just before spring training broke and they got a couple veteran infielders to come in, so they sent me back to Triple-A.

I just kept playing winter ball. At that time, they moved the Baltimore players that was in Triple-A to Richmond, which became the Triple-A franchise. Lee MacPhail was the farm director, who later became the American League president, and he was trying to get me to manage while I could still play in the minor leagues. I didn't wanna do that because I'd have to take a big cut in salary because I was bringing more money home from playing winter ball than I was playing over in the States. You could play winter ball and they would pay your expenses over and back and pay your expenses while you were there, so you could save a lot more money there than you could in the States.

You had to be invited to go over to winter ball; they sent people from their clubs over to scout players and they'd fill in in Cuba and the Dominican Republic and Puerto Rico and those places. They'd fill their clubs; they didn't have enough good players over there to make a good strong league; I think back at that time you could invite about seven or eight foreign players—you know, like Americans—to go over there and play. They'd come over and scout the players at positions they wanted on their club. I signed to go over and play one year and I had a pretty good year there so I kept going back every year for, I dunno, about six-seven years, I guess. I either played in Cuba or the Dominican Republic.

It was a pretty good league in those days because there was a lot of players over there playing in their home country and a lot of 'em played in the major leagues then. A lot of blacks went down there and it was a pretty strong league. I enjoyed playing there.

In 1944 with Boston, you were an everyday player. You hit a lot of doubles but only one home run. Do you remember it?

I wanna think I hit the home run against Pittsburgh, but I don't remember too much about that. I was more of a line drive–type hitter. I could hit the ball to the opposite field or I could pull the ball or hit straight-away. I was more of a hit-the-ball-where-it's-pitched-on-a-line hitter. I didn't lift the ball too often with home run power. I was a pretty good hit-and-run man. I could hit-and-run — you know, the runner starts and you hit behind him.

I guess the most home runs I ever hit was in Milwaukee. One year there I hit 15 or 16, I think. I wasn't really a home run hitter. I was more of a line drive hitter and that would've fit my overall playing as a shortstop more than a third baseman. If you hit like that playing third, you have to consistently hit for a high average, but if you can hit for an adequate average and play shortstop well, as an overall player you're better.

When I left Boston and they sent me to Milwaukee I didn't really wanna play third base. I didn't really wanna play third base in Boston, but I'd play anywhere in the big leagues, you know. *[laughs]* I just wanted the chance to play. But that fit their program they thought, so I played a lot of games at third base, even though I played some at short.

The shortstop in Boston, Whitey Wietelmann, was a notoriously weak hitter and had no other position. That must have been the justification for putting you on third.

Well, I guess. Far as I know. Of course, back in those days hopefully I can stay in the major leagues and I'm not questioning anybody about why they're doing anything. They preferred to put me there and gave me a chance to play. I started out hitting real well in the first half or more of the season, so I just stayed there. As I say, I filled in [at shortstop] some-time when he would be taken out for a few days, then I'd move back to third. All I wanted to do was play in the major leagues wherever I could play, but I would've preferred to have played shortstop because my best position was shortstop, I felt, and it went along with my other overall hit-ting and playing and everything.

I wasn't a power hitter for the corners, like first base and third base. That wasn't the kind of bat stroke I had. I was a much better hitter when I hit the ball either through the infield or on a line. That's why I hit a lot of doubles.

Does one game stand out?

One game that would stand out according to what happened, and I didn't even know it happened 'til I went in the clubhouse and the writers told me about it, I tied a record for assists that was set back in 1880-something at third base: 11. I remember the game and I wanna think a fella named Jim Tobin, who was a knuckleballer, was pitching the game. I know a lotta balls were pulled and hit down in my direction.

I remember it well enough to know that there was one ball hit that had I come up with the ball I would've broken the record. It was a line drive to my left. I could remember the play because the writers talked about it. The last ball that I had a chance to play was a line drive to my left that kinda hit on a long hop. It was just one of those things that you move as quickly as you can and you either get it or you don't. As I moved to my left to get it, I can remember it hit kinda on the bottom — not the heel, but kinda the bottom of the pocket of my glove — and went right straight down to ground. If it had hit the ground and bounced I would have had plenty of time, I think, to recover and throw the player out, but it hit the edge of my shoe and bounced out between me and the shortstop. I can remember that play because we discussed it in the clubhouse with the writers. If I'da come up with the play, I'da broken the record. It's been tied since then.

In '44, were there any pitchers you liked or disliked?

I don't think that I would say there was too many that I really thought was just really terrible to hit, but they were all pretty tough; they all had pretty good stuff and to me they were certainly major leaguers. There's a lot of 'em back there that I probably don't even remember now.

Who was the best?

I don't know. I'd say *two* of the best, because I played on the club with 'em in Cincinnati, were Bucky Walters and Paul Derringer. To me, when I got over to Boston and had to hit against those two guys— I knew they were tough playing on the club with 'em — and Derringer used to throw a real heavy-type ball. All the players used to talk about it. You know, he was such a big fella — his ball was real heavy and, boy, if you didn't get it on the center of the bat it just vibrated right up your arms. That was one thing that made him tough.

Bucky Walters, 'course, he was moved from a third baseman to a pitcher — had a good frame and a good arm — and he just had pretty good overall stuff, had some pretty good years in the major leagues.

A lot of people think both of those guys should be in the Hall of Fame. What do you think?

Well, in my book they should be 'cause I thought they were great. What I know about 'em, they were just tremendous. They seldom ever went out — at the time I knew anything about it, when I either played on a club with 'em or against 'em — and really pitched bad. They might have lost games here and there but mostly they were just so consistent. They were tough. They were good competitors and, boy, they just pitched pretty well, even when they lost.

Who was the best player you saw?

I guess I'd have to say the best one I knew enough or played against was probably Stan Musial. He was another guy who was so consistent. It was just *amazing* how he could *hit*. We talked about it a lot while scouting; if you see a kid out here with a stance like he had, you'd say, Lord, he'll never hit. But he just got the good part of the bat on the ball so consistently. He was just tremendous.

And, 'course, there were a lot of others. Tommy Holmes was a good hitter. He was consistent. Both these guys were good contact hitters. They were just tough at the plate. They could swing the bat.

You mention contact hitters. To what do you attribute the great increase in strikeouts today? It's certainly not the pitching.

What I think it is, having been out and scouting, there's so many players today who swing the metal bat. The bat is so light and will still drive the ball well if you get it out there properly, or close to it, even small, young players are out on the end of it, swinging like they're going for the home run every time they swing. My feelings are that kids grow up doing that and, I guess, nobody ever tries to change 'em. To me, there are some players who should forget about ever hitting the ball against the fence or over the fence. They're just not that type of hitter, they don't have that kind of power. In my lifetime I might have been big enough to have done it but that wasn't my natural feel or swing and I never really tried to hit home runs. I never tried to swing like that. I tried to hit the ball on a line wherever it was pitched and that's why I could hit to right field, right center.

I think there's a lot of players today who should be doing that and are not and they go through high school and college. I see some kids that I scout in high school and they go into college and they're doing the same thing in college. I guess when they get in pro ball they do the same thing with the wooden bats and, I think, they overswing and they pull the bat off the line to hit the ball properly. And naturally they strike out a lot. Some of 'em who are pretty good-sized guys who really have some decent power,

I don't think they ever trained or schooled themselves to first try to contact the ball properly. Even when they were young boys, they were just wailing away at it and naturally they miss a lot of pitches.

I don't think the pitching [today] is all that great. Man, they had some tremendous pitchers. You know, when you go back to 16 teams compared to 30 now, you walk in a park to play and you're a hitter, you're gonna face more good pitchers more consistently. I'm not saying there's not some good pitchers now, but once you get past those, the second line is not necessarily all that good, I don't think. They're spread too thin.

It has been said that the increase in population should take care of the increase in teams, but it just doesn't do it.

It's not doing it. I used to think when this first hit me that this is what happened, "Well, I'm getting old," or, "Heck, in my day they did this and they did that," but I don't think that's really what's happened. You say, "Well, there's a lot more population," but there's not that many more good ballplayers but you still have 30 clubs with players to play. If they were to cut it down today to 16, I think you'd see a lot different type of play at the major league level.

The caliber that, in my opinion, overall has dropped a lot as far as the skill of it. Overall I'm talking about; I'm not talking that there isn't some players up there who could've played *any* years. If you go on to an area where there's a new team, for instance, and the team isn't that good in talent, if they can just kinda compete and hold their own against some other teams that's not quite that good, to the fans that's okay, there's no problem — as long as the competition's there. It's only the people who have been around a while and they understand the difference in the finesse and the skill and the way they do it and the way they execute it and all that sort of thing — if they've *seen* that and they see it today, they're gonna see the difference. At least, in my opinion.

Wes Westrum made the greatest statement I believe I ever heard. He said, "Baseball is like church. Many go but few understand."

I think that's right. The fans just get the surface and the competition and whether you win or lose. But back in the days when they had 16 teams, boy, I'll tell you — you better know how to execute and you better know how to play or you're not gonna stay there very long. And today they are developing 'em in the big leagues and consequently they're gonna have some struggle.

Back in the years when I was younger, I know I saw it happen. You come to the major leagues and you don't have the know-how to use the mechanics properly and play, you're not gonna stay there very long. The manager's gonna say, "Send this player out and teach him how to play!" You had to learn how to play before you got to the big leagues.

It seems like this day in time it doesn't matter if it's the major leagues or Triple-A or college or what. It's a different approach to it all. They just do it differently. Yet, if they went back to 16 teams, which they're not gonna do and I understand why because people want major league in their area and I understand that, there would be a difference. Perhaps some day way down the road there will be, but right now there's not enough good players to make it what it was years ago when there was 16 teams. I think everybody in baseball that's been there very long understands that.

There's different areas that's wanting baseball right now, wanting expansion and wanting to get into it and I guess eventually they're gonna have to do that. They're gonna have to satisfy those people and move in there and do it.

If you're gonna play at even Triple-A back then you better know how. You better know how to execute; if you don't, you're gonna have trouble competing up there against the people who do know how. It may be gone forever, what we knew back years ago—the way it was executed. Whatever you're doing, there's a *right* way and that's just the way it is. It's not that somebody's suddenly said that; it's just over the years of trial and error it's been proven. They may come up with something new here and there, but basically that's what it is.

What about these guys who come out and say they're not going to play as hard because they lost arbitration or can't renegotiate their contracts?

I don't think you'd've found anybody back when I was younger who would've said that, no matter what, because there was a lotta people who should have been getting paid more than they were getting and everybody, including them, knew that but they weren't. But they didn't stop in the way they played when they walked on the field. There was just something about it, back in the years I played, if you put on that uniform you played to win.

Alvin Dark said if he'd gotten $100,000 he's not sure he could have played hard enough to justify that much money.

Yeah, that was part of it and I think the reason was that it mattered to a player, when he walked in the ballpark—especially if you'd been able to get to the major leagues—that what you did today mattered. You didn't want an opposition player to know you were out there not giving everything you had. You didn't want *any*body to think that you weren't giving everything you had. I'll make a guess: There were hardly any players that ever played in that time, when they walked out to start the ballgame, that their purpose was to give everything they had. There was an old saying back there: If you give everything you've got and it just doesn't work that day, that's all you can do. Come back the next and give everything you've got the next day. I think that was just the makeup and the attitude of people who played back in those years.

I played when I was younger on a club with some young fellas who, maybe they were a little older than I was and they may have reached the point where they thought, "I'm not gonna get too much higher," and they'd goof off here and there. But when you got up to the major league level and most places, even Triple-A, everybody was a good player and proven to be in Triple-A. They *could* play major league if they had an opportunity, back in those years, because they learned how by the time they got to be a Triple-A player. There were fewer jobs and you had to execute and you had to learn how and you had to know how to keep your job year to year. To me, it was the same way in the major leagues. That's just the way players played when they went out to play.

In those years, you know, you played a pretty fast game; there wasn't all this wasted time you see today because you were taught how not to waste time. It helped you keep more alert and it helped the game move more and whenever it's moving you're more alert. If you're an infielder and you're standing out there waiting for a batter to get in the box and the pitcher to walk around the mound and all this, pretty soon you'll catch yourself not as alert and as quick to move on balls that are hit. You get a little lax if it moves so slowly. If the game went extra innings that's one thing, but just the routine of playing inning to inning, they just went about it in a much more businesslike, faster way.

Did you save souvenirs from your career?

No, not really. I wasn't a collector. In some ways I wish I had now. I don't think it occurred to guys in my time. There might've been a few scattered around who did that, but overall I doubt there was a great number of 'em.

I've had some people write me about that sorta thing. I was amazed that they were doing that when I first started getting some of those letters. The only thing I had was two uniforms they had given me at Baltimore. I guess when I was in spring training with 'em at Yuma back when the Browns moved over there: '55. That's about the only thing I had that amounted to anything and I gave those to somebody that wanted 'em; I don't remember who now — a friend of mine.

Damon Phillips, 1942.

Do you get much fan mail?

I still get it along. I get 'em — not a big pile of 'em — but I get 'em along during the year every year. I might average one or two a week. They're maybe from a kid who saw me or from somebody who says, "I must be about your age because I remember seeing you play" in Boston or Cincinnati or someplace, or somebody who says, "I'm collecting this or that" and they send me something to sign.

I sign and most of the time I try to write 'em a note and thank 'em for sending it. I don't know, it's just playing baseball was a big thing to me when I started out as a kid and I was lucky enough to get up to the major leagues for a while. I just think anybody that would write me a letter and want an autograph I should say, "Thank you. I appreciate it." I never even dreamed anything like that would be taking place.

I know some of the stars, they can make so much money out of the autograph sessions. I don't know how many players would do it today, but if there are kids around or people that see you somewhere and want you to sign something for 'em, Lord, I just can't see anybody saying they're not gonna sign.

When I was a player and people asked me to sign, as long as I had time I would sign. Some kids would come up with just a piece of paper and want your name on there because everybody was doing it. If they wanted that, fine, I'd do it.

Whom have you signed as a scout over the years?

Let's see, without going in and trying to remember which ones got to the big leagues. I guess the fellas that did the best were Don Baylor — out of an Austin high school and he's had a pretty good career in baseball — and I signed Davey Johnson, who now manages, out of [Texas] A and M University at College Park, Texas. I'd say they have to be the two best players I ever signed. I signed some marginal players that got up there. I signed two Davey Johnsons from Texas. One of 'em was the pitcher — righthanded pitcher — that got up there for a while. He stayed up there three or four or five years, I think.

I've got a fella now named Scott Livingstone. See, I left baseball in '82 — didn't think I'd ever come back and then I knew some people like Bill Lajoie, who was over in the Detroit organization, and he knew me and knew my work and they needed somebody down through this area. They talked to me about coming back so I came back to scout in '87 and then I signed Livingstone and he's gotten up there – been up there a few years. He's a pretty good hitter. I thought he might hit a few more home runs than he's hit, but I talked to him one time about it and he said, "Well. I'm in and out of the lineup and under those conditions I just wanna be sure I contact the ball. I'm not trying to go for long balls or anything, just trying to hit the ball solid." So he's hit for a pretty good average the years he's been there.

Do you have any regrets from your baseball career?

No, I don't think so. I'd tell each one of the kids I sign no matter what happens when you go out to play, if anything happens – you're disturbed or whatever – don't ever let it affect you when you put on a uniform and walk on the field. Let it disturb you when you're off the field, not on it. Just dismiss it from your mind, walk out on the field, and give it everything you've got, and then *whatever* happens you can never look back and say, "Well, if I'da done so-and-so, maybe this'd happen." I just try to make it a point to do that because *I* did that.

I don't have any regrets. I certainly don't have any regrets over what happened to me during the war years because I've had people say to me, "If you hadn't had to go in the service, you might've stayed there a long time." Well, maybe I would and maybe I wouldn't. I saw in the Philippines, especially, numbers of guys that I was with in a big tent camp place there that had been over in the islands in the war. They'd been in the jungles over there; some of 'em had jungle rot, some of 'em had their foot shot off or their hand or something. I said when I saw all that, man, I was lucky enough to get back alive; whatever happened to me in baseball is just beside the point.

I'm just very lucky that I was in the service. I was up close enough; they had about 25- or 30- or 40,000 Japanese, I guess, backed up in some hills when I got there. I was in the Army and we could see the planes coming over dropping supplies, we could hear the artillery shooting, and all of us there thought we were gonna be in the fighting. I don't know what happened — they pulled me back and put me into a big camp where they had about 50-70,000 troops there and I was supposed to help with the recreation program there because I'd been in sports all my life.

By the grace of God, I could've been on the line shooting at those Japanese and them shooting at me, same as a lot of other kids were. Boy, I came back healthy and okay and could continue whatever career I had and I was thankful for that, so I didn't give it much thought that I had to take two years out of my playing and all. I don't know if I'da stayed there two or three more years or one more or none or whatever. I just never got too concerned about that. It didn't work out that way, so it didn't work out that way.

But I learned other things in baseball and I've been in it all these years and made a good living, so I don't have any complaints about anything.

Would you do it again?

I probably would. *[laughs]* I guess I would. My mother used to say, "You don't even come in to eat. You'd rather be out playing." I played basketball, baseball, tennis, track, whatever. If it was sports I was into it. The only thing I didn't play was football.

But really, I always thought I was a better basketball player than I was a baseball player. In fact, I hadn't played enough baseball like I had basketball because I didn't play baseball in school. We didn't have a team. I was a little leery when I went to the camp down at Beaumont that maybe I may not have played enough baseball to even make it down here. I was just lucky enough it kinda fell in place and they kept me. I had a pretty decent year my first year so I kept going back and it worked out pretty good. But I'd played a lot more basketball than I had baseball. I think the basketball helped me in baseball, too, because it's a quickness game.

Yeah, I think I'd do it again.

The subtitle of this interview is "Double or Nothing." In his only season as a major league regular, Damon Phillips led NL third basemen in double plays with 22 and doubles with 30.

He told about his record-tying game at third base. His 11 assists tied a 54-year-old record and in the nearly 60 years since it has never been bettered. Here are the major league third basemen with 11 assists in a game.

Deacon White, BufN	5-16-1884
Jerry Denny, NYN	5-29-1890
Damon Phillips, BosN	8-29-1944
Ken McMullen, WasA	9-26-1966
Mike Ferraro, NYA	9-14-1968
Chris Sabo, CinN	4-7-1988

DAMON ROSWELL PHILLIPS

Born June 8, 1919, Corsicana, TX
Ht. 6'   Wt. 176   Batted and Threw Right

Year	Team, Lg	G	AB	R	H	2B	3B	HR	RBI	BA
1942	Cin. NL	28	84	4	17	2	0	0	6	.202
1944	Boston, NL	140	489	35	126	30	1	1	53	.258
1946		2	2	0	1	0	0	0	0	.500
3 years		170	575	39	144	32	1	1	59	.250

Bill "Lefty" LeFebvre

First Pitch (1938–1944)

Bill LeFebvre is one of the many major league ballplayers turned out by Holy Cross over the years. It is not a school one would expect to be a source of baseball talent due to its location (Massachusetts), but as many as *six dozen* major league players have come out of its program.

Bill LeFebvre was a standout pitcher at Holy Cross and the Boston Red Sox signed him on his graduation day in 1938 and the next day he was in a Red Sox uniform in Fenway Park. That same day he played in his first game and when it came his turn to bat he hit a home run on the first pitch he saw. Even though he was always listed as a pitcher on the rosters, he became one of the game's top pinch-hitters.

You were a pitcher but you broke in with a bang as a hitter.

I graduated from Holy Cross on a Thursday, June the ninth, 1938, and on a Friday I went to Fenway Park.

The Red Sox helped me through college; they paid half of my tuition. When I tell people how much it cost me to go to Holy Cross they think I was nuts, but when I went in in the fall of 1934, room and board, tuition, and the whole works at Holy Cross was $800 a year.

Jack Barry was the baseball coach at Holy Cross. He had played with the old Philadelphia Athletics and he was a great friend of Eddie Collins [Red Sox general manager], who played second base [with the A's]. Jack Barry managed the Red Sox a couple of years and then he came to Holy Cross. I got in there at Holy Cross a little late in the season and he could only offer me a half-scholarship, which was $400. At first I didn't want to go because I didn't think my parents could afford it. That was in deep Depression. But my father said, "You go ahead. We'll get the money somewhere." We had six kids in the family and I was the youngest. My father was working then making 20 bucks a week and I had three sisters working and they were making 15-18 dollars a week.

I went down to the Cape Cod League and played in 1935 and I won 12 and lost none down there. They invited about 25 guys in the Cape Cod League to go to Fenway Park and work out. We would work out in the morning from nine to twelve and then we'd watch the Red Sox play in the afternoon. After we worked out for ten days, Eddie Collins called me up to the office and asked me if I wanted to play pro ball.

I said, "Yeah, but I want to finish school."

He said, "All right, we'll pay the other half of your tuition."

I said, "Well, I owe 'em for the first year."

He asked how much and I said $500, so he gave me five $100 bills, which I had never seen, and I paid $400 [to Holy Cross] and I kept a hundred bucks. That was my bonus. *[laughs]*

So I graduated on June the ninth, 1938, and went right to Fenway Park the next day, June the tenth, and signed a major league contract. Eddie Collins said, "Go down and see Joe Cronin in the clubhouse and he'll see to it you get a uniform."

My first major league contract was for 600 bucks a month. That's what they were paying then.

The first day I was there we were playing the Chicago White Sox and Monty Stratton was pitching for the White Sox and the Red Sox were getting beat like 12-to-1 in about the fifth or sixth inning and Cronin motioned to me to go out to the bullpen and warm up.

I said, "Who, me?" and he said, "Yeah. Hurry up!" I couldn't believe it. I was sitting on the bench there with guys like Jimmie Foxx and Bobby Doerr and Joe Cronin and Ben Chapman, Roger Cramer, Lefty Grove — guys like that. Pretty good ballplayers; most are in the Hall of Fame right now.

In about the sixth inning I went into the game and it was my turn to bat about the seventh or eighth inning and Cronin said, "Go up and hit, kid," and I went up. The first ball that was ever thrown to me in professional baseball I hit over the left field wall there in Fenway Park. I was a lefthanded hitter; I swung a little late. Monty Stratton was a pretty good pitcher.

Cronin said, "Listen, kid, you might be my pinch-hitter for the rest of the year," but I only stayed there for about another ten days and they sent me to Minneapolis, Triple-A ball.

On the ballclub in Minneapolis in '38 were Ted Williams and Stan Spence and Jim Tabor, guys like that. I played with Ted that summer and the following year I went down to spring training with the Red Sox and right after spring training they sent me to Louisville. They had just bought that ballclub for their Triple-A affiliate. Pee Wee Reese was on that ballclub. That was '39. In the middle of the season they brought me back up to Fenway Park and I finished the season with Boston.

That was Ted's first year and he got $7500. He had a hell of a year. They doubled his salary to 15,000 the next year. He had another good year and then in 1941 when he hit .406 he was getting $25,000.

They sold me to San Francisco. I went to San Francisco with two other guys for Dominic DiMaggio. 1940. I was with the Seals for a half season and then I went from there to Little Rock, Arkansas, then Scranton, all in one year.

How did the Senators acquire you?

I was with Minneapolis in '43 — I was there in '42 and '43 — and Washington bought me [in '43] and I played there half of '43 and all of '44. Then I went in the service. I was in the service in 1945. I came out at the end of '45 and went to spring training with Washington. They had about four or five young lefthanders; I was considered an old man; I was 31 years old. They sold me back to Minneapolis.

I more-or-less finished my career there. I hurt my arm at the end of the year. In those days they didn't even know what a rotator cuff was.

I went to teaching school. I taught school in Rhode Island for 27 years but I also coached at Brown University at the same time. I could get out of school at 2:00 in the afternoon and I'd go coach at Brown. I was born in Pawtucket, Rhode Island, and taught school there. Brown is in Providence, right next door. I coached there for 16 years.

When did you begin scouting?

I was scouting for Washington for about ten years— from '48 to '60 — as a part-time scout. I was with Houston for three years, in '61, '2, and '3 — their first three years. Then I managed a ballclub in the Cape Cod League for the Red Sox at Chatham in 1965. Then I went with the Red Sox in '66 and I was with 'em ever since.

Bill "Lefty" LeFebvre, 1944.

In 1944 you led the American League with ten pinch-hits and you had a career .375 average as a pinch-hitter. You played first base a couple of times. Did you ever consider switching positions?

I should have done that when I first started, but after I played up there a few years it was too late for me to switch around. We had Mickey Vernon and Joe Kuhel playing first base with Washington so I could've never beaten those guys out. And, of course, with Boston Jimmie Foxx was there. I would've had to play first base because I couldn't run that good to play the outfield.

I pinch-hit 29 times in 1944 and got ten hits, I think. If I was playing today I'd probably be making two million dollars. [In my career] I won five and lost five as a pitcher and I hit, I think it was .276. I pinch hit 32 times and I got 12 hits, I think it was.

Other than your first game, does one stand out?

After I hit that home run in '38 I didn't go back to Boston again 'til '39 in the middle of the season. The first time I went up there we were playing Cleveland. I started and won the game. That's when they [Cleveland] had Lou Boudreau and Ray Mack and Hal Trosky and all those. The first time I went up I thought I hit another home run. It hit the top of the screen in Cleveland and bounced back on the field. Another two feet and I think I'd had another home run, which would have been two home runs in the first two times at bat. That was a great thrill.

I remember pinch hitting against the Yankees. I think I pinch-hit against the Yankees about ten times in 1944 and I think I got six hits. One double header at Yankee Stadium I pinch-hit twice and got two basehits. I used to be able to hit pretty good. I look at these guys on TV now. I know I was a better hitter than these guys.

Guys in the old days, if you were an outfielder you had to be a *good* hitter. I mean, for average and power. And the first baseman had to hit, and usually the third baseman. Today I see guys going up to the plate hitting a hundred and forty-three or else .222 and they're batting third and fourth. Not that I'm criticizing what's going on now; I'm just saying if these guys were playing in my day with these averages they'd be playing in Double-A or Triple-A or even A ball. The real good talent is spread out pretty thin now.

I remember Jumping Joe Dugan, the third baseman on the '27 Yankees. He was a Red Sox scout so we got to know one another pretty well. He was telling a story one day. He said, "We started a game and Earle Combs was the first hitter. He opened the game up with a triple and then

Mark Koenig, the shortstop, hit a double. Then Ruth hit a home run and Gehrig hit a home run and Tony Lazzeri hit a double and Bob Meusel hit a triple. I was the seventh hitter and I came up and got a single and they booed me." *[laughs]*

Who was the best player you saw?

The best hitter I ever saw was Ted Williams, without a doubt. I think Joe DiMaggio had to be the best all-around ballplayer I saw. I didn't see Willie Mays; he was after me. Or [Stan] Musial. But in my time, Joe DiMaggio could do everything. He was a great outfielder, great arm; he could run.

In those days nobody stole too many bases. When I was with Washington we had George Case, an outfielder. I think he led the major leagues in stolen bases for about five years in a row, but he stole only 55-60 a year. I think the most he stole in one year was 61.

You see guys running when they're behind like 5-to-nothing or 5-to-1 or something. In the old days you never dared do that. If you were more than two or three runs behind you wouldn't dare try to steal a base.

I think the pitchers were different in the old days. They could hold the runners on better. Today, they've got that big kick like [Dwight] Gooden. These guys are getting a big jump over there at first base. By the time he releases the ball, the runner's taken about 15 steps. They're hard to throw out. The catchers can throw but they can't throw 'em out because they've got such a big lead. I think they're coming back to where they've [the pitchers] got the short stride now. The pitcher's got to release the ball fast.

Who was the best pitcher in your day?

Lefty Grove had to be one of the greatest. Bob Feller was only a young kid when I was playing. He was just starting out. Boy, he could throw 95 or 100 miles an hour easy. What made him effective, when he first started he was wild. I remember Jimmie Foxx. He had that left foot in the bucket a little bit. He said, "He's not gonna hit me in the head!"

And, of course, when I played they didn't have those [batting] helmets. I was a pitcher and I didn't mind brushing a guy back under the chin but, geez, you would never aim for his head. You'd kill the guy. But I think if they would have had those helmets in those days you wouldn't mind lowering the boom on a guy.

They more-or-less expected you to knock 'em down. If you got a guy 0-and-2, you know the next pitch was going to be right under his chin. High inside. Then you'd try to curve him low outside. You didn't want him to hang over that plate. Today they give these warnings. If you knock a guy down, right off the bat they [the umpires] go out to the mound and say, "Don't do that again."

Guys like Sal Maglie, Early Wynn — I played with him — and [Don] Drysdale — guys like that — they'd be thrown out of the game by the second inning if they were pitching today. They were saying, "This is my bread-and-butter and you're not going to take it away from me."

Do you receive much fan mail today?

I probably get two or three a month. I got a letter from a kid in Saudi Arabia the other day — wanted my autograph. I don't see why I'm not on a baseball card. When I was playing they'd take a picture of you, like a postcard.

Did you save souvenirs?

Not much. I gave most of the stuff away. I had a uniform from the Houston Colts, which is probably worth some money today, but I gave that away.

This had only started in the last few years— signing autographs, trying to get things to be sold. Some day I might try to dig out a lot of stuff. I know I must have some stuff around here. I've got an old record, one of these regular phonograph records, of Babe Ruth. He's talking on there.

I get a lot of letters from guys who write me. They would come right down to my house here. Some of these fellows live in New Jersey and New York. They want to buy what I have.

I do have a lot of old press guides. And I've got three World Series rings that Mr. Yawkey gave us, even though they lost he still gave us some rings. I gave one to my son and I gave one to my grandson and they're wearing 'em. From '67, '75, and '86. The '86 is a diamond ring.

Would you be a ballplayer again?

After I got my diploma. I'd want to go through college. I'd love to play right now.

The minimum salary's so much. When I played, at the end of their careers, after playing for years, Ted Williams got $100,000, Joe DiMaggio got 125, I think. And Stan Musial and Al Kaline and guys like that had to play 15 or 20 years before they reached a hundred thousand.

If a guy's got ten years in the big leagues now and he leaves it in there 'til he's 65 he gets more than $100,000 a year pension. You can take a pension out at age 45 now, even if you played *one* year in the big leagues. When I was with Washington, if I'd have stayed there another year or so,

I'd have a pension. You had to wait five years then; now its *one year*. At age 45, with just one year, you can get yourself a couple hundred bucks a month. But if you leave it in there, it accumulates. It's a different ballgame. But I had a lot of fun playing the game. I really enjoyed it.

Do you have any regrets?

Oh, no. No. No regrets at all. I've had a good life. I played ball, I taught school, I coached college, and I've been scouting. I did everything I like to do all my life. I always liked doing what I was doing.

It may be the dream of every kid who has ever played baseball: to hit a home run in his first major league at bat. The trouble is, each man who makes it to the major leagues, and it is a *very* small percentage of those who want to, only gets *one* first at bat.

Thousands of major league players have had that first at bat over the last 100-plus years and fewer than 70 have homered, so the odds are very much against it. And what about the odds against homering in one's first *two* at bats as Bill LeFebvre almost did? Way up there. Bob Nieman did it for the St. Louis Browns on September 14, 1951, and he is the only one.

As rare an occurrence as homering the first time up is, one would think it would be particularly singular for a pitcher to do it. Not so, however; about one out of every seven or eight times it has been done, a pitcher did it.

Only 11 times has it been done on the first pitch a man sees, and three of those were by pitchers. On 11 occasions, also, that first home run was the *last* home run the man hit. Five of these were pitchers. And with such an auspicious beginning, one might think that great things would come for the player, but only two went on to Hall of Fame careers (Earl Averill and Hoyt Wilhelm, and Wilhelm is not there for his hitting).

So here is a rather restricted list, those pitchers who homered on the first pitch of their first at bat and then never homered again.

Bill LeFebvre	BosA	6-10-38
Don Rose	CalA	5-24-72

WILFRED HENRY (BILL, LEFTY) LEFEBVRE

Born November 11, 1915
Ht. 5'11½" Wt. 180 Batted and Threw Left

Pitching record

Year	Team, Lg	G	IP	W	L	Pct	H	BB	SO	ERA
1938	Boston, AL	1	4	0	0	—	8	0	0	13.50
1939		5	26.1	1	1	.500	35	14	8	5.81
1943	Was., AL	6	32.1	2	0	1.000	33	16	10	4.45
1944		24	69.2	2	4	.333	86	21	18	4.52
4 years		36	132.2	5	5	.500	162	51	36	5.03

Batting record

Year	Team, Lg	G	AB	R	H	2B	3B	HR	RBI	BA
1938	Boston, AL	1	1	1	1	0	0	1	1	1.000
1939		7	10	3	3	0	0	0	1	.300
1943	Was., AL	7	14	0	4	3	0	0	1	.286
1944		60	62	4	16	2	2	0	8	.258
4 years		75	87	8	24	5	2	1	11	.276

CARL SCHEIB

A Major League Minor (1943–1954)

Who was the youngest player ever to appear in a major league baseball game in the 20th century?

That's an easy question. Everyone knows it was Joe Nuxhall, on June 10, 1944: 15 years, 10 months, 11 days.

Now, who, before Joe, was the youngest in the 20th century? He's still the youngest ever in the American League. This one is a little tougher.

The answer: Carl Scheib. September 6, 1943: 16 years, 8 months, 5 days. He pitched for the Philadelphia Athletics in the second game of a doubleheader against the New York Yankees.

Joe got racked for five runs in two-thirds of an inning; Carl gave up none in one and one-third.

Joe's second major league game came eight years later. He just wasn't ready in '44 — too young. But Carl's second game came a few days later. And he stayed with the A's, except for a command performance by Uncle Sam, for more than a decade, before experiencing minor league ball, until 1954, after his arm had left him.

This was a bad period for Connie Mack and his Athletics: five cellar teams, only two first division finishes in Carl's 11 years. But Carl had some good years in there: 14-8 with 15 complete games in 1948; 9-12, 11 complete games in '49; 10 saves, second in the league, in '51; 11-7 in '52.

133

Carl could hit, too. He may have been the best hitting pitcher of his time. As a 17-year-old in 1944, he went three-for-ten with two doubles. In 1948, he batted .298 (31-for-104) with eight doubles, three triples, two home runs, and 21 RBI. He even played two games in the outfield. As a pinch-hitter that season, he was 7-for-16 (.438). In '51, he walloped the opposition at a .396 clip (21-for-53) with two doubles, two triples, and two home runs. For his career, he batted an even .250 and as a pinch hitter his average was .263. If the A's had had a pitching staff, he may well have been converted to a full-time outfielder.

But the A's needed all the arms they could get in those days, so Carl remained on the mound. His 11-year record is 45-65, but it would have been interesting to see what he could have done on a decent team.

Once his arm went, he left the major leagues and tried the minors, but the arm wouldn't respond and he retired from baseball at the age of only 30. He dropped anchor in San Antonio, where he played his last game, and still lives there.

His name will forever be in the record books; the days of 16-year-old major leaguers have passed. But he was more than an item in passing in the records; he was a legitimate ballplayer.

Did you go directly from high school to the A's?

I quit high school and went to Philadelphia. I had been there for a tryout when I was 15 and he [Connie Mack] said, "Get back here as fast as you can next year." I went to school and as soon as the club came back from spring training I quit school and went down there and stayed with the club just pitching batting practice for a long time. Later on, I started making road trips with them and then in September I signed a contract.

Were you a pretty big kid?

Oh, yes. I was very big, very strong. I think I was six-foot; I weighed about 185.

You stayed in the major leagues for 11 years before you ever saw the minor leagues.

I left Philadelphia early in the '54 season. I went over to the Cardinals for about a month and then I finished that year out in the [Pacific] Coast League with Portland, Oregon. Then I played out there the next year and then I came down here to San Antonio in '56 and '57 and then I quit.

Carl Scheib as a 16 year old rookie, 1943 (courtesy Carl Scheib).

That's how I ended up in San Antonio; I liked it here and I just decided to move here.

Talk about your first game.

The first time I pitched in relief. It was against the Yankees. In fact, it was the same day I signed the contract. Of course, my parents had to sign. And after I signed the players were out on the field already. He said, "Get out there and get your uniform," and somebody said to go to the bullpen, which was very exciting. I was sitting there and somebody said, "Warm up."

Then somebody said, "You're in there." I didn't have time to get excited. *[laughs]* It was only an inning or two, but if I remember right I think I got them out. We were losing, which we did quite often.

They just kind of fed me relief jobs through '44 and then I went in the service in '45-'46. In '47 I came out and got kind of relief jobs again until he decided to start me.

I pitched [started] my first game in Detroit, which I won. Well, I won my first three and then the roof caved in. I wound up winning four and losing six, but I pitched some good games. My first game was a shutout. I beat Detroit, 4-to-nothing or something like that.

I lost my first one against the Yankees. I remember that was a very good game. [Vic] Raschi pitched against me and I think he had a one- or two-hitter and I had about a three-hitter. They got two home runs off of me and I think they beat me, 2-to-1.

You didn't have much of an offense behind you.

No. You can say we had a loose ballclub for all the years I was there. I think we ended up fourth once. But maybe you can say you contributed to it, too, you know.

It gets pretty despairing when you go out there and you give up a run or two and you already believe that you've lost the game because it was hard for us to get runs. And it always seems when you're on a losing ballclub, if you get five runs, why, they get six. You get one, they get two—always a little short.

I wish, in my career, I would've been traded off to another club. I would've liked to go to Detroit or Boston. I almost made it once. Detroit wanted me and Eddie Joost and they [the A's] wouldn't let him go so it fell through. I wish I could have been traded, though, just to see if I could have done any better.

I always pitched good ball against Detroit and I liked to play in that park for some reason. I used to like Detroit a whole lot. That's where I wish I went.

In '48 you went 14-8 and the A's finished fourth. They were the fewest games out that they'd been in 20 years.

Yeah. We should have won the pennant that year. We had a good pitching staff; there were three or four others who had as good a record as I did or better.

Going into September, I think, the first four teams were percentage points apart. I remember, we came home from Boston and Eddie Joost had bruised his hand real bad and he had had a good year leading off. He had around 20 home runs. We dropped, I think, something like seven games right quick, which sank us in fourth place.

And then we had to play at the end of the year to cinch fourth place, which I was lucky enough to pitch and I think I beat Detroit again. No, I beat the Yankees.

You had a pretty good year the next season [9-12], but then you had a couple of pretty rough years [3-10 and 1-12].

That 1-and-12 was a pretty good year for me, even though I lost so many games. They had me in relief a lot and I got a raise the next year, so they thought it was pretty good.

You were second in the league in saves to Ellis Kinder.

They didn't count them [saves] at that time. It didn't mean a hill of beans at contract time. You know, wins and losses is about all they ever had an argument on.

Then the next year [1952], they reported I'd be relieving again because I'd done fairly well. That was good, just so I knew what I'd be doing. Soon as the season started, I was a starter again, then relief, then start. He'd done a lot of that with the pitchers, but it hurt us. And I guess you have to do that with that kind of a ballclub; you've got to try to find somebody.

I know every year he stuck with me as a starter I had fairly good years. It was hard to keep your rhythm — you were a long reliever, sometimes a short reliever. Anybody that was available went in there.

Does one game stand out?

Well, nothing too exciting happened. I was pretty pleased one time in '48 when I beat Chicago and hit my first home run. You know, pitchers always like to hit. It was a grand slam. Of course, I always did like to hit.

That was my next question. For a pitcher, you were probably as good a hitter as there was. You pinch-hit a lot and even played a couple of games in the outfield.

Yeah, I played the outfield a little bit and I did quite a bit of pinch-hitting and was pretty successful. One year I won a couple of games in the ninth with two out. I felt like I could hit. I had confidence hitting.

Did you ever consider switching positions — going to the outfield?

Oh, Lord, I wish they would have! They talked about it so many times, but they needed pitchers so bad. I've known times when we only had two pitchers available to pitch. Everybody had sore arms.

One of those times I was pitching in Chicago and I think they scored seven or eight runs off of me in the first inning. They were just little bloop singles here and little singles there and one through the infield. I came into the bench and we had no pitchers and he asked me if I could finish the game. I said yeah and I shut them out the next seven innings and I think in the ninth inning they scored a run or two on an error. I got one of the biggest hands from the Chicago fans I think I ever got in a ball-game. Charlie Harris— he was a tall old boy from Florida — and I were the *only* two pitchers available. Everybody else had sore arms.

In fact, I was on the disabled list one time in my later years and stayed home off a road trip and they called me up to come pitch in Cleveland. With a sore arm. I lasted about three or four innings.

I had a good strong arm, but looking back over the years I think I hurt it in the service and it never showed up until the latter years. It started that year I was relieving because I think I was in about ten straight games— some were eight innings, some were one inning — and then I think I was off a day and then I was in six more days. And that's not even counting what I threw in the bullpen. It seems like after that I just started going downhill. It never did come around. I had a hard time in spring training sometimes. One year I went barnstorming with Danny Litwhiler and I hurt it again in that cold weather. From then on, I was just hanging on.

One time in the service I was pitching over there and they were getting to me pretty good, so I started throwing harder and harder and I hurt it then. I was so young I didn't think much of it, but later on, looking back, I think that may be when it started. I tell you, it's no fun having a sore arm.

Pitching has changed a lot since you began.

Yes. They don't care as long as a pitcher goes five or six innings. In our day, the only argument we had was winning and losing. If we got into the eighth or ninth inning in a close game, they wouldn't dare pull us out. We were going to win or lose it ourselves. Now they'll pull him in a minute and if the reliever loses you always wonder whether the change should have been made or not. Now they've got relievers and the short men and like that; that's a big change.

Of course, we old-timers sit here and say, "Nobody pitches nine innings," but it's what you've been geared up for; if you're taught all you need is five or six, that's all you'll throw. Today you can bear down from the start, knowing all they have to go is five or six innings. Back then we had to pace ourselves and only bear down when we had to.

Sometimes a guy is pitching a one-hitter and they don't hesitate to take him out. *[laughs]* That's pretty hard.

Another thing I don't like is that designated hitter. I think pitchers ought to hit for themselves. I think most of them could hit better if they knew they had to hit.

Who was the best hitter you saw?

Oh, there were some *real* good hitters around in those days. Of course, there were some that would always give certain pitchers a fit, like Johnny Mize. I could never get him out. It seemed like his bat looked about 40 inches long and about as wide as a two-by-twelve. Guys like [Ted] Williams were a lot better hitters and he beat me, you know, but he never gave me much trouble.

Yogi [Berra] would give me trouble. He was the kind of guy that was hard to pitch to. He could hit a ball anyplace — over his head. He was just so well balanced and so quick with his arms. He'd say, "Throw it and I'll hit it."

[Mickey] Mantle came in pretty late, when I was getting out, but he was improving. He hit a couple out on me in Shibe Park — rattled the deck up there. *[laughs]*

Who was the best all-around player?

Take guys like Billy Martin; he was a hustler. Phil Rizzuto. Those guys could hit, they could bunt, they could field.

Joe Gordon. Lou Boudreau was a good one. Very good. I'm talking about all-around. You've got some that were great hitters and then a little lax in the field. But Lou Boudreau was a great one.

Old Vern Stephens was pretty good — better than most people thought. That darned Boston team had some hitters. We went in there to play a four-game series one time and they scored 40 runs off of us! They were devastating. They had [Walt] Dropo on first and Bobby Doerr was there, and Ted Williams and Stephens and Dom DiMaggio. They were tough to beat. We never beat them in two years in Boston.

There was a game I felt pretty good about. I got hooked up with ol'

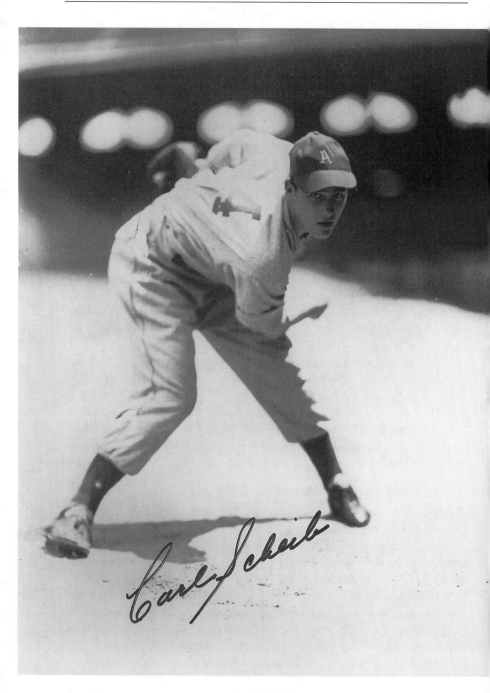

Carl Scheib.

Diz Trout — he just got traded from Detroit — in an 11-inning game and I beat them. Trout started and big ol' Al Benton relieved. I got more publicity out of that game than most others.

That winter, Trout and us went hunting up in Maine and he never did let me forget it. "If I hadn't been so damned old and run out of gas, I'd have won!" He was in his final years; he was a good pitcher, too. He and [Hal] Newhouser were together in Detroit. They were tough.

Who was the one best pitcher?

Cleveland had a pretty good pitching staff a lot of years. It's pretty hard to pick just one.

As a hitter, was there anyone you particularly enjoyed facing?

Yeah, anybody that threw hard. I was geared up for a good, hard fastball. The harder they threw, the better I liked them.

[Bob] Feller had a real good curve in later years — that big old roundhouse. I beat him one time in the ninth inning in Philly. I pinch-hit and he threw me that big old curve and I hit it straight down the right field line, which was pretty lucky, but it won the game. But he had a *heck* of a curve. I hadn't seen him pitch in his early years, before we went in the service, but I know afterwards he had a hell of a curveball.

One good pitcher was Newhouser for Detroit. He was always business out there — good curveball, good fastball, pretty hard to hit. He was a long time getting in the Hall of Fame; he's about as good as any up there. It had a lot to do with publicity through the years. Kind of being a character helps. To be remembered, you've got to be kind of a character. Take the New York clubs with the big press; they always build them up and you remember them more.

Do you sign autographs for the fans?

Oh, yeah. It's an honor to sign them — just glad people kind of remember me a little bit.

If you went back to the age of 16, would you do it again?

Oh, yes! I did it to leave. I decided I had to go; everybody who stayed where I was raised were either farmers or miners.

Schooling was almost unimportant at that time. I shouldn't say that; it's a bad thing to say, but the people raised there who stayed there ended up working in the mines or on the farms and I said, "Hell, I'm going to get out and do something else."

My daddy left it up to me. He said, "You can either finish school or go play ball." Of course, that's a dumb thing to say to a guy who wants to play ball. *[laughs]* I knew I should go back and finish, but I got too much time under my belt and never did.

I would do it again, the same way. I left home to go play ball, only I believe I would try to get with a different club or go to a different position. I would have loved to play the outfield; I always thought I could play there.

I played a couple of games out there and I guess the good Lord wasn't with me because I didn't get any hits. I hit the ball; I didn't strike out. But if I'd played three or four more games maybe I'd have broke loose; you can't tell, but that's life.

I had an awful lot of confidence in hitting. I just believed that any pitch a man could throw I was going to hit someplace. That's really why I was pinch-hitting with the club — because I didn't strike out. Connie had seen so many guys go up there to pinch-hit and they would *take* pitches and then stand there and take a third strike. As young as I was, I knew the only reason you went in to pinch hit was to *hit*. I swung and I believed I could hit the ball — and I did. It may have been back to the pitcher or it may have been a basehit, but I very seldom struck out. If you can put it in play, you're going to get hits sooner or later. I felt confident.

As far as playing the outfield, pitchers are always shagging fly balls out there. There was no worry about playing the position.

How did you come to settle in San Antonio?

I played here last in '57. We lived around Philadelphia, but I told my wife if I ever get out of baseball we're going to someplace where it's warm. I always liked spring training — it was warm. We kind of liked San Antonio so we went back and put our home up for sale. We came down here and bought a piece of land. Now I wish I was out in the country; I'm in the middle of town now. It's grown so fast around here; we *were* out in the country. *[laughs]*

What do you think of the baseball salaries today?

I'd even play for nothing just to get the pension. We old-timers have tried to get a little of that, but the union said no. There's so *doggone* much money in there. I know there's some ballplayers, including myself, that a hundred bucks a month would mean a hell of a lot to them.

Dick Fowler, a good friend of mine, has passed away and his wife hardly gets anything out of that pension — not enough to get by on. She's been having a hard time for years. The way I see it, the pension's worth more than anything. They won't have to go to work, that's for sure.

There's a lot of changes. We used to get six dollars a day for meal money. And tips came out of that. We'd go on road trips for 20 to 30 days, which meant we had laundry bills and stuff like that. And taxi fares. But in those days, a meal in a good restaurant was only about four dollars.

It's good for the players, but I think the guy that invests in a ballclub ought to be able to make some money, too. They're taking a risk.

And I think they need ballplayers. There's not too many good ones out there. You see guys that you think are through that hang on for four or five more years because there's no one to take their places. Back years ago they had some farm teams that were awfully good teams. The Yankees had Kansas City; they had as good a ballclub as two or three teams in the majors.

And a lot of guys preferred to play in the Coast League; they were making more money than they would in the big leagues. But today, the guys that would finish their careers out there are hanging on in the majors.

We have said that Carl Scheib is the youngest player ever to play in the American League and Joe Nuxhall is the youngest major leaguer of the 20th century. But Joe is only the second youngest of all time, and Carl ranks down at sixth.

The youngest major leaguer of all time was Fred Chapman, who was 14 years, seven months, and 27 days old when he took the mound for Philadelphia of the American Association in 1887. Nuxhall was next, then comes Joe Stanley, another pitcher, who was 16 years, five months, and nine days old in 1897 when he debuted with Washington of the National League. Willie McGill, yet another pitcher, was 16 years, five months, and 29 days old in 1890 when he first pitched for Cleveland of the Players' League.

World War II was the reason for most of the real young players appearing. Five of the 11 who played major league ball before they were 17 years old did so in 1944 or 1945. The next youngest was Tommy Brown, a shortstop with the Dodgers, who was 16 years, 7 months, and 28 days old in 1944. Then comes Scheib.

The last 16 year old to play in the majors was Jim Derrington. He was a bonus baby of the 1950s who was 16 years, 10 months, and one day old when he pitched for the White Sox in 1956.

Carl Alvin Scheib

Born January 1, 1927, Gratz, PA
Ht. 6'1"   Wt. 192   Batted and Threw Right

Pitching record

Year	Team, Lg	G	IP	W	L	Pct	H	BB	SO	ERA
1943	Phi., AL	6	18.2	0	1	.000	24	3	3	4.34
1944		15	37.1	0	0	.000	36	11	13	4.10
1945		4	8.2	0	0	.000	6	4	2	3.12
1946	Military service									
1947		21	116	4	6	.400	121	55	26	5.04
1948		32	198.2	14	8	.636	219	76	44	3.94
1949		38	182.2	9	12	.429	191	118	43	5.12
1950		43	106	3	10	.231	138	70	37	7.22
1951		46	143	1	12	.077	132	71	49	4.47
1952		30	158	11	7	.611	153	50	42	4.39
1953		28	96	3	7	.300	99	29	25	4.88
1954	Phi., AL-StL, NL	4	6.2	0	2	.000	11	6	6	14.85
11 years		267	1071.2	45	65	.409	1130	493	290	4.88

Batting record

Year	Team, Lg	G	AB	R	H	2B	3B	HR	RBI	BA
1943	Phi., AL	6	5	0	0	0	0	0	0	.000
1944		15	10	1	3	2	0	0	0	.300
1945		4	2	0	0	0	0	0	0	.000
1946	Military service									
1947		22	45	4	6	0	0	0	3	.133
1948		52	104	14	31	8	3	2	21	.298
1949		47	72	9	17	2	0	0	10	.236
1950		50	52	6	13	0	1	1	6	.250
1951		48	53	9	21	2	2	2	8	.396
1952		44	82	4	18	0	0	0	7	.220
1953		35	41	4	8	0	0	0	4	.195
1954	Phi., AL-StL, NL	4	2	0	0	0	0	0	0	.000
11 years		327	468	51	117	14	6	5	59	.250

ROY PARTEE

If Only the Throw
Had Been Good (1943–1948)

The distance from Class B to the major leagues is a lot longer in talent than it is in miles. Roy Partee made that jump in 1943 and didn't miss a beat. It's a huge jump and one that can no longer be made. Classes B, C, and D no longer exist, but 50 and 60 years ago, the level of play in B was probably every bit as good as it is in AA today.

Partee was a major league catcher for five years and a part of baseball for half a century. The last half of his time in the game was spent as a scout, where he built a reputation for being one of the best at evaluating young talent.

Many of today's fans aren't familiar with his name, though, but most have seen his photograph, although they aren't aware that they have.

Every baseball fan knows the story of Enos Slaughter's mad dash around the bases in the final game of the 1946 World Series. The picture of him sliding home with the Series-winning run shows the Red Sox catcher waiting in vain for a throw that was both too late and off-target. That catcher is Roy Partee.

❖ ❖ ❖

How did you get started in professional baseball?

Originally, the Los Angeles Angels [PCL] signed me at a tryout. I used to go down and catch batting practice at Wrigley Field when I was only a sophomore or junior in high school and I knew Truck Hannah [Angels' manager] — I mean, he knew me — and I used to go down and put the gear on and catch for him, and then, soon as I graduated [1937], I had already filled out a questionnaire and at the end of my school year I went to Catalina Island for I guess it was about two months. $70 a month. They had a semipro team over there made up of Peanuts Lowrey and quite a few fellas that the Angels signed eventually. Then I came home and they offered me a contract to go out the next year.

I went down to Bisbee. It was in the Arizona-Texas League — Bisbee and Tucson and Albuquerque. It was only four clubs— short trips. The trip from Bisbee to Albuquerque was a pretty long trip. I made another $75 a month by driving the bus. That was a big bonus for me, but I lost a lot of sleep 'cause I used to have to drive the bus all night and then park it. The guys would go up in the rooms in the hotel and they'd sleep and catch about two or three hours' sleep, but I had to be back with the bus to take 'em out to the ballpark for a night game.

You must not have needed much sleep. If you'd have been rested, there's no telling what you would have done. [Roy batted .365, drove in 107 runs, and scored 106.]

Yeah, I might have gone to the big leagues. *[laughs]*

You weren't Angels' property long; you played for the San Francisco Seals three years later.

What happened, I went out the next year and I played under Goldie Holt [in St. Joseph, MO, Western Association]. We didn't get along. I had gained a few pounds, getting married. He second-guessed me 'cause he was the second baseman. I was in and out; I was just really disgusted. Bert Barkelew was one of our pitchers who went into the Coast League the following year. We had a pretty good ballclub, but Goldie Holt was a terrible manager. He couldn't handle young fellas— didn't have the patience — so when I came home —'course, I was supposed to go to the next club; I don't remember which one, but I think it was somewhere in the Texas League — I waited and waited and finally Earl Hamilton — he was president of the ballclub — wrote me and said, "I'm gonna have to give you your release 'cause the Angels don't have a position for you." So I had about a month to go before spring training and I was out of a job. This was at the end of '39.

That ended that year and the followin' spring I was lookin' around. There was Dan Crowley, a jeweler workin' part-time on his own down in Los Angeles; he called me and said that Salt Lake City was lookin' for a catcher, so I contacted them. I went up there for a quick workout and they signed me, so I stayed in Salt Lake City that year and that's when the owner of the Seals, Charlie Graham, came in and saw me play five games and decided to buy my contract from owner Eddie Mulligan, a great major league infielder. That was in the Coast League, so I jumped from a Class C league up into Triple-A the next year and I sat the bench under [Lefty] O'Doul. I think I got into maybe 30 ballgames. I only caught the guys that threw too hard and [Bruce] Ogrodowski and [Joe] Sprinz didn't wanna catch 'em. I had to do the dirty work and ended up with swollen hands and bumps all over me because these were old-time catchers and, 'course, I wanted to play and I got beat up a little bit catchin', but I thought I did pretty good.

Tony Lazzeri was on the ballclub and he was the second baseman and he could see I wasn't gettin' a good chance, so what happened, the following year he managed Portsmouth, Virginia, and he talked Mr. Lawrence, the owner of the ballclub, into buyin' my contract from the Seals. So from Triple-A I go down to a B league in Portsmouth in the Piedmont League.

With Tony Lazzeri's help and enthusiasm and all, he said, "You keep goin'. You're havin' a good year." And I did have a good year [.290]; I hit the ball real well and I played with sprained ankles and so on. He brought me in near the end of the year and he said, "What club would you like to go to if they buy your contract, the Red Sox or Philadelphia [Phillies]?" I said, "The Red Sox." Tony said, "We'll see what we work out."

So, anyway, I was sold from a Class B league and went up to the major leagues and reported to the Boston Red Sox in spring training of '43. I got off to a good start and stayed there ands I think I hit .290 or somethin' like that, which was pretty good comin' out of a Class B league. Mr. Frank Lawrence [Portsmouth owner] mailed me $1500 for Christmas as a bonus for my sale to the Red Sox. He was a real gentleman as it was not in my contract.

You were Boston's number one catcher in both '43 and '44.

Yeah, but I think that's when Hal Wagner, a lefthand hitter, came over from the A's [in 1944]. They made another trade 'cause we had Ed McGah that played a little bit, but he never got anywhere in the Red Sox organization. He was a bullpen catcher, but he couldn't stand the heat; he'd fall flat on his back. He was from the Bay Area and he collapsed a couple

Roy Partee, 1946.

of times and I had to go in and relieve him catchin'. He wasn't much of a prospect as far as I was concerned and they didn't think so, either.

I caught the remainder of that year and the Army was after me, so I skipped around. I had my papers transferred back and forth during that whole season. Then they give us our physicals back in Boston 'cause they were after all the pro ballplayers. They figured if they could play ball, they could go in the service, so there was Bobby Doerr and [Bill] Conroy and myself; there was about five of us that went down and faced the board. We were told before we took our clothes off to get a physical that we were in the Army because we were ballplayers. I had a spur on my back with which they rejected me, and another one—[Leon] Culberson—had a knee spur, Bobby Doerr had a busted eardrum and they rejected him, so when we stood there we all were rejected for little ailments, but one week later we were called in again for an Army physical.

We were told by a yeoman before we took our clothes off that we were in whether we were 4-F or not because of the feelings from Washington 'cause they sent a colonel down and he told us, "Sorry, but we can't help it because of the newspapers and people writin' in and their sons are in the Army and you're not; you're playin' ball and all that stuff." So when we stood there before this captain, he just stamped all our papers "Accepted." That was just about the time of the invasion in '44, so I was headed for the Army and was supposed to be in the training camp back East, but that winter I traveled across the United States five times.

I was married and had three kids at the time and that deferred me, but I still was accepted and I was finally in uniform and I went through two six-week trainings in the infantry. We were gonna go to Europe — to Germany — and then they changed that so I came back across the United States to the West Coast and I ended up getting on a boat to go to the South Pacific and I ended up on Leyte Island. I was in there for a year — all the rest of '44, all of '45–then I busted my butt to get out of the service.

I was on Leyte Island and they informed me I could go home on the next boat and, man, I'm telling you, I got my stuff together and got on that boat and I arrived home and I had eight days at home to buy some civilian clothes and get on a plane and report back to Boston and I reported to Boston on Opening Day of the American League. They always opened in Washington, D.C., and I was in Boston workin' out, playin' catch with one of the other fellas that just got out of he service, and they won that opening game and then they came home that night and that's when I got to meet the ballclub. I walked out on the field the day after the season opened as a Boston Red Sox player. That was in '46.

Then we got in the World Series. We won the pennant by 16 or 18 games and it was a breeze. Really. We had a great ballclub and everything was goin' our way. You know, when you win a pennant you got all the breaks, too. That's what hurt us for the World Series is that the Cardinals ended up in a tie and they had to play it off, so we didn't do a thing except play exhibition games and work out in 40-degree weather in Boston. We were waiting for them that whole week and then we were gonna open up the following Monday or Tuesday for the World Series. The Cardinals won it [the playoff], of course, the last day. We opened up back in St. Louis. My folks drove all the way from California to be there.

We weren't *really* primed because we'd sat on our tail end too long, but the Cardinals were still hot from the playoffs. I'm not usin' that as an excuse, but it was just that you have to face the facts. They had a pretty good ballclub, defensive and all, but overall I think we had a better ball-club.

Ted Williams, in the exhibition game, he got hit with a fastball from the pitcher on Washington, Mickey Haefner. He got hit on the elbow and they iced him up. He started in the World Series with that elbow. He was in pain and he couldn't really swing the bat like he did without the injury. He was handicapped and, of course, he hit a couple of line drives, but they were caught. I felt for the guy and that was one reason he couldn't get a ball in the air. And they pitched around him.

Rudy York was on that ballclub. I probably learned more baseball than I ever did in my life from Rudy York. A good man on a ballclub. He hit a home run, I think, in the second game up into the hot dog stand in St. Louis, which won the ballgame. In fact, I think one of his rooters was eating a hot dog and it knocked it out of his hand. *[laughs]* He was standing in front of the hot dog stand out in the left field bleachers and I'll never forget it. He said, "My idol knocked the hot dog out of my hands." He was tryin' to catch the ball. *[laughs]*

But, anyway, Rudy York, I thought, did *wonders* with the ballclub. He had everybody on their toes and like stealin' signs and inside baseball, which I never realized, playing against him, that he knew so much about baseball. He used to pick up pitchers' weaknesses of maybe throwin' a fastball or a curveball. Maybe he'd telegraph it. Rudy taught me — and the whole ballclub — quite a bit about knowing inside baseball. I would have to say he was one of the smartest men on the ballclub or in the league. He was really great.

Talk about Slaughter's run in Game Seven.

The score was tied and we were in the bottom of the eighth and Slaughter walked and there was two outs. Then [Harry] Walker came up to hit and Klinger — Bob Klinger — was pitching, so with two outs and a man on first base, I figured, well, we better pitch away from this guy a little bit 'cause he wasn't a long ball hitter, number one, and he was sort of a punch-and-judy type hitter. What we heard was that we didn't have to worry about him hittin' the long ball, so I signaled for Klinger to keep the ball away from him 'cause I didn't want him to hit a ball in the hole and pull the ball by Rudy York at first base and then he [Slaughter] would go to third base if there was a base hit.

I gave Klinger the signal and he nodded. I think we had the count 2-and-1 — two balls and one strike. Klinger didn't have a big curveball; he had a good sinker and a slider-type curveball, so I moved on the outside corner and I said, "Well, I just gave him my signal to keep the ball away and up a little bit," so in case it was a ball he would take the pitch and at the same time, if it was a ball outside and high, I'd have the chance to throw Slaughter out if he was stealin'. I just *knew* that he was gonna go. I didn't want him to pitch in so he could pull the ball, so I moved out a little bit on the outside of the plate and the ball *was* high and away from him, but it was still not close to the strike zone. Klinger made a good pitch.

And, sure enough, he stuck his bat out and he hit this little blooper a little bit towards center and Culberson had gone into centerfield at the time for Dom [DiMaggio] because Dom had pulled a leg muscle. Culberson runs in and, of course, he can't catch the ball and when the ball was hit Slaughter broke for second base, runnin' like a son-of-a-gun. On the pitch he was runnin', which I anticipated he was gonna do, and Pesky's runnin' — all I can see is his number — and the ball drops in front of Pesky and in front of Culberson and Culberson came in and kinda went to scoop the ball up and he kinda fumbled it a little bit.

A lot of people don't realize it, but this is what *I* saw. I remember seein' the ball roll into his glove and roll out and then he picked it up and instead of comin' up and pickin' out Slaughter running — he should've seen Slaughter runnin' at the time of the pitch, he should've picked that up — and Doerr is yellin' at Pesky and Culberson and he's yellin', "Home-home-home!", and, of course, Culberson can't hear Bobby Doerr because of the crowd yellin'. If DiMaggio was in center field I don't think Slaughter would try to score; if so, he would have been out at home by 20-30 feet.

It was just a constant roar and so Culberson came up and he just flipped the ball overhand to Pesky. Pesky got it and he turned and he started his run in and he took a step and a two-step and he brought up his arm to throw the ball, but he didn't know where to go. He didn't see Slaughter going *into* third base and then Slaughter just put his head down and I could see that and Doerr could see it and Doerr had his hand up to his face and he was yellin', "Home-home-home-home!", and, like I said, nobody could hear him.

So then Pesky comes up and he takes a little hop — a skip — and he threw the ball to me, but the ball was so high. He didn't have a real strong arm, like [Eddie] Pellagrini; if Pellagrini had been playin' shortstop, Pellagrini would've thrown him out by ten feet because of his arm; he had a rifle and Pesky had a blooping-type arm. He never threw a ball on the line with somethin' on it to first base; it was always soft-tossed-like, but he'd always throw runners out, but on this he reared back and he threw it sky-high and I looked at the ball up in the air and I could see Slaughter out of the corner of my eye and the ball was hangin' in the air, and I said, "Oh, God," you know, to myself. He's got the play beat; I can't do a thing about it because it's too high and it's up the line, it's up third base. If I'd've let it hit the ground and stayed at home plate and tried to block Slaughter, which I could've done, it would have been interference.

If you've ever seen the picture of it, I'm up the line and Slaughter is sliding across home plate. Slaughter is across home plate, but, like I say, if I have the ball — if Pesky had kept the ball down in the dirt towards me — I'd've had a better chance. But I'm standin' there waitin' for the ball to drop out of heaven, for criminy sake! *[laughs]* It just kept hangin' up there and there was no way, but if he'd've thrown the ball down *low*, say about the height of the pitcher on the mound — at that height — I'd've had a bet-ter chance of catchin' the ball and blocking the runner at the same time, but there was no way. I could tell from experience; I said, "If I have home plate, he's gonna score anyway. He's just got the play beat, the ball's hangin' up there, so I better block it and take a chance."

So I did; I ran up, oh, say, ten feet and blocked the ball on the first hop. I fell down on one knee to block it so it wouldn't get through me because I had to keep the runner from goin' from second to third base — Walker — 'cause he was on second base. If I'd've let the ball get by me, he would've ended up on third base and that might mean another run. The only thing I had left to do was block the ball and keep Walker from goin' to third base because Slaughter had the play beat because the ball was so high in the air. And that was it: the end of the game. *[laughs]*

Bobby Doerr afterwards — we were in the clubhouse and we were sad sacks, I tell you — Bobby said, "I yelled at Pesky to go 'Home-home-home.'" I said, "I know you were." I remember Bobby runnin' and he was in back of second base and running towards second and yellin' towards Pesky and he had his glove up and he kept sayin', "Home-home-home!", and I *knew*, 'cause he glanced at me a couple of times, he knew Slaughter was gonna not stop at all — he was gonna be comin' home — and Bobby knew that. He was tryin' to tell Pesky. Pesky couldn't hear him! Couldn't hear him because of the crowd roar.

He [Pesky] should've, on the play, he should've seen — playin' short-stop — Slaughter break for second base and then with the crowd roarin', he should've assumed that he's tryin' to score 'cause that's the winning run. He should've assumed that and instead of even hesitating, he should've whirled and fired the ball to me, low, where I could handle it. I would say that Pesky flubbed the dub just momentarily and, like I say, I knew he did-n't have the arm, but he could've maybe cut down one step and then throw low and it would've helped maybe by three or four steps in order for me to catch the ball. Somebody would've had a broken bone somewhere, either Slaughter or myself, if we'd've collided because I've had very few guys score when I've got the ball in my hand. I've been cut and my shoes have been ruined and I've been bowled over.

You had some momentous collisions.

Billy Johnson [Yankee third baseman] knocked me over. I rolled over twice after he hit me. He was about a hundred-and-ninety and I'm stand-ing there sort of blind-sided one time and I'd just caught the ball and I turned around and he had his shoulder down and he hit me on the right side 'cause my back was to first base and he was comin' down and he just put his head down and I tagged him out, but I rolled over twice on the ground from him hittin' me. I've got a picture of that that shows me; my feet are off the ground, my butt is about three feet up high. *[laughs]* All you can see is my number; I remember that 'til this day. *[laughs]*

The reason I'm laughin' is what happened later on in a play that was in Boston after that one series. They came into Boston and we had a play at home plate and once again I took the throw from Rudy York and I know that Johnson's tryin' to score, so I had my right shoulder towards home plate 'cause I wanted to catch the ball and I figured I had a chance to tag Johnson and what I did, I saw him outta the corner of my eye goin' into a slide and I threw my body in front of home plate and I had the ball in my right hand and I reached in back sideways and tagged at him. I don't know that his feet are already comin' towards me, but by the time I went to tag him, his belt buckle was there and I tagged him from the belt buckle right up under his chin and across his nose. I've got a picture of that. *[laughs]*

I didn't know that I did any harm to him at the time, but he comes out the next day, says, "Hey, Roy!", and I looked at him and he's got this big swollen lip, big scab comin' up on it, all bruised. He said, "Now that's one-and-one. We got one more to go. It's tied." *[laughs]* Boy, he had a lip that wouldn't quit. His whole upper lip was swollen and that's where I tagged him with the ball.

First time when he bowled me over, he did it with his shoulder. This time, he tried to slide under me 'cause I guess he knew I was gonna be layin' across the third base line in front of home plate, so he started to slide earlier and when he hit the ground I caught the ball and I just tagged in back of me. I didn't know where he was; all I know is he was down close to the line. I backhanded at him. I didn't do it on purpose, but I knew I had to tag the guy and hang on to the ball. It was funny. We both laughed about afterwards. He was a pretty good guy. He took it all as a joke. It's baseball, what the heck.

You were traded to the Browns for the 1948 season.

That was a trade of ten of us. Ten of us went to St. Louis for Jack Kramer and Vern Stephens and ... was it Denny Galehouse? I think there was one more pitcher. It was ten for two or ten for three. Stephens was the one they really wanted because goin' into Fenway Park with him as a pull hitter, you know. He could hit a ball nine miles.

Pellagrini was my roommate when we went over to the St. Louis club. Gerry Priddy was on the ballclub — he was traded from Washington — so we didn't have a bad ballclub. Pellagrini and Gerry Priddy made a good

Roy Partee (courtesy Roy Partee).

double play combination. We had Chuck Stevens at first base and Whitey Platt was out in the outfield. Les Moss was the other catcher. We didn't have that bad of a ballclub.

Wasn't pitching the problem?

We had some guys that could throw pretty good. Fred Sanford. Ned Garver was new, but they didn't expect him to do so much, but he turned out to be our best pitcher. I think he won about ten ballgames. Cliff Fannin could throw pretty good.

Ned Garver—it was his first year. When the season ended we got off the bus at home. I remember this: He came up and he said, "Say, Roy, before you leave, I wanna tell you somethin'." He said, "You know what? You got me more strikes than any catcher I've ever pitched to." I said, "What are you talkin' about?" He said, "You caught the ball close to home plate." In other words, if it was a little slider or a breaking ball, I caught the ball before it got too far back for the umpire. I never realized. I knew that to try to get strikes you have to try to cheat a little bit on the umpire, but I didn't realize I was cheatin' *that* much.

Your reputation was that you were outstanding at calling a game and were one of the top handlers of pitchers.

I was told that several times and I know that I had a lot of friends in pitchers. *[laughs]* They liked the way I caught 'em and I appreciated what Garver told me, but I never personally realized that at the time. I knew I could get strikes on certain umpires by catchin' the ball and holdin' it out away from me and holdin' it close to the plate as I could. I'd kinda backhand the ball a little bit and I'd turn the glove and I'd try to catch all the balls close to the webbing.

Anyway, I always *taught* catching to put the thumb at one o'clock with the catcher's glove instead of what they do now. They turn the glove upside down and catch. They catch like a first baseman. They turn the glove all the way over and the webbing is on the ground. You don't catch that way.

There's so many catchers I see, they don't know how to shift. They got all the weight on their right foot and they can't move to their right on a wild pitch, on a curveball or a breaking pitch in the dirt.

The way they're holding the glove, even if they can shift they can't get the glove in position to catch the ball.

No, because it's upside down. I've noticed that.

I've helped Spalding and Wilson as far as goin' to lunch with a couple of the [glove] designers in St. Louis. Harry Latina was the glove maker there and he invited me out to lunch to explain my theory of a glove. I sat there with two other fellas and I said, "Start shavin' it down around the top there and only have one layer of felt in the middle." I said, "I take a razor blade and I cut the felt — slice it — not all the way through, but I slice it all the way over and I rethread the felt itself." They have about five, six rows of felt and I'd remove two or three of 'em all around the tip of the fingers and all the way down. I'd keep it a little heavy around the bottom of the glove. Other than that, I'd relace it with the string that was inside of the glove and get the felt real tight and then shave the middle piece of felt in the center.

Oh, I used to shave the thumb down, too, and shave it down on the ends towards the webbing more, so there'd be an opening there so the ball *could* go into the webbing and stay — wide enough to stick in the webbing. I would shave the center of it so when the ball starts hittin' it would splinter up that webbing because I sliced it all and it would move into the crevasses of the rest of the glove and fill up the vacant spots.

I'd take a brand-new glove and unlace it and do it, but — geez — the way they're got 'em laced up nowadays you have to be a mathematician. I fixed all my gloves that way.

The Browns traded you to the Yankees after 1948.

I didn't even report [to New York]. I went to the Kansas City [Blues]

team to play ball. [George] Selkirk was the manager of that ballclub —
a real fine man, one of the nicest guys you'd ever wanna play ball for.

We got in the Little World Series with the International League. I
think it was a Cardinal farm club — Columbus [Ohio]. It was about 30-
40 degrees below zero *[laughs]*, but we lost a heart-breaker due to a couple of mistakes base-running.

Then the next year, I'm with Syracuse, which was a farm club for the
Yankees — International League — and I stayed there. I sprained my back —
threw a disc out — and I've had back problems ever since. I was in and out
of the lineup.

I finished up in '54 in the Northwest League. I wanted to get a few
games and I had a chance to manage up in the Northwest, but I turned it
down and I managed in the California League in Stockton — '55, '56.

Did you play at Stockton?

Heck, yeah. I promised Jack O'Keefe, the chief of police, that, if he
wanted me as a manager, I'd catch a hundred ballgames. And I caught a
hundred, even though I had a broken finger. *[laughs]* I didn't even know
it was broken 'til I got home after a ballgame and the thing was purple and
white and I went to a doctor. It was my index finger on my left hand —
the glove side — and I had caught I don't know how many ballgames with
that. It was a split bone, it wasn't across. I finally had to take two weeks
off, but I used a great big thick sponge to protect it. I still caught a hundred ballgames.

What was your last active year as a ballplayer?

Let's see. Fifty-nine I managed in the Giant organization and I caught
one ballgame in Eugene, Oregon. [Hal] Luby — he was the business manager — he wanted me to catch more ballgames and I said, "No, I can't
because I've got two prospects the Giants want to develop that are catchers," but he thought that I was supposed to catch.

[Later] I had Bobby Bolin — remember him? — and he'd only won, I
think, nine games in a season in three years with the Giants [system] and
I asked Bolin, "What's been your trouble?" 'cause he could throw b-b's.
I'm watchin' him pitch and Johnny Orsino, the catcher — big Italian from
New York — and I said, "Are you callin' for fastballs?" and he said, "Yeah,
but he's throwin' me curves." I said, "What are you talkin' about?" The
ball wasn't really curvin', but it was movin'. What it was was sailing. I
didn't tell Orsino because he didn't know a sailer from a curveball.

So I asked Bobby Bolin, I said, "How you holdin' the ball — with or
cross seams?" He said, "Well, Gene Thompson" — the pitching coach of

the Giants—"says to hold the ball this way." And it was *with* the seams. In other words, you held the ball across those two seams, but you had the smooth part of the ball on each side of the ball when you threw it, instead of cross-seam. He had all the pitching staff in the Giant organization pitchin' that way, with the seam, and the ball would sail. I mean, to this day, as bad as my arm is, I can make the ball move about a foot or two to the left by just comin' overhand and havin' the fingers on the seams of the ball, but they didn't know this. They kept thrown' balls and, if you come right overhand, that ball *will* sail. An old-time catcher with Boston, Tom Daley, showed me that years ago and I always remembered it. He said you gotta turn the ball over and have all four seams goin' for you.

I told Bolin, I said, "Hold the ball this way, where all four seams are gonna be turnin' against the barrier of the air." I said, "It'll feel like the ball is larger. You practice on it." And then I said, "I want you to throw it three-quarters delivery." So he said, "Okay, Skip."

So about two weeks later he came in; he said, "I wanna try it your way." He's pitchin' against Winston-Salem and, god, he goes out there and he only struck out 24 or 26 and he pitched a one- or two-hitter. They had some pretty good ballplayers on that team and he's blowin' the ball right by everybody. The ball's takin' up; instead of the ball letter-high and sailing away from a righthand hitter for a ball, the ball is now up and *in*, under the righthand hitter's chin. And they're chasin' this ball. They can't touch it because that ball's jumpin' so much. He started at the waist-high and it was right between the letters and the waistline by the time his fastball got past 'em.

Geez, I remember Bill Brenzel, a scout for the Dodgers; we finished the ballgame and I'm walkin' into the clubhouse and I hear, "Hey, Roy!", and here's Bill Brenzel, who was a very close friend of mine, and he's got his glasses off and he's got his handkerchief and he's cleanin' 'em! He said, "Did I see what I really saw with these glasses?" *[laughs]* And he's cleanin' 'em.

And I said, "Billy, you saw it. This guy can throw it!"

The best year he ever had I think he won 24 ballgames for me and he thanked me a dozen ways. I said, "When Gene Thompson comes around, don't tell him that you changed the grip on the ball. Just say, yes, you're throwin' like he says and forget about it because he'll screw you up again." *[laughs]*

And the righthander that they gave a lot of money to that was from up north — Herbel, Ron Herbel — I tried to teach him a few things and, god almighty, I'm tellin' you! In fact, I caught a ballgame to catch him and I said, "Now I want you to keep throwin' just like you are, but," I said, "I want you to throw what *I* want," because I'd already talked to him about the fastball and all 'cause he could throw pretty good, not quite as hard as Bobby Bolin, but he had some life to his fastball.

So we're ahead, 2-to-1, and we're goin' into the eighth inning and he got a little wild; he'd get a little wild throughout the ballgame and I'd settle him down and he'd get the team out. This time, he's got the bases loaded and he's got two outs and he's got two strikes on this Puerto Rican third baseman that couldn't hit me.

I want a fastball. I want a good hard fastball and he shook me off, the first time he'd shaken me off all night. I give it to him again — I give him the clinched fist and then the fastball — and he just said no. He wanted to throw the curveball, see. *[laughs]* I gave him the fastball again and he finally nodded. I didn't wanna cause a scene and walk out there. He finally got back on the mound and he pitched. He threw this half-speed ball and the Puerto Rican hit a home run, a grand slam home run. Later he [Herbel] apologized. He put his hand up to his neck, he said, "Sorry, Skip. I choked."

When did you start scouting?

I joined the New York Mets when they came into the league. Their first year was, let's see, '62, so I guess I started in '61.

Who were some of the players you scouted?

Well, if you wanna talk about Tug McGraw and Buddy Harrelson. Oh, I've got about 20 that went to the big leagues— or more. I can't think of 'em all.

There was the long-legged giraffe from Utah, played the outfield. He only played a few years due to a dislocated hip goin' into the left field wall after a fly ball for the Mets. George Theodore. Everybody said, "Who in the hell signed this guy?!?" *[laughs]* When he walked out on the field, he was all legs! Legs and arms, but he could play and run and hit. At one time, I had five guys on the major league roster. Theodore was there, and Buddy Harrelson and Tug McGraw.

In fact, the best ballplayer was the first one I signed. That was *Hank* McGraw. He was the best ballplayer I ever signed, but he just waited until his brother made the big leagues and then he just gave up. He quit. He was the best athlete I ever signed. Tug's brother. I signed him just as he graduated. He was the first player I signed. He could catch, he could play the outfield, first base, shortstop; he was quite an athlete. He had 19 scholarships for basketball, about 20 for football when he was in this Catholic school over in Vallejo. He was probably one of the best athletes that ever came out of that whole area — southern California.

Roy Partee (courtesy Roy Partee).

Do you know what Tug's son is doing?

He's thumbin' a gee-tar.

Tug had recognition in New York several years ago. He invited me and the Mets sponsored the whole thing and Tug came in there with all his family. His son I met for the first time. "That was from my other love," he told me. I met his wife several times and then I met this fella and he didn't look like any of the family, but Tug told me the story: "He's a musician." Tim McGraw. He's had a lot of number one country songs.

Matt Williams — I drafted him — the third baseman. The Giants drafted him number 426th when he was in high school south of Reno — Carson City. He went to a little high school down there and I saw him play in a tournament as a sophomore and I put a follow on him. I got a card and drafted him outta high school, but I know the baseball coach at the university down there and I knew he was gonna get a full ride, but I drafted him anyway. I think we offered him 40,000 and he was worth it at the time outta high school. Of course, I didn't know that he'd go like he has been.

Criminy, I knew he had the power and all, but I was always leery of a certain area he was havin' trouble with the pitches. I figured he could correct it, but he still gets into that rut when he goes after that pitch kinda tight on him and low. If it's up in the area where he can hit it it'll be gone, but you can pitch around him and then throw him that hard slider low away and he chases it, but don't get it too close to him 'cause he's got that long-arm swing and he can pull that outside ball. If you've ever noticed, he hits most of his pitches to center field or left field, but he *can* hit a ball to right field with power. I saw him do that in high school.

I said he could play shortstop in my report. I saw him play shortstop-third base in high school. I said in my report he's a two-way shot. Move him to shortstop if you think he can't hit, but, hell, he swings that bat. *[laughs]*

Back to your playing days, is there one game that stands out, other than the World Series?

One game? Oh, I guess when I hit the home run in Fenway Park. They were gonna call the game because of darkness and it was the Yankees and the righthand pitcher that could throw b-b's. That was in '44. We're in Boston and the game is gonna be called because of darkness and there was no lights, of course, and [Joe] Cronin had a remarkable string of at bats, you know, pinch-hitting and hitting home runs. He had several in a row and he went up to hit for the seventh hitter.

Atley Donald, he was pitching [for New York] and [Mike] Garbark was catchin'. Cronin goes up — there was still a crowd in the stands, they wait there in Boston — to hit and there's one out and he pops the ball up and everybody groans. They get up; they start gatherin' their blankets and coats *[laughs]* — the game's over. I mean, they're gonna call it because of darkness.

I'm the next hitter. I'm hittin' eighth and I walk up and I'm thinkin' to myself, I said, "I've never gone for a home run." I'm thinkin', "I'm gonna swing from my butt up. I'm gonna try to hit one out." I actually thought that 'cause Garbark said, "Com'on, get the ball over!" Myself, I said, "He's gonna throw me a fastball. It's gonna be a strike right down the middle and I'm goin' for it!" And you can believe this or not, I've *never* said that to myself, I've *never* said I'm gonna hit a home run, but Cronin didn't hit one and I figured, well, *some*body's gotta hit one now. I see the ball comin' and I swing *blindly*, but I remember hittin' that ball and I know it's out in the screen goin' to first base. *[laughs]* Everybody started runnin' back into the ballpark when I'm roundin' the bases to see me touch all the bases. *[laughs]*

I go down and everybody's standin' there shakin' my hand and everybody starts yellin' and clappin', "Atta boy, Roy!" I gather all the catchin' equipment — the mask and the shinguards and my glove. That was my routine all the time. I always did that. I walk into the clubhouse and there's Cronin standin' there; he said, "What in the hell's goin' on!?! Aren't they carryin' your equipment for you?" *[laughs]* He said, "Well, draw one!", and when he said that, they all went and got a beer. When we won, he'd say, "Draw one, it's on me."

I'm sittin' there and I said, "I actually did it! I actually won the ballgame with a home run!" I hit against a pitcher that had a reputation of throwin' the ball by everybody. That's why they had him in there; it was dark, they figured we couldn't see the ball. That was it. That was the highlight of my career, I guess.

Would you go back and be a ballplayer again?

Oh, sure. I mean, not with what I know is going on now. *[laughs]* If I had the same situation and the same playing conditions and the same type of people, I'd go back in a minute.

What I see now on the playing field and some of those hot dogs and how they take charge of the whole ballclub and talk back to the manager with no respect. They think they're number one because they're makin' a few million dollars and they think that they can do anything they want. That's what bugs me and, to tell you the truth, I very seldom watch a ballgame. If I wanna see one particular ballplayer, I'll turn it on to see him, but as far as the enjoyment of watching a ballgame, it's not there. I might want to watch to see [Barry] Bonds strike out ten times. *[laughs]*

Roy Partee's rookie year was 1943. That season, 19 major league catchers had 250 or more plate appearances. Partee batted .281 while making the big jump from Class B to the major leagues, only Bill Dickey, Walker Cooper, Ernie Lombardi, and Buddy Rosar, among major league catchers, batted higher.

Roy Robert Partee

Born September 7, 1917, Los Angeles, CA
Died December 26, 2000, Eureka, CA
Ht. 5'10'   Wt. 180   Batted and Threw Right

Year	Team. Lg	G	AB	R	H	2B	3B	HR	RBI	BA
1943	Boston, AL	96	299	30	84	14	2	0	31	.281
1944		89	280	18	68	12	0	2	41	.243
1945	Military service									
1946	Boston, AL	40	111	13	35	5	2	0	9	.315
1947		60	169	14	39	2	0	0	16	.231
1948	St. L., AL	82	231	14	47	8	1	0	17	.203
5 years		367	1090	89	273	41	5	2	114	.250

World Series

Year	Team	G	AB	R	H	2B	3B	HR	RBI	BA
1946	Boston, AL	5	10	1	1	0	0	0	1	.100

WHITEY LOCKMAN

Breaking in with a Bang (1945–1960)

On July 5, 1945, 18-year-old Whitey Lockman, just up from Jersey City, was penciled into the New York Giants starting lineup for the first time. Manager Mel Ott had him batting third against the St. Louis Cardinals.

Conventional managerial strategy today might not have had him in the lineup at all that day, or maybe he'd be batting farther down in the order. Lockman, you see, was a lefthanded batter and pitching for St. Louis was George Dockins, a lefty-throwing rookie who was turning in a stellar first year.

In the bottom of the first inning, in his first time to the plate in the major leagues, with one out and one on, Lockman took Dockins' pitch into the upper deck in right field in the Polo Grounds. That was more than 50 years ago now, and Lockman remains today the youngest man ever to homer in his first major league at bat.

That was only the first of many highlights of a 15-year major league playing career, most of which was spent as an important member of the Giants. He was a major contributor to his team's two National League championships and 1954 World Title. On October 3, 1951, his double knocked Don Newcombe out of the game and the Dodgers brought in Ralph Branca to relieve, setting the stage for the next hitter, who was Bobby Thomson.

Whitey Lockman as an 18-year-old rookie, 1945.

Then in 1954, Whitey's Giants were in a tough battle with the Brooklyn Dodgers and Milwaukee Braves. On September 11, third place Brooklyn was playing second-place Milwaukee while league-leading New York was hosting Cincinnati, a team that had defeated the Giants the day before. The Dodgers won their game, moving past the Braves into second place.

Meanwhile, in the Polo Grounds, the Reds were leading the Giants, 5-3, entering the bottom of the seventh. A New York loss would have brought the Dodgers to only three games behind with two weeks still left to play. With two out and the bases loaded, Lockman was sent in to pinch-hit for catcher Ray Katt. He belted a grand slam and New York prevailed, 7-5. Neither Brooklyn nor Milwaukee was within four games after that.

Lockman was the first baseman on these championship Giants clubs, but he had begun his professional baseball career as an outfielder. The usual cause for an outfielder to be shifted to first base revolves around foot speed and glove work [not much of either], but such was not the case here. In 1948, his first full season, Lockman played center field for New York and led the National League in putouts and was second in total chances per game [TC/G, or range] and fielding average.

But the Giants were rich in outfielders and in 1951 became richer when they brought up young Willie Mays. That gave the team, in essence, five regular outfielders: Monte Irvin, Don Mueller, Mays, Thomson, and Lockman. Before Mays arrived, manager Leo Durocher experimented with Irvin at first base because he was the least adept of the four in the outfield, but it wasn't working.

When Mays came, Durocher made some pretty bold moves. He placed the rookie in center field, moved Irvin back to left field, placed Thomson at third base [where he had played in the minors but it had been five years since he'd last played the position], and told Lockman he was a first baseman.

The move eventually paid off with a pennant and Lockman became one of baseball's premier first sackers. He led the National League that year in TC/G at his new position and the next year (1952) probably would have won a Gold Glove, if such an award existed in those days. He led the league in putouts, double plays, and TC/G and was second in assists and fielding average. And he was the starting NL first baseman in the All-Star game.

On May 8, 1973, Lockman was the Cubs' manager and history was made, not once but twice. In a 3-2, 12-inning victory over the San Diego Padres, Chicago pitcher Bob Locker pitched in his 500th major league game, all in relief. It was a new record. Then Whitey was ejected and he told coach Ernie Banks to take over for the rest of the game, making Banks baseball's first black major league manager, if only for a short period.

The Giants signed you at the age of 16.

Yes. I was signed like in early May of '43 and my seventeenth birthday was the latter part of July of that same year, so I was 16 but closer to 17.

Due to the war?

No. I just happened to graduate from high school. In my school, which was a county school in North Carolina, there were 11 grades, not 12 — seven and four — so that I graduated in '43–in April — when I was 16. I had played high school baseball, had played American Legion baseball and there had been some scouts around. Actually, the coach of my American Legion team happened to be a birddog for the Giants' scout and apparently he recommended me to him and he came and worked me out and signed me.

You didn't waste much time in the minor leagues, less than two and a half years.

Correct. The year I signed in '43 I actually joined the Jersey City team in the International League; Gabby Hartnett was the manager. I spent about a week or so with them, although I didn't get in a game, and then they determined I needed to go down lower, so I went to Springfield, Massachusetts, in the Eastern League.

So I went down and played for about six weeks, I think, and then was recalled by Jersey City and finished '43 there and spent the whole season of '44 there. I enlisted in the Merchant Marines at the end of the '44 season and spent about six months in that and then came out and played in the spring of '45 at Jersey City and then was called up to the Giants in July of '45.

You broke in with a bang. You're the youngest man ever to homer in his first major league at bat.

I remember the home run. It was off a fellow named George Dockins, a lefthanded pitcher with the Cardinals. There was a man on; it was a two-run homer. I was batting third in the lineup. Mel Ott was batting fourth, protecting me. *[laughs]* I remember it was a curveball and I remember I hit it in the upper deck in the Polo Grounds. Wasn't a long blast; as you know, the right field foul line in the Polo Grounds was fairly short, but then it was not hit down the line. It was out from the line a ways and went in the upper deck, so it was hit pretty good.

In spring training of 1947, you broke your ankle and missed all but two games of the season.

This happened a week before the regular season was to begin in a spring training game in Sheffield, Alabama, a game against the Cleveland Indians. The diamond was a skin infield — hard, concrete almost — and I was on first and our manager put the hit-and-run on. I took off, there was a — oh — medium speed ball hit to [Lou] Boudreau, who was playing short for Cleveland. I misjudged this thing; since I was running, and I could run pretty good, I didn't figure Boudreau was gonna make a play at second, but at the last second he under-flipped the ball to Joe Gordon and I tried a late slide. The spikes of my right heel caught in the hard ground and my body kept going and my ankle stayed there. It was like a reversed dislocation and a broken fibula. Kind of a mess.

Is this why you moved to first base?

I was a center fielder at that point and then when I recovered and came back I was still a center fielder. I was an outfielder until Mays came up in '51.

That was a good reason to be moved.

I don't think so. How could they do that to me? *[laughs]* I was a pretty good outfielder.

As a matter of fact, Durocher said — and this is a couple years later — I remember him being quoted in the paper, said, "If anything happens to Mays, I've still got a pretty good center fielder." And they go, "Who's that?" *[laughs]* He said, "He's playing first base." I always appreciated that. I always considered myself a pretty good center fielder and then when Mays came along I realized I was not quite as good as Mays.

The Giants certainly weren't hurting for outfielders. They had Bobby Thomson, Don Mueller, Monte Irvin, you, and Mays, and Hank Thompson could play out there if necessary.

That was the problem that Durocher had at that point. With Mays in the picture, there was no doubt that he was gonna play center field, you know. So now there's Bobby Thomson, Monte Irvin, Don Mueller, and myself. Hank Thompson's not really considered in that picture; he was more of a third baseman. But there were some pretty good outfielders there that Durocher had to make a decision on, so one day in St. Louis, I believe somewhere in the first part of May, he tossed me a first baseman's glove — I didn't even have one — said, "You're playing first today." This was during the regular season. That's how it came about.

The one thing, I think, that eased the transition was that, during pregame practice beginning early on in my career in the big leagues, or even in the minor leagues, too, I used to fool around in the infield but not at first — at shortstop. I had a fantasy about being a major league shortstop and I used to take a lot of ground balls, make throws, and do all that stuff in the infield, so that helped give me a sense of what infield play was like a little bit.

It was not an easy transition for me, neither mentally or physically. For example, taking throws from the infielders in games, I would get over there and not have either foot on the base and just kind of go with the flow where the throw was; I would kind of shift. So one day we got into Boston to play the Braves when they were still there and they had a first baseman named Earl Torgeson. Earl Torgeson said to me, "I've watched you play a couple of games now. You know, you're gonna get hurt." *[laughs]* I kind of thought he meant a ground ball's gonna jump up and hit me. He said, "Can I give you some advice?" I said, "Yeah."

So he said, "You're righthanded, I'm lefthanded. As a lefthander, when I go to first base to take a throw from an infielder, I put my left foot on the bag and take the throw, except on a throw from the catcher or the pitcher down the first base line." And he said, "Then it depends on where the throw is. But you're righthanded so put your right foot on the base and take your throws from the third baseman, shortstop, second baseman with your right foot on the base."

So I started working on that a little bit the next day in pregame and it made a lot of sense and it helped me a lot. From that point on, I wasn't as clumsy, as far as trying to shift.

[Earl Torgeson enjoyed a solid if not spectacular 15-year major league career, appearing in two World Series ('48 Braves, '59 White Sox). He had a reputation of being gruff but he went out of his way repeatedly to help younger players, teammates and foes alike, adjust to life in the big leagues.]

Your early desire to be a shortstop paid off. You eventually played a couple dozen games at second base.

I'm not sure how many, but I played some. Not until, I think, during like '58.

Our problem was that Davey Williams, our regular second baseman, had a real severe back problem after being steam-rolled by Jackie Robinson at Ebbets Field, so during the winter after he got hurt I wrote Bill Rigney, who was the manager at that point, a letter stating that I'd be glad to take a shot at playing second base. The reason for that was we had some people coming along, like McCovey and Cepeda. There was a guy on the scene at that point named Gail Harris, who they thought was gonna be the heir-apparent to first base. I figured, what the heck, maybe I could keep my regular playing alive by switching positions again, so I wrote Bill Rigney a letter and he took it seriously. He wrote me back and said we'll see in spring training, so I worked out there some in spring training in '57, I think it was, but I didn't play any there that year.

I didn't play a lot of games there, but in '58 when I did play there, we had a pretty good year that year and were in contention. It was kind of a shame that we were in a position that I had to fool around at second base. If we'd have had an experienced second baseman, why, we'd have had a better chance probably.

I remember watching a game in '58 and you didn't start. Danny O'Connell started at second and he was pinch-hit for and you came in. I was amazed.

[laughs] I was, too.

Everyone knows the story of 1951, but I suspect if you went up to 100 baseball fans and asked, "Who knocked Newcombe out?" I doubt if two or three would know. That was you.

Well, this was obviously the third playoff game of that series and Newk had started the game. I don't know how many pitches he had thrown up to that point, but, as you know, it was the ninth inning and he did get into trouble by Dark singling and Mueller singling. Then Irvin popped up and he was a little bit out of the woods, but he had runners at first and third with one out, you know, and now he's facing a lefthanded hitter.

I think there was some concern at this point about whether he was tiring a little bit and this and that, but, actually, as I recall, the pitch that I hit for the double was thrown as well as the earlier pitches in the game that he threw. I don't think he had lost any of his velocity at all. I had already had my mind set when I walked into the batter's box that I would try to hit the ball out of the ballpark in right field. I was not a dead pull hitter, so it had to be from the middle of the plate in for me to do it, but he threw a ball on the black outside — a fastball — and just kind of muscle memory and instinct caused me to hit a line drive down the left field line.

We get a run in and runners at second and third and I'm the tying run; they've got an open base and there's always been some speculation as to whether they should've walked Bobby Thomson to get to the guy on deck, who was Willie Mays. But they chose not to and to change pitchers at that point and bring in Branca.

We were all pumped, you know, in this contest. A strange thing, I never had a conversation about that game or any part of it with any of the Dodgers that participated in it until somewhere around '80 or '81 when the Winter Baseball Meetings were held in Dallas. It so happened that one night several of the Dodgers and myself — I was with Montreal at that point as a major league scout and Pee Wee Reese, Duke Snider, Dick Williams, who was on the that '51 team — were all at this table in a restaurant at the Marriott Hotel in Dallas and I was seated next to Pee Wee. We were just talking about general things and, as I mentioned, it had never come up and I'd been around some of these guys before, but Pee Wee said to me, "Whitey, when you came up in the ninth inning of that playoff game, were you nervous?" And by the time he got through making his comment, it was quiet at the table and everyone was listening to my response. *[laughs]*

So I said, "Pee Wee, to tell you the truth, I was not." And then there were some chuckles from Snider. He kinda giggled and said, "Oh, come on!" I said, "No, I'm telling you." And then I went on to explain to 'em that during the course of the last 44 games of the season, in which we won 37, there were so many cliffhangers and so much at stake as we got on down towards the end and every game was so important and we couldn't afford to lose, that I said, "I think I was really immune to being nervous by the last week of the season." So I think I convinced 'em that that was my true feeling, that I wasn't nervous, that I was probably keyed up and so forth and pumped, but nervous — no.

Then we went on and talked about how *they* felt. It was a very interesting conversation.

The other thing that I distinctly remember is that I don't remember the feelings that it was over when we started the bottom of the ninth. The game progresses and there are a lot of games that you play. You have certain feelings at certain points of some games that it's gonna be difficult to overcome a lead or whatever, and this certainly was a game in which it didn't look good for us, obviously. I remember when the bottom of the ninth began and Newcombe went to the mound to take his warmup tosses and the infielders were all taking their warmup tosses. Before the catcher threw the ball to second, Jackie Robinson jogged in to the mound, patted Newcombe on the back like, "You got 'em, kid," you know, and that irked me. *[laughs]*

You were full of clutch hits. Your home run in Game 3 of the '51 World Series was the big hit for the Giants in the 5-run fifth.

Right. Off Raschi. It was a line drive in the lower deck down the line. We won that game, 6-to-2.

In 1954, the Indians supposedly had the greatest pitching staff in the history of baseball, but the Giants' staff was as far above the National League as Cleveland's was above the American League. How do you think you guys stacked up to the Indians before the Series?

Well, you know, we were a little in awe of the fact that they won like 111 games or whatever it was. There's another thing here: every spring, starting in 1947, we played each other for a couple of weeks. In the early days—'47, '48; I'm not sure how much longer it went — we were the only two teams in Arizona, so we played each other because there is nobody else to play. We really got to know each other, not only on the field but off the field.

So by the time '54 rolled around, there was a kind of seven-year deal going on here that we knew these players on the Cleveland team better than we knew any other team in the American League and better than some teams in the National League. They had a good book on us and we had a good book on them and there was no question about the quality of their '54 team, not only in their pitching but their offense and defense and everything else. To win that many games can't be luck, obviously.

Let me inject something here that, personally, the biggest thrills I had in baseball were being on the '51 pennant winners and the '54 pennant winners and, subsequently, the '54 World Champions, so that once the regular season of '54 was over I felt elated and happy that we'd won the pennant 'cause we beat a tough Dodger team.

Going into the World Series, I don't know what it is; I mean it's important, it's not anticlimactic — it's important to win the World Series, you got a shot at it so you try to win it — but we were certainly aware of how good they were. But I don't think a lot of people realized how good *we* were. I think they really expected it to be the other way, that Cleveland would sweep us, in view of their pitching staff and offensive power and all that stuff.

As it turned out, the first two games obviously could have gone either way. If they had, it could have been the other way around — they could have swept us — but we got the breaks and had Dusty Rhodes came through in a phenomenal fashion pinch-hitting and we got decent pitching that you mentioned before. Our pitching wasn't that bad — [Johnny] Antonelli and those guys — and our bullpen was probably better than anybody's, with [Marv] Grissom and [Hoyt] Wilhelm, so that we had some things go for us and we got some breaks.

Once we won those first two games in the Polo Grounds in the fashion that we did with Rhodes and the good pitching, we got to Cleveland. Lemon, Wynn, and then Garcia started the third game in Cleveland. I didn't do much; I think I got two hits in the four games but one of 'em was the first pitch of the third game, which was a single to center, and I think it had some sort of an effect because you could just kinda see 'em sag and moan.

In the first game, what did you think when Vic Wertz hit the ball that Mays caught?

I thought it was a hit. I'd seen a couple of home runs to center field there in the Polo Grounds and from the crunch I thought it had a chance. I was heading to my cutoff position — you know, behind the mound — because I thought it was a hit. And so did everybody.

Throughout your career you were hard to double up. Why?

I guess speed and being lefthanded — closer to first. I didn't hit a lot of ground balls to second base. I probably hit more ground balls over toward shortstop area to where it's a little harder to turn it than it would be like second-short-and-first. I really don't know [why]; I've never really analyzed it.

You were frequently the leadoff hitter. Wes Westrum batted eighth and he was walked a lot to get to the pitcher, so you must have come up an awful lot of times with either Westrum or the pitcher on first base. It would seem that the front end of the double play was there waiting for them, so you must have been doing something.

Well, maybe I was concentrating on hitting the ball in the air — who knows? — but I was not a fly ball hitter, either.

[In 15 seasons, Whitey hit into only 68 double plays or one every 87.4 at bats. It's the eighth best in history for players with more than 6,000 plate appearances.]

You didn't strike out often, even early on as a young player.

I think the thing that probably helped me most was my first year as a professional. I hadn't turned 17 actually, and at Springfield, Mass, in the old Eastern League, I had a manager named Spencer Abbott. Spencer Abbott was brash and yelled a lot and for a 16 year old to come up against

Opposite: Whitey Lockman attempts to tag Red Schoendienst of the Cardinals after taking a throw from catcher Wes Westrum.

a guy like that was kind of frightening, due to the fact that I'd never been out of North Carolina in my life and all that stuff.

But he did give me some sound advice, which was, after having seen me play for however long it was—a week or two—said to me one day privately—thank goodness—he said, "Kid, you're not Babe Ruth, you're never gonna be Babe Ruth. Don't try to hit home runs. Just try to get the bat on the ball no matter where it's pitched. If it's outside, don't try to pull it to right field. Go with it no matter where it is. That's the best advice I can give you." And it was good advice and I stuck to that and became kind of a spray hitter and was able to jerk one out occasionally, depending on where the pitch was. That was the best advice I got as a hitter.

You were a legitimate .290 hitter.

A lot of guys who are regular players in the big leagues do better as regulars. As my career started to wind down I didn't play as much and it's difficult to keep an average up, but, yeah, I was a .290 guy. I hit .301 one year, I think; '49 I think, then .295, .290, .286—right in there.

Other than the two World Series, is there one game that stands out in your memory?

I think probably my first game in '45 when I hit the home run. I got another hit, I think, in that game, and I don't know how many runs I drove in; we lost to the Cardinals eventually so it doesn't matter. And then the '51 playoff game. Those are the two I remember most about, I guess.

What about the 1952 All-Star game?

Not so much. I did start it and I think I played the whole game. It was a rain-shortened one, I think the only one in history. Hank Sauer hit a home run that won it, 3-to-2 or something. I'll tell you, the biggest thrill for me was being around the guys like Musial and Campanella and Robinson and some of those big guys that I admired a lot.

Who was the best player you saw?

Mays. I've thought about it over the years and this is kind of a tricky area to talk about because, obviously, I didn't see some of the great players in the American League, having spent my whole career in the National League except for a half a year with Baltimore in '59, so there are discussions about other players—Mantle and so forth—being comparable to Mays. I'm sure they are, but to me, to analyze and evaluate Mays' ability, take each point of it—the hitting, the running, the throwing, the fielding, the power—and stack that up with any player, Mays comes out ahead to me. A great, great athlete and particularly a great, great, *great* baseball player. He had not only all the physical tools, but he had the instincts for the game and the desire to play it and enjoyed playing it. He was the best all-around player that I saw.

Who was the best pitcher you saw?

That's a little tougher question. There's two sides to this coin: one would be who was the toughest for me to hit and then who probably was the best pitcher overall.

In my era, I think if I had to pick a pitcher to start a game — a crucial game — it would've been [Ewell] Blackwell. That may surprise you a little bit 'cause he didn't have a long career, but when he had it going in like '47, '48, he was the toughest guy that I saw, not only against righthand hitters. He had this whipping throwing action that he came from third base — I mean, really wheel and deal — and righthand hitters bailed out on him. But his ball had such great movement on it that he was tough on lefthand hitters, too, that could follow him a little better from the mound into home plate. To me, he was the toughest pitcher that I saw.

Alvin Dark said Blackwell was the only pitcher he tracked. He'd check the Cincinnati scores and hoped Blackwell pitched the day before his team was to play the Reds so they wouldn't see him in a series.

I can believe it. Dark was a righthand hitter, but Alvin was able to read some pitchers. I don't know if Blackwell was one of 'em, but Bob Rush, for example, with Chicago was a tough righthand pitcher for a while, but Alvin could read him and he hit him good.

A surprising thing about Blackwell: Walker Cooper, who was a catcher on our team in '47, '48 — somewhere in there during Blackwell's time — hit Blackwell like he owned him and Walker Cooper was a righthand hitter. After a while, I finally went up to Coop and I said, "Hey, there's gotta be some reason that you're hitting this guy and I think I know. You've picked up something in his delivery or his release and you know what's coming."

He said, "No." I said, "Then what is it?" He said, "Watch me the next time I hit against him and you will see that I'm bailing out and he's making mistakes and throwing the ball inside and as I'm bailing out, now it's in my wheelhouse and I'm taking a poke at the first one." *[laughs]* "I don't take any strikes off this guy!" And that turned out to be the case.

The toughest guy for me to hit was Curt Simmons, who was a lefthand pitcher for Philadelphia, and the main reason why is that I just could not pick the ball up. This guy's a cross-firing guy and he could throw hard.

Some guys throw heavy balls, some guys throw lighter balls; his ball was a heavy ball and even when I hit it, I felt like I hit a rock. He's the only pitcher in my big league career that struck me out four times in a game. That happened once and I was embarrassed. *[laughs]* Of course, my teammates were on me almost the whole time.

When you start looking at records, Warren Spahn — I mean, the guy's incredible! And then Sandy Koufax? If I had to pick one guy, I think, from all eras — and I didn't see Koufax as a hitter that much — I would say, at his peak when he had it going there with the Dodgers in the early '60s, he was the toughest pitcher I saw.

People talk bout Nolan Ryan's hits-to-innings pitched; Koufax may have given up another quarter hit per game but Koufax wasn't walking all the men Ryan was.

That's exactly right. It was a crying shame to watch Nolan Ryan throughout his career and all the pitches he threw that didn't mean anything. He had a great arm, great desire, great body.

We mentioned Alvin Dark. If you look at his record, every team he went to, as a player and as a manager, improved when he joined it. He was a steady performer and probably lost 10 or 12 points a year off his average giving himself up for the team. Does he belong in the Hall of Fame?

Yes, I think he does. He's one of the best athletes I've ever seen. He could do a lot of things on a baseball field and could have done 'em on a football field, I would imagine, if he'd have gone that route. Or as a golfer. There was, first, his athletic ability; second, he was a fellow who used his head probably better than most athletes during the course of battle; three, he took very good care of himself physically. He was always in good physical condition, didn't dissipate, didn't drink or smoke, got his rest. He was just the consummate professional athlete with ability.

I don't think people appreciated how good he was 'cause he was up against Reese and some other people. As far as I'm concerned, he's deserving [for the Hall of Fame]. Even as a manager he had the same work ethics he did as a player. He used those managing and he was very good at it.

Speaking of managing, how much did you pattern yourself after Durocher?

I didn't consciously try to emulate him. I'm sure that some of the things I learned from him as a player and his managing techniques in the area particularly of motivation I probably used, but by the time that I became a manager in '72 I had played for not only Durocher, but Mel Ott and Fred Hutchinson and Paul Richards and Bill Rigney, so I had been with some pretty good baseball people as managers.

You learn from those experiences with each of those people and how they went about their business, but when the bell rings and you're faced with a situation that all those guys were faced with, whether it be strategy during the course of the game, as the game starts, before the game trying to get a team up and ready for the game, whether it be a pitcher that's gonna pitch that day or whatever, you're on your own. Maybe all that stuff comes into play subconsciously somehow, but you've still got to make the call and do it.

I really enjoyed my time as a minor league manager and major league manager. The situation when I was manager of the Cubs, we had a good team and there was some underlying stuff, front office-wise, ownership-wise, going on at that point that was distracting. When I took over in mid-season of '72 from Durocher, we went 15 over from that point on and we had a good year. It was just that Pittsburgh was tough; they won by ten. We were ten behind when I took over and we finished up ten behind, even though we went 15 over the last half, so we just couldn't make up any ground on 'em.

But '73 may be one of my most disappointing years in baseball because it appeared to me that we had the best team in the league and we struggled and things happened that year, like Montreal coming through and being contenders and the Mets winning and the Cardinals being good, and all that stuff, and we just fell by the wayside. [Ferguson] Jenkins had won 20 games five years in a row and won 12, I think, in '73; [Milt] Pappas had won 17 or 18 the year before and won less than 10. It just was one of those years you cannot explain. We just fell apart and I was disappointed. I managed into '74 and then left and went back into player development.

Would you have liked to manage some more?

No. I had an understanding with Mr. Wrigley, the owner of the team, when I took over. We had kind of a heart-to-heart and you know the first thing he said to me? He said, "The general manager wants you to manage the team. Why would you want to manage the team?" *[laughs]* You know, here's the owner of the ball team asking why I would want to manage. What do you say? You have to go trough the whole thing. I said, "I'm a career baseball person and my ambition, since I quit playing, was to manage in the big leagues."

I don't know if he really ever understood it, but then he said, "Well, I don't understand why people want to manage, but you're very important in your job as player development director. When you get through

Whitey Lockman as Cubs' manager, 1972.

managing, we would like you to continue that." That's kind of the way the atmosphere of the thing was, so that's why I went back into player development after managing.

Would you have liked to manage the Giants earlier?

You know, I thought I might have a shot at it one year, about 1969. I was managing Tacoma in the Pacific Coast League for the Cubs and we were playing well and eventually won the Coast League championship that year. Sometime during the middle of that season we came into Phoenix to play the Phoenix Giants and Tom Sheehan, who was kind of a right-hand man to Mr. [Horace] Stoneham, was at one game. He came down after the game was over and caught me before I went into the clubhouse. He said, "The old man would like to talk to you." He said, "He's here in Phoenix and he's doing fine. Can we have lunch together tomorrow?" I said, "Sure."

We set up like a 1:30 P.M. appointment date for the next day and I showed up about ten minutes early and sat down in the restaurant and they never showed up. I waited until about quarter-to-two and called Mr. Stoneham's house and got no answer and never heard another word about it. *[laughs]* We had to leave the next day.

I've often wondered. I never got a chance to talk to Tom Sheehan or Mr. Stoneham about that, but the Giants at that point were not doing well and I've wondered to this day whether he had some interest in me. I'll never know, I guess.

Do you still receive fan mail?

I get about two or three [autograph] requests a day. I have a slip of paper made up and on the paper it says, "Due to the time required to sign autographs, there is a charge of $10, which goes to the Muscular Dystrophy Association." We have a son who has that. I return the request with that slip in it and invariably people will send the $10 back.

I've never attended [a card show]. My business is to spend time with my family. When you're in this business, you bounce around an awful lot, particularly during the summer, obviously, with the road trips. In the winter when they have the card shows on and I get requests to attend 'em, I just don't feel I should take the time. I don't want to take the time.

Did you save souvenirs from your career?

World Series rings. I think I've got an old Giant uniform. That's about it.

Do you have your baseball cards?

A few that my kids have picked up over the years, but I have not collected them.

Would you play baseball again if you were a young man?

Yes, I would. The only thing I would do different is I wouldn't smoke. I was a smoker and you just can't stay in proper shape and smoke. But I enjoyed playing the game. Yes, I'd do it all again.

Way back at the beginning of this, we said that Whitey Lockman is the youngest player ever to homer in his first major league at bat. Here is a list of those players who accomplished this feat before their 21st birthdays.

Player	Team	Date	Age (yr-mo-day)
Whitey Lockman	NY (NL)	7-5-45	18-11-11
Ted Tappe	Cin (NL)	9-14-50	19-7-12
Clyde Vollmer	Cin (NL)	5-31-42	20-8-7
Jay Bell	Cle (AL)	9-29-86	20-9-13
Buddy Kerr	NY (NL)	9-8-43	20-10-2
John Kennedy	Was (AL)	55-5-62	20-11-7

CARROLL WALTER "WHITEY" LOCKMAN

Born July 25, 1926, Lowell, NC
Ht. 6'1"   Wt. 175   Batted Left, Threw Right

Year	Team, Lg	G	AB	R	H	2B	3B	HR	RBI	BA
1945	NY, NL	32	129	16	44	9	0	3	18	.341
1947		2	2	0	1	0	0	0	1	.500
1948		146	584	117	167	24	10	18	59	.286
1949		151	617	97	186	32	7	11	65	.301
1950		129	532	72	157	28	5	6	52	.295
1951		153	614	85	173	27	7	12	73	.282
1952		154	606	99	176	17	4	13	58	.290
1953		150	607	85	179	22	4	9	61	.295
1954		148	570	73	143	17	3	16	60	.251
1955		147	576	76	157	19	0	15	49	.273
1956	NY-StL, NL	118	362	27	94	7	3	1	20	.260
1957	NY, NL	133	456	51	113	9	4	7	30	.248
1958	SF, NL	92	122	15	29	5	0	2	7	.238
1959	BalAL, CinNL	90	153	17	37	6	2	0	9	.242
1960	Cin., NL	21	10	6	2	0	0	1	1	.200
15 years		1666	5940	836	1658	222	49	114	563	.279

Year	Team, Lg	G	AB	R	H	2B	3B	HR	RBI	BA
World Series										
1951	NY, NL	6	25	1	6	2	0	1	4	.240
1954		4	18	2	2	0	0	0	0	.111
2 years		10	43	3	8	2	0	1	4	.186
All-Star										
1952	NL	1	3	0	0	0	0	0	0	.000

ED WRIGHT

50 Years Too Soon (1945–1952)

Back in 1991, the Braves were nearly World Champions, but the rarefied atmosphere of the World Series was something to which the franchise had never grown accustomed. That Series marked the end of a 33-year dry spell for the Braves in whatever city. Earlier, way back in Boston, the team had endured a 34-year period of frustration and in both intervals "second division" was the most fitting description of the annual finishes.

In 1945 the team was still in Boston. The offense was Tommy Holmes, the pitching was nonexistent. The previous year they had made a legitimate run at the cellar, avoiding it by only three and a half games. It appeared in this final year of the war they would not be denied; with 60 percent of the season completed, the club was in seventh place and floundering.

While the Beantown hurlers were struggling, minor league veteran Ed Wright was pitching for Indianapolis in the American Association and having his best season. It had been eight years since he became a professional, but it was only his first season in a classification that high. Several things had occurred to slow his progress: illness, league collapse, job freezes brought on by the war.

Through July, 1945, Wright had a 13-5 record for Indianapolis and

Boston bought him. He made his first appearance as a Brave on July 29 and from then to the end of the season he won 8 games and lost only 3 with an ERA of 2.51. Not coincidentally, the team moved up to sixth place.

His 8 wins in two months were second on the team [9 led] and his ERA would have been third in the National League if he had had enough innings to qualify. Counting his record with Indy, his record for the year was 21-8, 2.83.

He followed that brilliant rookie performance with a 12-9, 3.52 season in 1946, but injury, illness, and management pretty much ended his career after that, even though he pitched professionally through 1953.

Ed was on the rosters of two pennant winners in his major league stay, but was not a contributor to either. He was with the Braves for a short time in 1948 and spent some time with the 1950 Whiz Kid Philadelphia Phillies.

In 1938 you're listed as playing for Jackson in the Kitty League, but there's no record in the books.

I'd won two games and lost one and my appendix ruptured. That was the first of June and I didn't play no more the rest of that year. Then in 1939 I was in the Northeast Arkansas League with Jonesboro and I won a couple of games—I don't even remember for sure—and boils come up all over me—my arms, my legs, and everywhere. I come home and the next year—19-and-40—I signed with Milwaukee—they were in the [American] Association – and I went to their training camp, but they sent me to Paducah [Kitty League].

You had a real good year there.

Yeah, I believe it was 16-10. I really won 17, but they took one game away from me on protest or something. I don't remember now just what it was.

Then in '41 I went to training with the Memphis Chicks and stayed in spring training with them and in the first month of the season and then they sent me down to Greenville in the Cotton States League. I believe I won maybe 15 down there. [15-10]

In '42 I went back to training with the Chicks and I didn't make it then and they sent me to Meridian, Mississippi, in the Southeastern League. And I didn't make it down there.

I come back home and I got my old job back here at a fabrics company and I agreed to play with Jackson again in the Kitty League. In the meantime, Ellis Kinder was pitching for Jackson and I was owned by

Ed Wright (courtesy Ed Wright).

Memphis, so they traded me to Jackson for Ellis Kinder. I told 'em I wouldn't report over there unless I could keep my job and work, too, and that's what I done. You know, the cities was close around here and I could work and then make the game at night. I'd won four games and hadn't lost any that year and the league folded up. [Ed's 1942 record: 4 games, 37 innings, 4-0, 2.68.]

Then in '43 I was out of baseball. That was a war year and they were freezin' the jobs and everything, but I did go down to Memphis and pitch amateur ball for the Kroger Company down there. We won the city championship there.

In 1944 I wrote Earl Mann a letter in Atlanta and he said to come on down to spring training. I went down and made the club. Kiki Cuyler was the manager, but he knows as much about pitchin' as a little leaguer does. I won four games and lost three there in the Southern League and he sent me to Norfolk in the Piedmont League.

I went on up there and had a good year. I got with an old major league pitcher, Garland Braxton, and he taught me a few things about pitchin'. I went 8-and-3 up there [with a 1.69 ERA].

Eddie Popowski, used to be the Red Sox coach [and manager], was the manager of Roanoke in that Piedmont League and he recommended me to Indianapolis in 1945. I belonged to Atlanta and they [Indianapolis] traded Eddie Morgan, an outfielder, to Atlanta for me. He didn't report, but I was havin' such a good spring trainin' at Indianapolis that they just bought me.

I started off good — won nine straight there 'fore I ever lost one. I had a no-hitter in that. Casey Stengel was a manager of Kansas City at that time and that was against his team. I went and had 13-and-5 and then Boston bought me in July. I went on up there and won eight, I believe, and lost three.

Next year, in '46, [Billy] Southworth came over from the Cardinals. I started spring training and down there in Fort Lauderdale in fielding practice I stepped on a ball and popped my ankle and I missed a lot of the spring trainin'. It threw me behind some, but I did go ahead and win 12 games that year.

I told Southworth I could have won 20 games just as easy as I did them 12 if he'd have pitched me. See, he had his pets. 'Course, Spahn and Sain was there. Before Southworth come, that other manager [Del Bissonette] pitched me every fourth day. It didn't matter if it rained. The other pitchers took turns; if it rained theirs out he'd start me and I was winnin' for him. Southworth come over there and bring ol' sore-armed Ernie White and Johnny Beazley and them that helped him in 19-and-42 [with the Cardinals].

That was in '47. That year, Sain pitched the first game and Spahn the second and I pitched the third to open the season. I was subject to tonsil-litis and after that first game I pitched my tonsils swelled up and bursted and I was out five weeks. I tried to get Southworth to have 'em out and he wouldn't do it.

During that year I had three spells with my tonsils when I didn't pitch nothin' hardly. I won a couple, I guess; I don't even remember. [3-3, 6.37] That was the trouble — my tonsils. I'd lost a lot of weight and it affected my arm, too; I didn't have no strength in it. But he wouldn't have 'em out, but right at the last — two weeks before the season was over — he agreed to have 'em out. *[laughs]* In '48 I come back and had a pretty good spring trainin' yet he sent me down to Milwaukee. I went down there and I think I won 9 and lost 12.

Bissonette was the manager of Boston when I went there; he ended up being the manager at Toronto, so he recommended they buy me from Milwaukee. I went up there and started off the '49 season with him and had a good record there. At one time, I had 8-and-3.

The Phillies called up the second baseman, Mike Goliat, and then our best hitter broke his leg and where I was winnin' some close games I was losin' 'em then. I think I ended up 11-and-9 there.

I was with the Phillies for a month in 1950, the year they won the pen-nant. I didn't get in any games 'cause they had [Robin] Roberts and [Curt] Simmons and [Russ] Meyer and ol' Jim Konstanty if they needed him. What happened there, I had the club made in spring trainin' in Florida. Andy Seminick was the catcher and he told me the manager liked me. I was pitchin' against Washington that day and Russ Meyer pitched the first four innings and I was pitchin' the last five. I think it was the ninth inning and we had 'em beat, 13-to-1.

I tried to sidearm Sam Dente and my elbow popped. I called the catcher out there — it wasn't Seminick, it was ol' Stan Lopata — and I told him I believed I hurt my arm. It burned all the way down to my wrist. I had two outs and he said, "Aw, go on. You can get this hitter out." He talked me into finishin' the hitter and that done it. It was three months 'fore I got to pitch and that's the reason I didn't pitch when I was with 'em the first month.

I went to Toronto and it was a lot colder up there. Before I'd go out to pitch a game I'd have to take 20 minutes heat on my elbow. I didn't do too good that year. The elbow come back. After that year I didn't have no more trouble with it.

In 19-and-50 when I went back to Toronto I won a game or two or somethin'. They traded me to Minneapolis, back in the Association. Up in the season Minneapolis traded me to Ottawa, back in the International League. I think I had about a 5-and-6 record there at Ottawa in '51.

Ottawa belonged to the Philadelphia A's, so the A's invited me to spring training in '52 and I made the club, stayed with 'em the whole year. I didn't start a game, but I relief-pitched some. I think I won two and lost one. I saved some games, but they didn't count saves then.

That ended it up there. At the end of '52 they sold me back to Memphis, where it's close to home, and I pitched a few games for them and they traded me to Chattanooga. They pitched me a little bit there and I was disgusted anyway.

Hopkinsville [Kentucky] got back in the Kitty League then and I managed Hopkinsville the last part of '53 and part of '54. It shut down again in '54, so that ended me in baseball.

I went into the service station business and that's where I've been ever since. I've enjoyed it, but I still keep up with every out and hit and everything else in baseball. It was a shame I was born 50 years too soon.

I had a pretty good earned run average in '46 when I won the 12 games: 3.52. In '45 when I first went up when I had 8-and-3, it was two-five-one. Overall, all of it up there, I believe it was four.

In '46, you also batted .305.

I'm prouder of that than I was my pitchin'. I was a pretty good hitter; I got some timely hits at times. I hit two doubles one time off of Johnny Vander Meer. 'Course, he wasn't the no-hit pitcher he'd been, but he could still throw.

Talk about Southworth as a manager.

He wanted to think for the *whole* ballclub. He didn't give nobody credit. For instance, when a club would come in town we'd have a meeting — the pitcher and the catcher. We'd sit down with him and he'd give us the scorebook — how to pitch to every hitter. Before we could discuss the first hitter, he had the book out of our hands telling us how to pitch instead of talking it out. Johnny Sain, he never would take the book; he never would have a meeting with him.

He was a good manager, but he had his pets. I remember Johnny Hopp dressed right beside of me, the next locker. He'd come in, he'd go over and pat Johnny on the back, talk to him — me sittin' right there dressin' and never say one word to me.

Hopp was another of Southworth's old Cardinals.

Oh, yeah. He was from St. Louis. They helped him years before, but they was through when they come up there [to Boston].

I thought [Tommy] Holmes was gonna kill Hopp one time. Holmes won that battin' title in '45 and the next year Hopp was there. Hopp batted in front of Tommy and if he was on first base and Tommy hit a dribbler to the infield, he'd loaf it to second base to get throwed out so Tommy wouldn't get a hit. Tommy'd get mad.

That's the way he [Southworth] was [with his favorites]. Earl Torgeson didn't like him. *[laughs]* Frank McCormick played with lefthanded pitchin' and one day against, I believe it was [Ken] Raffensberger from Cincinnati, he put Torgeson on the bench and during the game Torgeson laid down like he was goin' to sleep. Southworth didn't say a word.

On the train that night — we was leavin' for a road trip — Torgeson, me, and Tommy Holmes was settin' in the booth talkin' or playin' cards or somethin' and Southworth walked up. He was drunk. He looked at Torgeson a minute and he said, "You let me down today, didn't you?"

Torgeson says, "I don't know. Why, Bill?"

"Dammit, you laid down on the bench and wasn't in the ballgame!" And one thing led to another and Torgeson jumped up and was gonna hit him, but we got between 'em. I sent somebody to get Ernie White. Ernie was the only one to do a thing with Southworth.

There was just things like that. One time in spring trainin' down in Bradenton, him and a bunch of sportswriters come down the street and we was all sittin' on the porch out at the hotel. Southworth was drunk and he slowed down real slow drivin' along by us and cussed every one of us out. Crap like that.

I told him when he sent me out, "Bill, if you'd have pitched me like I was pitchin' when I came here, I could have helped you."

He said, "I was countin' on you more than I was Johnny Sain in '46."

I said, "If you'd have pitched me, I'd have won 20 games, too." I mean, I'd go out and pitch a good game and then maybe next time I wouldn't do too well so I'd sit on the bench and miss two or three turns. I had to pitch every three of four days to be sharp.

Southworth was a successful manager, but eventually it seems as if his teams rebelled.

He'd make us play a ballgame in the mud up there. Pour gas on that field and he'd get out there and work like them groundkeepers. He'd work just as hard as they did to get that field in shape. He just hated to not play. He'd always tell us, "Always *think* you're gonna play. Don't get lax and think you're not gonna play and then have to go out and play." That was good advice.

He was a fiery manager, but his son [Billy, Jr.] was drowned in a plane crash [in 1945] and he never was the same after that.

Who was the best pitcher you saw?

There's several of 'em. Vic Raschi was one of the best *pitchers*, but you talk about throwers and Bob Feller was about the best. Raschi was a smart pitcher. Early Wynn was a good pitcher. 'Course, Spahn was awful good with us.

And little Bobby Shantz. In '52 when he was the Most Valuable Player I saw him win every one of his 24 games that year. I saw him strike out [Stan] Musial and [Whitey] Lockman and [Jackie] Robinson [in the All-Star game]. None of 'em touched the ball but Lockman; he foul-tipped one of 'em. That little feller, he weighed 139 pounds. His fingers wasn't an inch long and you wouldn't have thought he could throw, but back then the Yankees offered [$]300,000 for him. That was pretty good money, but they wouldn't sell him.

Who was the best hitter?

The one who give me the most trouble was ol' Johnny Mize. I could have him two strikes and, dad gum, he'd manage some way to hit that ball. He was tough.

I never did have much trouble out of Musial or [Enos] Slaughter. They never hurt me too bad. One time I pitched a five-hitter against the Cardinals and Slaughter and Musial neither one didn't get a hit.

I guess Ted Williams was the best hitter I ever saw. I faced him several times in spring training. One time he broke his bat and hit a home run off of me. *[laughs]* It was Fenway and it was 300 feet to the right corner and it just got inside of the foul pole.

One time I was pitchin' against him and they played that shift on him. I threw one strike and he swung at it and missed it. The next ball he didn't pull it on me; he hit it right through the shortstop and the shortstop was over behind second base.

If he hadn't been such a powerful hitter, he'd have hit more home runs than anybody. He hit the ball *so* hard that it would go over the infield and it would drop just like a pitcher throwin' a curveball, so much topspin on it. It would just dive down.

He got all the breaks from the umpires. "Ted Williams got a good eye; he don't swing at nothin' bad," which he didn't, but sometimes some of those balls they'd call were strikes. The umpires leaned a little bit for him.

Is there one game that stands out?

Yessir, there sure is. The Cubs, in 1945 when they won the pennant, in about the first week in September — the season ended then right in the last few days of September — they was in first place then and I beat 'em, 2-to-nothin', on a five-hitter. The sportswriters got all over 'em: "Let an unknown rookie shut 'em out." *[laughs]*

The manager let me come home after that game — stayed three days— then I went on over to Cincinnati when they got there and I pitched two games there in four days. Pitched one on Saturday, they beat me 2-to-1; and then I pitched ten innings on Tuesday and beat 'em, 3-to-2. That manager pitched me. There's three games right there that I give up three runs and yet I lost one of 'em. But Southworth was different.

Another thing, if I hadn't have got out of the Southern League I never would have went anywhere 'cause Kiki Cuyler didn't know nothin' about pitchin'. He didn't tell me one thing or try to show me nothin'. I got to throw hard and that's all he wanted me to do was rear back and throw.

I got with Braxton over at Norfolk, then the best one was at Indianapolis: Bill Burwell. He just taught me a couple of things; I'd get out there and pitch nine innings and wouldn't even be tired. He was a coach with the Pirates when I went up there playin' against 'em.

Any regrets?

Nosir. I'd go over it again if I could. Only thing, like I says a while ago, I was just born 50 years too soon.

I had a lot of ups and downs that would have made anybody quit, but I liked it so well I just kept pumpin' it.

A few days after this interview was done, Ed called and said, "I know you asked me about the best pitcher I saw and the best hitter, but you didn't ask me about the best ballplayer.

"It would have to be Willie Mays. He was the complete ballplayer. I was fortunate to play with him at Minneapolis when they called him up in 1951. I've seen him make some unconscious plays in that outfield. Up there Minneapolis had an old park and the outfield fences had two-by-fours around it to nail the planks to, and I've seen him run and put his spikes up on those two-by-fours and jump higher than the fence to catch a ball. He made hard plays look easy. He and Joe DiMaggio could go get 'em, I'll tell you that.

"When he come up we used to have a lot of fun with him. We'd all play tricks on him and everything. He didn't know how to take us, but he learned. It didn't take him long.

"It's a funny thing. I don't know if you heard the story on him. The scouts heard about some feller down in Alabama. Willie was from Alabama. They went down to scout this guy and they let the other guy go and they signed Willie. They had never heard about Willie."

HENDERSON EDWARD "ED" WRIGHT

Born May 15, 1919, Dyersburg, TN
Died November 19, 1995, Dyersburg, TN
Ht. 6'1"   Wt. 180   Batted and Threw Right

Year	Team, Lg	G	IP	W	L	Pct	H	BB	SO	ERA
1945	Boston, NL	15	111.1	8	3	.727	104	33	24	2.51
1946		36	176.1	12	9	.571	164	71	44	3.52
1947		23	64.2	3	3	.500	80	35	14	6.40
1948		3	4.2	0	0	—	9	2	2	1.93
1952	Phi., AL	24	41.1	2	1	.667	55	20	9	6.53
5 years		101	398.1	25	16	.610	412	161	93	4.00

DON LUND

Baseball Over Football (1945–1954)

Bo Jackson played baseball for a living and football for a "hobby." Deion Sanders did something along those lines. Chris Carpenter considered looking into both sports as well. A few others—Vic Janowicz, Red Badgro, Ernie Nevers, etc.—also tried both. More recently, Brian Jordan did both very successfully.

One who didn't but certainly could have was Don Lund.

Drafted number one by the Monsters of the Midway themselves, the Chicago Bears, out of the University of Michigan in 1945, instead he accepted Branch Rickey's offer to join the Brooklyn Dodgers. He never became the star it looked as if he might become, but he enjoyed his professional baseball career and has remained associated with athletics his entire life.

You were the Associate Athletic Director with Michigan. How long were you with the university?

I was coaching with the Tigers and left to become the baseball coach at Michigan. I was here four years, '59 through '62, then I went back to the Tigers as farm director 'til 1970. In July of '70 I came back to Michigan as Assistant Athletic Director. Bump Elliott was Associate Athletic Director; he left and went to Iowa as their Athletic Director and Dave Strack moved up and I took Dave's spot. Then Dave went to Arizona and I moved up as Associate Athletic Director.

You were the Tigers' farm director when they had some pretty good teams. Who were some of the players developed under you?

I was really pleased with the '68 World Series team. Everybody except Norm Cash came up through the farm system. We got Cash in a trade for Steve Demeter with Cleveland. All the rest — [Dick] McAuliffe, [Don] Wert, [Ray] Oyler, [Mickey] Stanley, [Jim] Northrup, [Willie] Horton, [Al] Kaline, [Bill] Freehan, all the regulars—came through the Tigers' system.

We were down in the Series, 3 to 1, and came back and won it. A key play was that play at the plate with [Lou] Brock. Had he slid he would have made it. There was a basehit to left and Horton threw him out at home plate. It was just one of those things. If you review it in slow motion, you'll see Freehan had his foot blocking the plate and Brock misses and Freehan spins and tags him. The umpire sees it all.

How did Freehan compare to Johnny Bench as a catcher?

Bench changed the style of catching, doing it one-handed with that glove like a first baseman's mitt. Freehan never let a ball by him. Bench probably had a stronger arm than Freehan did, but Freehan's technique was so good that he would release the ball so quickly. I recruited Bill and we spent a lot of time with him. He was so good, especially on pop flies.

Their techniques were different. Bench was one-handed and I don't teach that, but you don't take a Johnny Bench and make him two-handed. But the pitchers should have taken Freehan out for dinner all the time. He had such good technique blocking the ball. He stopped so many wild pitches because he blocked them so well. He had the top fielding percentage in history at the time of his retirement. I don't know if he still does.

Bench's way — one-handed with the new glove — is more difficult and it's tough for kids to emulate him. It worked for him, but it's not for everyone.

Freehan also coached baseball at Michigan.

Yes. He always wanted to coach. When he retired from the Tigers he was in the range of 75- or 80,000. In the off-seasons he had prepared himself

Don Lund as a rookie with Brooklyn, 1945.

as an automobile rep. I think the Tigers probably wanted him to manage but he couldn't afford to do it. If he went, say, to a Double-A club he'd get 15,000, maybe 20 max. So instead he went into business but stayed in the game by going to spring training and working with young catchers. He always wanted to coach. Today, if he were playing, he'd be making, what, two million a year?; so he could afford to stay in the game.

He's a loyal, dedicated Michigan guy; he's got the Maize and Blue in him. When we recruited him that's the first thing we did; we had him bend over and we used a big long needle with Maize and Blue in it and hit him in the butt.

He was a good Catholic and always wanted to go to Notre Dame. When he visited Notre Dame they talked about spring football. He asked about baseball in the spring and they said when football was over he could play baseball. We told him if he came to Michigan he could do what he wanted. If he wanted to go out for football I had no objection.

He was the best football player we had. He played end and I'm sure he would have been an All-American if he'd stayed. But then there was no draft in baseball and the offers got so high he had to take one. He left after two years of college.

How important is college to a baseball player?

Statistics show those who drop out before two years usually won't finish, but that increases by about 50 percent after two years. With the draft today after the junior year, statistics show that most boys will finish.

If boys sign out of high school and show talent they'll be sent to the Instructional League and then end up getting married and never get to school. My recommendation is that you go to school first. Kids mature and are better mentally prepared to face the world. They can still play ball but they can get away from home and adjust.

Of the boys that sign, only about three percent make it to the big leagues, and most of them for only a short time. The odds are against them. When I was the farm director I'd have to release kids who should have gone to college. The scouts' job, and I'm not knocking them, is to sign ballplayers, but these boys should go to college if they can. Look at Will Clark, for instance. Or Tom Seaver. These guys played well in college and things went well.

And [Barry] Larkin. He was the best defensive back in the state of Ohio but he never played a down of football here. He was drafted out of high school but came here and matured. He had a chance to play here and for the Olympics, I believe. Then he was drafted his junior year and signed. And he made it to the big leagues quickly.

How about Chris Sabo, another Michigan product who became Rookie-of-the-Year?

He could run pretty well. I'm amazed that it took Cincinnati that long to realize he could play. I think he was a hockey goaltender in high school in Detroit. He was a tough, hard-nosed kid.

Let's talk about you. You were a college football star. Did you have a chance to play professional football?

Well, I wasn't a star, but I played for three years. I was the number one draft choice of the Bears.

Why did you choose baseball?

Pro football wasn't like it is now. Our football coaches didn't advise us to go pro and the money certainly wasn't what it is now.

But I'd always wanted to play baseball. George Sisler was a Dodgers' scout and he saw me play one game and liked what he saw, so I went to New York to talk to Mr. Rickey. [Rickey had been baseball coach at Michigan; in fact, he had coached Sisler there.] He said, "Son, what do you want to sign?" so I told him and he said okay. I should have asked for more.

You joined the Dodgers straight from college.

Yes, but I only stayed a little while and I went to St. Paul. I struggled a bit that first year.

You went from the Dodgers to the Browns to the Tigers and had a good year in '52 at Buffalo.

Yes. I hit three-something and the Tigers bought my contract.

You were the regular right fielder for the Tigers in 1953.

Yes. I think I played about 135 games. It was great. In those days we only played 14 night games. It was a good routine.

What was your top salary?

I got up to about $9,500.

Was 1954 your last year?

As a player, yes. Then I scouted and worked with the farm system — ran tryout camps. Then I joined the big club as a coach.

Who were some of the best players you played with or against?

The best player I played against was Mickey Mantle. He had as much ability in his body as anyone who ever put on a uniform. He could run, he was strong; he could do it all. It was unfortunate he had those injuries.

And then playing against Joe DiMaggio was a real thrill. He did everything so gracefully.

Another would be Stan Musial. You'd always stop warming up before a game to watch him in the batting cage. Ted Williams, too; he was the best hitter I ever saw. I played against Willie Mays when he was with Minneapolis before he went up.

Guys I played with — I guess Al Kaline. He was kind of a weak kid when he joined us out of high school but you could see him mature and develop and he did everything so well. He always did everything correctly, took nothing for granted. So fundamentally sound in the outfield.

A good hitter was Harvey Kuenn and a guy who had a great year for us was Ray Boone. He drove in a lot of runs.

And his son, Bob, was a great kid. He worked harder than anyone. At 40 or 41 his body was like a kid of 30 or 28. Great shape and he worked at it. That's the reason he could continue to catch. He seemed to be swinging the bat better than ever. His mother, Patsy, used to be a stand-in for Esther Williams. The whole family is health-conscious. She and Ray look great.

What are the major changes in the game from when you played?

Uniforms and equipment have had a big change. The metal bat for the amateurs has been a big change.

Do you think the metal bat will ever be used in pro ball?

I don't think so. When you scout now and see kids with power they don't have it when you put a wooden bat in their hands.

Another change: so much night ball today.

What about the quality of play?

The quality, I think, is down. There's no question that the kids are bigger and stronger today, but they just don't play ball properly. Complacency, I think, figures in here. Attitude. A sign of the times. Attitude is so important if a team is successful, if an individual is successful.

Take a kid like Alan Trammell; what a great attitude, played hard. He was hurt a little — his back — but he was always trying. Then take another kid, [Lou] Whitaker — great ability, but he was in and out of the lineup. Sparky [Anderson] commented a little sarcastically, "He plays when he tells me he wants to."

"Well, what do I have to prove?" he said. He has to prove that he's a professional baseball player and every game you play you give your best. Jim Campbell [former Tigers' general manager] said he'd probably have a big year one year because his contract was running out. So he hit 25 home runs. "What do I have to prove?" He had to prove he's gamer, he wants to play. Look back a little to his youth when he was hungry. The attitude change is amazing.

One day the scorer gave him an error. His big concern was about that. He should have caught it. Here's [Jack] Morris out there busting his butt and if everyone doesn't bust his butt the pitcher pays the price.

This is a general statement, though. There are some guys who play hard all the time.

Are there any changes that should be made in baseball?

Maybe they need to reach a point on how much they can pay and still stay in business. The owners today are a factor. It used to be they were in it and it was their livelihood. Now it's businesses and corporations and it's for tax purposes. They still want to win, of course, but they may not have to. Go back to the Griffiths and Connie Mack; they had to win to make money to stay in business. [George] Steinbrenner makes changes in management all the time. There's got to be stability. And you can't buy a team.

And the number of guys on the disabled list! It's amazing. The Tigers traded [Tom] Brookens to the Yankees for [Charles] Hudson. Hudson's running in the outfield and pulls a hamstring! That seems to me you're not in shape.

Nobody today wants to play all the time. You get a guy like [Cal] Ripken who plays a lot of games in a row and it's big news. But he's a gamer; he wants to play.

And the pitching! A manager says, "Give me six good innings." Then he goes to the bullpen. I say, "Here's the ball. See you after nine." If a guy's thrown a lot of pitches, that's different; take him out. But mentally today they're just set to pitch six innings. What's remarkable is a guy like [Nolan] Ryan. The right attitude, a great body. And Morris.

Talking about the attitudes today, what do you think of the players charging for autographs or not responding to requests?

It's been brought about by the merchandising of products. The agents tell them not to sign, to wait for the card shows. It's hard to blame the players.

Opposite: Don Lund with Detroit, 1953 (courtesy Don Lund).

And baseball cards are better than the stock market. I've got a Mickey Mantle card; it's not mint but it's pretty darned good. It's worth more than $300 or so. And I've got one of Duke Snider and one of Jackie Robinson, but it's not in real good shape. And I've got the complete '62 Topps set. It's never been out of the box. I don't know what it's worth.

Do you respond to fan mail?

Oh, sure.

How many letters do you receive?

It varies. Maybe several requests for autographs come at once, then several months go by with only a very few. But I always sign. If it makes them happy, it's fine with me.

Were you a collector of souvenirs?

Not really. I've got a couple of Tiger caps and some bats. One was when they retired Greenberg's and Gehringer's numbers. And I've got one from the '68 Tigers which all the players signed, and a bat from the College World Series when I was coaching. A couple of baseballs, too, but that's about it. My wife kept a scrapbook from high school, college, and pro, but I don't look at it much.

Given the same situation, would you choose baseball again?

Oh, yes! Sure would! The best time was playing, then I enjoyed coaching.

I think I had some aptitude to become a manager. When I went back to the Tigers as farm director I probably thought I might have been a manager. That's probably what I should have done. There's a lot of time and effort in being a farm director and the rewards are not the same. It's a while to see your results and the pay's not much.

Did you enjoy your work at Michigan?

Oh, yes. I enjoyed coaching because I love working with kids. I ran a baseball school here for a while. That was fun. But my time at Michigan was enjoyable.

Right field for Detroit was Don Lund's for only one year. In 1954, they stuck a 19-year-old bonus baby out there and the position was pretty well sewn up for the next two decades. The kid's name was Al Kaline.

DONALD ANDREW LUND

Born May 18, 1923, Detroit, MI
Ht. 6'   Wt. 200   Batted and Threw Right

Year	Team, Lg	G	AB	R	H	2B	3B	HR	RBI	BA
1945	Brk., NL	4	3	0	0	0	0	0	0	.000
1947		11	20	5	6	2	0	2	5	.300
1948	BrkNL, StLAL	90	230	30	53	11	4	4	30	.230
1949	Detroit, AL	2	2	0	0	0	0	0	0	.000
1952		8	23	1	7	0	0	0	1	.304
1953		131	421	51	108	21	4	9	47	.257
1954		35	54	4	7	2	0	0	3	.130
7 years		281	753	91	181	36	8	15	86	.240

AL LIBKE

Versatile (1945–1946)

Al Libke was an imposing specimen on the mound or at the plate. Six-feet-four inches tall and 215 pounds, he began his career as a pitcher who could hit, but became a hitter who could pitch. Moved from the mound to first base with the Seattle Rainiers of the Pacific Coast League, he joined the Cincinnati Reds in 1945, became their regular right fielder, and led the team in hitting while batting third in the order.

He still had a pitcher's arm, though, and on four occasions as a rookie he was called in from the outfield to pitch. In four-and-one-third innings, he allowed only three hits and no runs. In the field, he led all National League outfielders in double plays and ranked fifth in assists.

The next year he was still in right field and it wasn't until the last game in the season that he pitched again. This time he started against the Pittsburgh Pirates. It was his first start since his days in the Coast League; nonetheless, he worked the first five innings and allowed only two runs and four hits in a game eventually won by the Reds, 3-to-2.

That was his last game in the major leagues. Rather than sign for a salary reduction in 1947, he retired and then accepted an offer from the Hollywood Stars back on the Coast and played two more years. He left behind a major league batting average of .268 and an ERA of 1.93.

❖ ❖ ❖

My first year in baseball was 1941. My uncle had taken me over to Seattle from Tacoma and I signed with the Seattle Rainiers and they farmed me out to the Wenatchee Chiefs, which was in an A league. I was 22.

I'd just been working in different jobs around. I helped my dad as a blacksmith's helper and I worked in a paint factory — all kinds of different things. And playing semipro.

I enjoyed playing wherever they put me. I apparently could have been a pretty good pitcher, but as I was starting to develop — I always had a very good arm — I was starting to pitch pretty well with Seattle and our first baseman was injured or something. I can't recall the reason, but all of a sudden he was gone, and Bill Skiff, the manager, said, "Al, would you play first base until we find someone?" He knew I could play a lot of positions. Well, as luck would have it, I started hitting pretty well and he just stopped looking. He said, "That's good enough for me." And after the end of that year, Cincinnati bought me.

When you joined the Reds in 1945, you were one of the top offensive forces on the team.

In those days, we had guys like Bucky Walters and Ewell Blackwell and Ewell used to say, "Just give me one run. That's all I need." Well, that's about all we could ever muster. *[laughs]* [The Reds scored the fewest runs in the National League in Libke's two years with the team.]

I always like to think of myself as either starting a rally, keeping it going, or driving in the final runs. If you did that, you were doing a good job.

You pitched four times as a rookie.

The first [major league] training camp I went to, the outfielders were doing a lot of the pitching for batting practice because the pitchers weren't ready yet and so I went out there to pitch some batting practice and Bucky Walters was there and he said, "What the hell are you doing in the outfield? You should be pitching."

I said, "Well, I've been a pitcher up until the last year." He said, "You should *still* be a pitcher."

Jimmy Wilson, the coach and a great guy — tremendous man — he also thought I should pitch, but they needed lefthanded hitting so that's where I played. But they brought me out of the outfield a few times and they didn't score on me.

You tailed off a little in your second year.

You know, I started off that year tremendously. We had gone down to Florida for spring training and I became acquainted with Ted Williams of the Red Sox when we traveled together up from Florida to Ohio prior to the season beginning. He, for some reason, took a liking to me and gave me a lot of advice and helped me out. I think for the first month I was leading all kinds of categories in the league. I was *really* doing well and then it just kind of tapered off.

I think, had I played with that guy, he'd've made a star out of me. He was a real good guy to me. There's been a lot of negative things said about him, but not by players. They respected his ability and he had it, I'll tell you.

You started a game on the mound that season.

That was the last game of he season. You know, your arm gets conditioned for pitching. I gave up the ghost in the fifth inning.

What happened in 1947?

[Manager] Bill McKechnie became ill and didn't return. They sent me a contract with a cut and I'd always promised myself that if I started going downhill I'd quit. I'd seen too many bums in baseball when I was in the Coast League and in the Western International League, so I said, "That's it," and I went selling real estate.

Well, a week before the Coast League season began, I got a call from Oscar Reichow, who was the general manager of the Hollywood Stars, and he said, "Al, if you'll come play with us I'll pay you what Cincinnati wouldn't. I've talked with them and they said that's agreeable with them." So I went down without any spring training at all. I hit very well in the Coast League.

It wasn't unusual for a Coast League team to pay better than a major league team in those days.

That's right. A lot of the players made real good money.

When you retired, you were only 30 and still a good ballplayer.

I could've been a real good ballplayer, I think, had I been able to play with someone who tried to help me a little bit. I could've been a good pitcher or good hitter, either way.

When you were with Cincinnati, the Reds were pretty much in a state of limbo from year to year. They had little talent and weren't making money.

Oh, man. A lot of times the players on the two rosters would outnumber the fans. It was terrible for a while.

How did you miss the war?

I was called up; my draft number was up. I was a big, strong guy—
I could do a lot of things—and I figured that I was gone. I made arrange-
ments to lease the apartment we were living in and get rid of our furni-
ture and went down to the reception center and went through the whole
thing. Because I had wrecked my left knee the last game of the 1941 season, but had it repaired that fall, the guy looked at it and said, "I'm gonna
put you in limited service."

I about died because I was the biggest and strongest kid at the whole
center there. It kind of hurt my feelings in a way, but then I found out
there were four or five requests from different commanders around the
country that wanted me to come to their base to play on their teams. Well,
I figured they'll get me at some point in time if this thing keeps going
on, so I did not play organized ball in '43. I played for a shipyard team in
Seattle.

Does one game stand out?

I've had a lot of real good games. I remember the last game I played
for Seattle. It was the last inning of the ballgame and it was a nothing-
nothing tie and I hit a home run in the last of the ninth and won the ballgame, one-to-nothing. My dad was there. It was against Sacramento; a
guy by the name of [Guy] Fletcher was the pitcher.

Who was the best player you saw?

I saw an awful lot of real good players, but I think the best hitter I
ever saw, of course, was Williams. I only played with him for the couple
of weeks that we were en route from Florida to Ohio. He was just a great
hitter.

There was an awful lot of players who had a *lot* of courage. I remember in Seattle we had a little roly-poly pitcher called Dick Barrett. He was
a competitor; he'd go out and win those ballgames. He had a great curveball.

I think in the majors, I admired Bucky Walters a great deal because
he was very supportive of me all the time. When he pitched, he said, "Now,
look. I want you to play back a couple or three steps over what you normally would. I don't care if they hit a single in front of you, but I don't
want any doubles over your head." And he was a first-class guy. There was
a lot of no-goodniks in the game, unfortunately.

I thought that Eddie Miller was a fantastic shortstop for us. He had
an old glove that he'd cut out the inside pocket. All he had was a piece of
leather between his palm and the ball. It was such a lousy-looking glove

he could leave it lying anywhere and nobody'd ever steal it. He could really go get 'em.

And I learned an awful lot from a little guy named Lonnie Frey. I used to go up and watch him hit batting practice. He'd hit the ball quite a way with just a very smooth swing. I thought, if he can hit 'em that far, as big as I am, if I just get a little smoother I should be able to hit quite a ways. You learn every day.

I was lucky enough to have a 21-game hitting streak. The guy that got me out was a guy that should never have got me out, but that's the way it goes. *[laughs]* [It was Ken Gables of the Pirates.] You know, you hit three or four balls right on the nose right at somebody. [That streak was the second longest in the NL in 1945.]

The first year when I hit .283 up there, I should've hit over .300 because I went 0-for-25 that last part of the season. My wife had left early and I was there alone and I was hitting that ball pretty good but right at people.

Would you be a ballplayer again?

Oh, yeah. I think with what I know now I would've done things a little differently. When you're that age and the way baseball was in those days, we didn't do an awful lot in the way of training or lifting weights and improving yourself in a lot of ways like they do now, or *can* do now. If you had natural ability, you were lucky.

One guy I remember in Seattle who *made* himself into a good player was a guy by the name of Al Niemiec. He was just an average player, but that guy practiced and practiced and practiced, and most of the rest of us did not practice that much. I always admired him for that. They'd hit him ground balls by the hour and he'd practice knocking the ball down and then picking it up with the first attempt. Just little things, but over the course of the season maybe half-a-dozen outs were created by him being able to do that.

What was your salary with the Reds?

I think it was somewhere around $3,500 for the [first] year. I talked with Jimmy Wilson and he had managed the Cubs for Mr. Wrigley and he told me that Mr. Wrigley wanted to put in a minimum wage of $5,000 a year, but everybody said, "Oh, no, we can't do that! That would ruin the incentive!" It was a heck of a lot better than working, and I'm assuming, had I continued on, I would have done better.

Opposite: Al Libke (courtesy Al Libke).

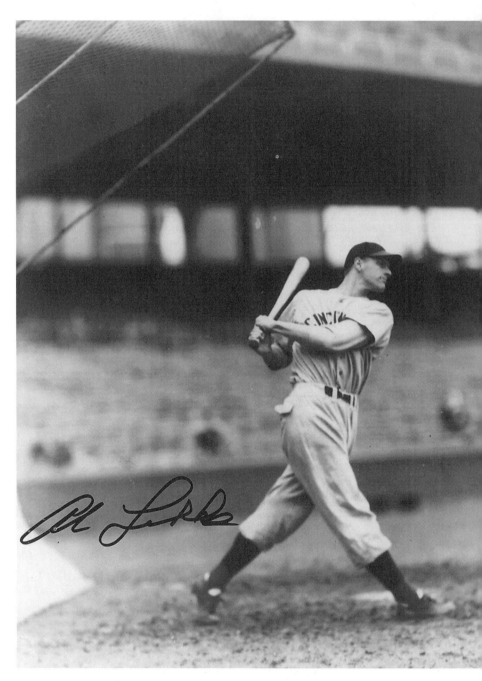

Al Libke (courtesy Al Libke).

I had no complaints about it because I pretty much accepted what they said. I know Mr. Giles called me into the office my second year 'cause I was doing so well the first month and he voluntarily gave me a raise. We didn't have agents in those days. I remember we had a meeting about a union and we just killed that quick-like. None of us were for that at all.

Do you receive much fan mail?

It's rather surprising, not having played for 50 years and I get four or five a month. I think that these guys that charge for autographs to kids — or whatever — are crazy. I don't believe it.

I even printed up some of my own cards. I wrote back to a card company that has my picture. The first time I wrote to 'em, they sent me a little packet of small pictures that I could send out to people that asked me. The next time I asked I didn't hear from 'em, so I just went to a printing company down here and printed up a bunch of my own. That's part of the game, in my opinion. We're supposed to be role models and be good guys and if the kids are interested in your picture or an autograph, heck, give it to 'em.

Any regrets?

No, no. Not really. It was a great experience and it stood me well in everything I've done because people sort of enjoy meeting someone who has played in the majors and knows something about it. I've always been active in the community here; I helped form the Little League here and coached in it for years, and the Babe Ruth League. I've been on the board of directors of the YMCA here for years and I'm a trustee of it now. I was an insurance agent/broker here for years and I won a statewide award for community service from the insurance industry, which I was very appreciative of. It's amazing how many doors it [baseball] opens for you.

Al Libke mentioned Dick Barrett, a name unfamiliar to most of those who are/were not fans of the PCL. Tracey Soutar "Dick" or "Kewpie" Barrett, around 5'9" and 170 pounds, spent 13 years in the PCL, ten of them with Seattle. He won 20 games seven times (and missed an eighth when he was 18-17 with 11 one-run losses), pitched a perfect game, and once won both ends of a doubleheader. He appeared in the major leagues with limited success, but he was a PCL legend. In 1942 when he went 27-13 with a 1.72 ERA he was named the *Sporting News* Minor League Player of the Year.

ALBERT WALTER LIBKE

Born September 12, 1918, Tacoma, WA
Ht. 6'4"   Wt. 215   Batted Left, Threw Right

Year	Team, Lg	G	AB	R	H	2B	3B	HR	RBI	BA
1945	Cin., NL	130	449	41	127	23	5	4	53	.283
1946		124	431	32	109	22	1	5	42	.253
2 years		254	880	73	236	45	6	9	95	.268

RED HAYWORTH

Rookie Series Catcher (1945–1946)

The 1944 St. Louis Browns won the only pennant in the team's history. Today that feat is discounted by many: "It was a war year," they say, and the team is dismissed as a fluke.

But c'mon, guys. Browns' players were not excluded from the war effort. Just as every other team did, the Brownies lost players to Uncle Sam. But the team that was assembled in St. Louis in the summer of '44 was the best in the American League and that's what it's all about: The best team wins.

The greatly underrated and nearly forgotten Vern Stephens supplied the punch and the team led the league in runs. Nelson Potter and Jack Kramer were the aces of the pitching staff and George Caster tied for the league lead in saves.

The staff ERA was 3.17, second in the league, and one must remember that ERA is as much a function of catchers as it is of pitchers. And the Browns had a very unlikely pair of catchers, especially for a pennant winner: two rookies, Red Hayworth and Frank Mancuso. And the fact that they were rookies was not the only unusual aspect of these two. Both were the much younger brothers of major league catchers who had also played in a World Series.

Red Hayworth was 29 years old, a little on the high side for a rookie.

He had been a Yankee property up until the 1943 season and the Yankees simply did not need a catcher — Bill Dickey was there — so Red stayed in the minors longer than maybe he should have.

During the regular 1944 season, Hayworth and Mancuso shared the duties behind the plate, but when it came time for the showdown with their co-tenants of Sportsman's Park, the Cardinals, manager Luke Sewell chose to go with Red. He started every game of the World Series, only the second rookie catcher ever to do so.

❖ ❖ ❖

Whiteline McCandless, Yankees scout, signed me in 19-and-36. I went to Joplin, Missouri, and I played out there with [Johnny] Lindell and [Johnny] Sturm and some of them boys. We had a winner out there that year. Bennie Bengough was the manager.

I played at Norfolk, Virginia, the next year, then I went to Augusta, Georgia, then I was in Dallas, Texas, in the Texas League, and I had a cold in the spring in my shoulder. I came back and played the next year there.

Let's see, when I was with the Yankees they dealt me to St. Louis in a deal in 19-and-42. I went there at Toledo in '43. That was in the American Association. 'Forty-four and '45 I was in St. Louis.

There just wasn't any room at the top in the Yankees' chain in those years.

No, but they were real nice to me. Real good. When I played in Augusta that year we got in the World Series, you know — a lot of the fellas I knew.

Gehrig was there and George McQuinn was one of the finest first basemen I ever saw. He got a chance to play with St. Louis and later played with the Yankees, but you didn't expect George to come in and play over Gehrig. George was a great fielder. He made contact, too. He was a great fella.

When you came to the Browns, you caught a World Series pitching staff as a rookie. What difficulties did you have in adjusting to a pennant race in your first year?

Well, I tell you, I was very fortunate. Our manager was Luke Sewell; he was a catcher. Our bullpen coach, Zack Taylor, was a catcher, and Freddy Hofmann, at first base [coach], was a catcher — an old catcher, used to be with the Yankees— so I had a lot of catchin' around me.

And my brother had told me a lot of things about catchin'. 'Course, when I started in school I was a first baseman; they made a catcher outta me first thing, just like they did my brother Ray.

Red Hayworth

I'd say I was lucky. I was catchin' some pitchers that pitched a year or two ahead of me in St. Louis, like [Denny] Galehouse and [Nelson] Potter and [Bob] Muncrief. I went up with Jack Kramer; he had a good year at Toledo. But that made it a bit easier on you and Sewell, too, bein' a catcher, he had a theory that I liked. He called the pitchers and catchers together first of the year and says, "Now listen. It's not what you throw, it's where you throw it. Let's get together now, you pitchers and catchers." And that's the way we went.

He didn't set over there and call pitches from the side, either, like some of 'em do. No, they let you run your ballgame because you know actually what the pitcher has — his best pitch and so forth — and after two or three innings his fastball may not be as good at first and then it gets more alive, you know. Or vice-versa. And a man can pick up and his curveball can get better or worse. They can tell more catchin' 'em than you can settin' on the side.

I think some of your best shots on TV are the ones right in back of home plate and you can see the rotation on the ball and so forth. Now your off-center shot out there where they have to do it in TV, you think a ball's a strike when it's not a strike. At that angle it makes it a little bit tougher, and, 'course, we've got a lot of announcers that second-guess the umpires on those. I don't like that because I think we have some good umpires.

I played when we had some great umpires and I really enjoyed 'em. Bill McGowan, used to umpire in the American League, he's one of the best. If I had a game to go, I'd like him to umpire 'cause he'd tell you. He was a good, stern man, and he wanted everybody to hustle on and off the field. He says, "If it's not on the black, it might as well be a foot off. It's a ball. An inch off, it's still a ball." *[laughs]* McGowan was a great umpire. I liked him; he was real good.

We sit and watch a game — Ray and I do — and he's got a theory that with two or three announcers all they do is read stats. *[laughs]* You know, 'bout what the boy did down at Podunk or somewhere else, and he'll just cut the sound off and watch the game.

We have some good announcers, too. [Tim] McCarver and the big pitcher at Baltimore, you know, he's a good announcer. Several of 'em are really good announcers; they call the game. Of course, we're spoilt to the fact that Dizzy Dean started in St. Louis when I was there and he just called it like it was, you know. That's what people like.

I think the fans, if you go up and sit down in the stands, the fans that you listen to, they wanna see you play. They don't care nothin' 'bout you puttin' on a show for 'em. They come out to see the *team* play.

'Course, the way they dress and the way they hit a home run and what they do, it'd be a little bit rough back in those days. If you did what some of 'em do now, I think Allie Reynolds and some of those other guys would have you on the ground pretty quick because they didn't put up with nothin' like that.

Talk about the '44 World Series.

It was a good Series. We had good pitchin' and they did, too. We managed to hold Musial down. It was a good Series, good fieldin' in it. The break that hurt us was on a bunt that [Don] Gutteridge was coverin' first base on a bunt. The ball was thrown [by Potter] a little bit to one side and he couldn't get off [the bag] to get the ball. It went to right field. Finally wound up in extra innings and we got beat, 3-to-2, when [Ken] O'Dea got a pinch-hit — a pinch-hit single.

It was a good Series. The Cardinals, 'course, had good pitchin', good fieldin' and we did, too, at the time. We had good experienced pitchers. It was a great Series to play in. We could've won that game *very* easy, but that's the way it goes sometimes. Things happen against you, you know.

You spent 1945 with St. Louis. Where did you play in '46?

'Forty-six I went — Mickey Owen and myself — to Mexico, played in the Mexican league. We could make more money. Workin' for [Bill] DeWitt, you wasn't gonna make much money in St. Louis. *[laughs]*

My brother told me I had a chance to go to Philadelphia — the Athletics — but they wouldn't trade me over there. I found out 'fore the year started, so I manipulated around and later I went to Mexico. Then the thing that helped me a lot, I went to Cuba in the wintertime, played winter ball. I was there with Sal Maglie and Lou Klein and several of those fellas down there and [Adolfo] Luque was one of the managers down there. That was a good league there in Havana — the winter league. Every day was like a World Series and you got a lot of experience playin' with experienced players, too, and I had that experience in St. Louis, but, still, I enjoyed playin' with 'em.

You guys who went to Mexico were suspended by the Commissioner's office.

Yeah, they were supposed to be suspended. I played with Max Lanier's All-Stars one summer, too, and I got to where I hurt my knee in my right leg — tore the cartilage out of it, torn loose — and 'course, I had that operated on. I was with Fred Martin and some of the rest of 'em that year — playin' with Max and them in exhibitions. We drew big crowds and all.

Then they reinstated us in the wintertime. I was 31 or -2, I believe it

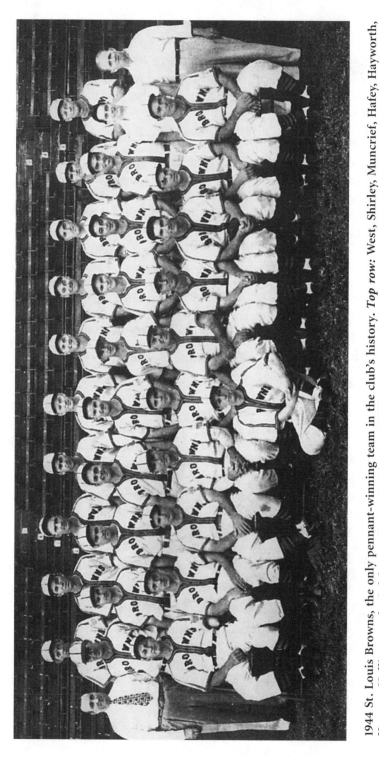

1944 St. Louis Browns, the only pennant-winning team in the club's history. *Top row:* West, Shirley, Muncrief, Hafey, Hayworth, Kramer, Hollingsworth, Galehouse, Kreevich, Jakucki. *Middle row:* C. DeWitt (traveling secretary), Caster, Baker, Potter, Zarilla, McQuinn, Laabs, Christman, Byrnes, Gutteridge, Bauman (trainer), Hanley (property man). *Bottom row:* Paul, Zoldak, Clary, Taylor (coach), Sewell (manager), Hofmann (coach), Moore, Chartak, Stephens, Mancuso, Scanlon. (Batboy in foreground.)

was, but I felt good; I'd taken care of myself. I still feel good. I'll be 85 in May — the 14th — if I'm livin'.

I guess Ray told you — the Mancusos and us are the only brothers — catchers — that played on different major league clubs and we all played in the World Series. I had never noticed that 'til a few years ago when our minister at church said somethin' about it to me. *[laughs]* I knew his brother Gus; he was a nice fella.

You had some memorable teammates in St. Louis. Vern Stephens.

Stephens was a fella that hit like DiMaggio — feet wide apart. The balls that they take now, which really are strikes — they call 'em balls — they'd never get them by people like Yogi Berra and Vern Stephens and them. They hit 'em — the ones right across your letters. He could hit a ball a *long* ways. He had good power, had a good arm as a shortstop. He played on a field that was terrible there in St. Louis because the Cardinals played on it and we played on it and when we wasn't playin' somebody was workin' out on it, so it's not like it is today. Never had an off day, that field didn't.

Vern had good power, he was a good fella on the ballclub. He'd be borderline [Hall of Fame]; he had good power and, 'course, he'd be made for Fenway Park. He hit the ball out in St. Louis when he'd get ahold of it. He played there when it was a long ways to left field — 'bout 360 to left field, you know, down the line. It's not like those 325 and -30 jobs you got now. We walked up there and hit the ball good and it'd be what we called "warnin' track power"; they'd just stand in front of the fence to catch 'em.

Sig Jakucki.

Sig Jakucki was an odd person. I liked Sig. You had to lead him all the time — you go right along with him, don't let him shake you off. He was a big, strong fella, had a good fastball sinker, not a bad hitter.

I remember one time the Yankees — they steal signs pretty good and they'd steal 'em off him, off his glove — and they said somethin' to him when he come into the bench about the way he was holdin' his hands. They were whistlin' on the curve and not sayin' anything on the fastball. The way Sig told 'em, he said, "Well, if I get it where I want to, they're not gonna hit it anyway." And that's just the way he was.

He was a big, strong, bold fella, very bold in everything he did. He told me one time he pitched in front of a hundred thousand people — the largest crowd in the country — when Ruth went to Japan and played one time. He was in the service over there and pitched against 'em. Jakucki was a kind of a raw type fella, but he didn't bother anybody at all. Didn't bother anybody. He was a big, rough character. *[laughs]*

George Caster. If you had a stopper in the bullpen, he was it.

George was the only knuckleball pitcher we had on the staff and he threw a knuckleball that didn't break deep, but he could move it. He did a good job for us when he relieved. 'Course, we didn't have as many relievers as we do now. Our pitchers then were geared to pitch eight or nine innings; now they're geared for five or six innings because they don't throw in between off the mound. They throw in the bullpen and do as they please.

Pitchers used to have to throw 12 to 15 minutes; they'd rest a day after they pitched and the next day they'd throw battin' practice, then they'd run, then they'd rest. That's the way they'd alternate in their pitchin' and they built their arms and their arms were a lot stronger than they are now. I've talked to a lot of coaches and all about that. You gotta use that arm to get it strong.

Al Zarilla.

Ol' Al did some scouting over there in Hawaii. Al was kind of a jolly-like ballplayer. He was a good hustler and if he was on base you better watch out. If somebody dropped the ball and he was five feet off he'd take off to the next bag. You know, he'd just get and run.

We was playin' the Yankees one time—I'll tell you this *[laughs]*—man on base and Al was hittin' and just as the pitcher started to pitch, well, McGowan at first base called time. Somethin' happened out there and he called time and Al hit the ball and flew out to right field. 'Course, McGowan stopped it and said, no, you have to play over—pitch over again. He was right; he had time called. And, you know, the nest pitch Zarilla hit it on the roof. *[laughs]* Things like that'll happen when you're winnin'.

He was a jolly fella, a real good fella. I'd like to see him. He was a good man on a ballclub—he was *lively*, you know. He was a dandy.

Who was the Browns' best player in '44?

We had some real good ballplayers at the time. 'Course, I'm partial to George McQuinn at first base. He's one of the few first basemen that can play the bag on the back side. He could play it like [Keith] Hernandez used to with the Mets—he could back up and catch the ball. And he knew what plays to make and he was just a cat over there around first base. I always felt like Stephens and Gutteridge could just pick up the ball and throw it towards first base, hopin' he'd come up with it, which it looked like sometime. He was really a good fella and a good man on a ballclub.

Who was the best overall player you saw?

[laughs] Well, you hit me between the eyes. I might miss somebody there, I believe. There was some good ballplayers around then. You know, Washington had some good ballplayers, too.

Incidentally, we were playin' Washington in September of '45 when Mr. Truman came out for the first game while he was president. He didn't get to come out in the spring; it was in September. 'Course, he'd been on our bench the year before he became president. He threw out the first ball and they lined up — Washington did — down from first base to home and we lined up from home to the stand. 'Course, we were gonna be the goats, but I knew he was lefthanded and when he motioned left and went over right and come back left, I broke out of the line. Al Evans or somebody hit the ball — hit their hand — and I scooped it up and I got it now. Mr. Truman signed it. He threw out another one and George Myatt got it, but all the boys said, "You hold that and don't let nobody else sign it but Truman." 'Course, it was full of senators and the Commissioner of Baseball and all was there, but they just wanted his name on it. *[laughs]* It's one of the balls I saved.

But speaking of ballplayers you played against, it just runs in your mind. Back then offhand I'd have to run them down and think about that 'cause there was some good ballplayers on all the ballclubs.

Ray played with 'em and I played against [Hank] Greenberg and [Rudy] York. And [Dizzy] Trout was pitchin' over there. I'd just go over each club; that'd be a hard thing to say which was really the best ballplayer.

The ones that liked to play and liked to beat you, like Bobby Doerr and those fellas— they came out to beat you. Joe Gordon. They hit .275 and you think they're hittin' .350. They beat you.

Joe Gordon was vastly underrated. When he was with New York they were winners and when he came over to Cleveland all of a sudden they were winners, too, yet he gets very little recognition.

Well, he was quite a ballplayer. He was a good friend of a lot of the fellas in the Yankee system that I knew real well. He was a ballplayer's ballplayer and I'd compare him a lot with Bobby Doerr with the Red Sox. He could beat you. He'd hit .260 to -75 and you'd think he's hittin' .350 'cause with a man on base he could really hurt you to both fields. Those fellas were good ballplayers.

'Course, the one that I *didn't* play against but everybody tells me and Ray tells me, one of the best ever lived was Charlie Gehringer. He just didn't make a mistake on that infield; he knew how to play all the hitters and everything. And he could hit lefthanders just like he did righthanders.

The best pitcher?

One of the good pitchers that I saw was with the Red Sox at that time: Tex Hughson, a big righthander. He was one of the best pitchers in the league, I thought — good fastball, good curve, good straight change, and about four or five times — maybe — in a ballgame he'd throw you a good knuckleball. Hardly ever threw it. Mace Brown lives over here in Greensboro — was pitchin' coach for the Red Sox, good friend of mine — we talked about him a lot when I saw him. I tell you, he was tough to hit at! He was really tough 'cause he had a good fastball, he had a good sharp curve, and he had the good motion on his change.

Later on we talked about it; they didn't throw enough straight changes. They were scared to throw 'em. It's one of the best pitches in baseball. It's really a good pitch. You got to perfect it in your delivery.

Just like in your catchin'. I was talkin' to some fellas; they was talkin' 'bout catchin'. I said, "Well, Atlanta's got a young catcher that I really like." [Javier] Lopez. He's got the short stroke with the bat, he's got a good arm, and he lets the ball come to him. That's the things that when I was scouting I talked about to minor league catchin' coaches.

We were talkin' up at Salem one day. The problem — they got these mitts and they wanna reach out and get the ball one-handed and they try to backhand balls where they don't shift their feet. It's a proven fact, if you let the ball come to you it'll get to you quicker'n you can reach for it and you can throw on the one-two count and the other way it's an extra step and an extra step is where they can steal a base on you.

'Course, they got some good young catchers that, if they do that, could really be dandies. And they got some that just go the other way. Like I said, I was fortunate enough; I broke in under a good receiver, Bengough. He could catch with anybody. He was the fella that hurt his arm when he was with the Yankees, you know, and couldn't throw but, boy, he could *really* catch and he could show you some things.

There's some good catchers around. The big boy [Rick] Wilkins that was with the Cubs, I saw him over here in Winston-Salem break in and he always had the good arm. He had the lousy soft mitt and he'll catch you two or three games and he'll look great and again he'll get a little careless — some of 'em get careless — and backhand the ball on the righthand side and it'll get away from him.

Now we couldn't catch that way when we was catchin'. Our foot went over there to block the ball. We blocked everything we could. It makes it better on your pitchin'. That's what the catchers are supposed to do.

[Ivan] Rodriguez down with Texas and the boy Atlanta's got — both of 'em are strong. And that boy who was with the Dodgers [Mike Piazza] —

he's strong, too. They're strong and they can catch every day. And they got the good quick release. They don't hurry their throws. A good catcher just comes outta there throwin' and he don't have to hurry himself. If you hurry, you kinda jerk, you know, and you don't have your rhythm, but he's got a good arm, too. We got better catchin' than we've had in a few years right now.

You hit a home run.

I hit it off Hot Potato Hamlin with Philadelphia in St. Louis. I believe it was USO Night in St. Louis. We were behind and Hamlin happened to throw the high curve — he was a curveball pitcher, you know — and he got it up in my eyes and, believe it or not, I hit it over the fence down that line. *[laughs]* It went 360; it went out there a little ways in left field.

Oh, I had a lotta fun outta that — hittin' that home run — because, see, I was a hit-and-run man. They taught me to hit-and-run in school. I'm like Alvin Dark — you could throw the ball right straight at me and I could almost hit it to right field, hit it on the ground. You've gotta learn to do that. 'Course, Sewell told me when I come over there, he said, "Don't worry about your average. You're not gonna hit as much; it's gonna cost you 20-25 points," but he says, "We want you to hit-and-run." I said, "Okay with me." So I been on winners doin' it so I kept on doin' it.

[Red was a good man for the hit-and-run; in 452 major league plate appearances, he only struck out 19 times.]

I set down at the ballpark at Durham with Eddie Mathews when he was workin' for the Braves and I was coverin' the Carolina League — that's what I did 'fore I finished, I did pro coverage — and he talked about fellas up there, walk up there to hit and the man led off with a double and 'steada hittin' the ball to right field they stand there and pull the ball to short or third, or if it was a lefthander they'd go with the ball away from 'em and hit it the other way. He said a lot of times he'd just cover the plate and be sure he could pull that ball to second or first — back when he played. He played to win, you see. And that's what he wanted them to do, but he said it's *hard* to get the young players to do it.

The young players won't give themselves up because it hurts their batting averages and they don't want that.

What if they played when you hit a fly ball to left field and the man scored, you still had a time at bat? They changed that, but that knocks off a few points per year, too. We never worried about that. I always talked to Freddy Hofmann, one of our coaches. I'd bet him, I'd say, "Get a man on third base with one or no out I'm gonna get him in." I just tried to hit a fly ball deep enough to score him, 'steada hittin' the ball on the ground.

Does one game stand out?

We beat the Yankees to win the pennant. The game ended, let's see, Stirnweiss popped up and George McQuinn come over and caught the ball. The most exciting thing was all kinds of hats and everything come out of the stands in St. Louis. People were so excited they threw hats away and everything. And, 'course, bein' in that ballgame that meant so much and really there was no pressure playin' it, I don't think, the way our club played all year. They talk about pressure, there's no pressure much. You got a job to do, especially if you're catchin'; you don't think nothin' about pressure. You gotta go out there and do the job. But that one there's the most exciting game to end that I was ever in. I had some good, close ballgames I played in, but that was just somethin' — a chance to get in the World Series.

When you get in there and get into a World Series, I don't care how good a ballclub you got or anything, everything's gotta go for you down the stretch. You gotta hustle and work for it and things gotta bounce just right for you.

Do you still hear from the fans?

It runs in clusters. Now some days I'll get two or three cards and in maybe a week I'll get something else. And I get pictures. The people are *very* nice; they send you self-addressed envelopes and they want you to sign cards or little pictures and different things. My wife is deceased now and that's one thing we always did — when they come in I sit down that night and I sign 'em and throw 'em in the mail the next day. I always do. The people are so nice to you and you get some of the nicest letters from all over the country.

It's nice to be remembered and I don't mind doin' it at all. I have the time to do it. See, I'm retired. I started in '36 and the end of '89, the start of '90 in January, I told the gentlemen down in Houston I just didn't believe I was gonna go out anymore — pro coverage, which I *liked* to do.

You scouted for about 40 years.

I managed one year when I was scouting and won the pennant over in the rookie league and I told Charlie Grimm, with the Cubs then, I says, "That's my year right there. That's my one year to manage and I'm not gonna manage any more." They used to put a scout in there to manage, you know. At the time, the people with the Cubs were nice people.

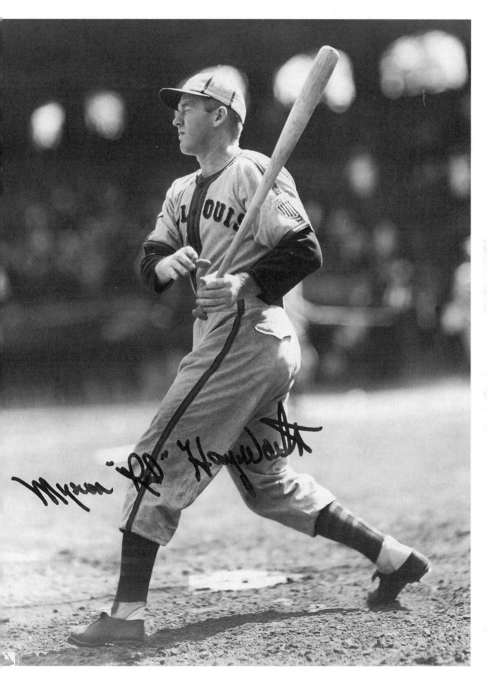

Red Hayworth (courtesy Red Hayworth).

Outside of playin', I did a lot of scouting. I put that uniform on for about, what, for about 17 years, I guess. 'Course, I played winter ball, too, in Havana, Cuba, which was a great place to play.

I enjoyed it all. I'm not against baseball. I'll stop over here to the college and see 'em play and different ones around here. 'Course, I got passes to the major leagues—if I wanna use them — from the Commissioner's office, American League and National League passes both, but I don't wanna go to Atlanta to see a ballgame. Like my brother Ray, I'd just as soon see it on TV here. If I had some friends goin' down I wouldn't mind goin' a day or two, but otherwise I wouldn't fool with it.

Would you do it all again?

I certainly would. And somethin' I wanted to do all my life was play and I'll tell the fellas, and I'm serious in this, when I was playin' there was a lot of ballplayers when I started in '36. My theory was to get to the ballpark early and get your uniform before somebody else got it *[laughs]* because, I tell you, there was a lot of 'em around wantin' to play. We wanted to play and I enjoyed every bit of it.

I was fortunate. I played under good managers. That's a big thing in baseball. I played under Johnny Neun at Norfolk, which was a great guy. You know, he used to work with the Yankees and manage Cincinnati some. And Johnny used to say, "Don't ever kick on it rainin'"—that you wanna play or something else. I said, "I don't kick 'cause I like to have that day of rest." I was catchin' every day. "Because," he said, "you can't beat the elements anyway. What's the use to talk about it?" So I always thought he had a good theory there.

I still enjoy baseball. Some people get a little sour on it. I don't see how you can get sour on somethin' that's been your livelihood.

Only the 1944 Browns reached the World Series with an all-rookie catching staff and Red Hayworth is one of only three rookie catchers to start every game of a World Series. The other two are Bill DeLancey of the 1934 Cardinals and Andy Etchebarren of the 1966 Orioles.

Myron Claude "Red" Hayworth

Born May 14, 1915, High Point, NC
Ht. 6'1½"   Wt. 200   Batted and Threw Right

Year	Team, Lg	G	AB	R	H	2B	3B	HR	RBI	BA
1945	St. Louis, AL	89	269	20	60	11	1	1	25	.223
1946		56	160	7	31	4	0	0	17	.194
2 years		145	429	27	91	15	1	1	42	.212

World Series

Year	Team, Lg	G	AB	R	H	2B	3B	HR	RBI	BA
1945	St. Louis, AL	6	17	1	2	1	0	0	1	.118

ADRIAN ZABALA

Done In by Durocher (1945–1949)

My family moved to the San Francisco Bay area when I was a small boy. There was a marvelous baseball team there called the Seals and I soon became a devout fan, and I remain one today, nearly a half-century after they ceased to exist. I still haven't forgiven the Giants. The franchise, no longer called "Seals," moved to a place totally unsuited for an aquatic marine mammal: the desert of Phoenix, Arizona.

Many former Seals' players still rank high on the list of my favorites: Jim Moran was a brilliant second baseman; Sal Taormina grew old as a Seal with never a shot at the majors; Johnny McCall; Leo Righetti, Dave's dad but a shortstop; Nini Tornay; Reno Cheso; Elmer Singleton, just to name a few.

Another was Adrian Zabala. He wasn't there long — a year-plus — but it seemed as if he pitched every day. I coerced my parents into taking me to maybe a dozen games in 1954, Adrian's only full season as a Seal, and I'll bet I saw him pitch ten times. He led the PCL in games (59) that year and probably in saves, too, but no one was counting them then. In my 13-year-old opinion, he was the best southpaw in the league.

Adrian Zabala pitched professionally from 1937 through 1956, missing only 1943 when the war took him away. He spent parts of two of those 19 active years with the New York Giants, where a disagreement with Leo

Durocher cost him more major league time. He began his career as a starter, a very successful one. He won 20 games once and 19 twice and only once in his first 15 professional seasons did he fail to win in double figures (and then it was nine wins). He made the adjustment from successful starter to successful reliever without missing a beat; he was first or second in appearances four years in a row toward the end of his career.

He was one of the jumpers when the Pasquel brothers offered big money to join their league in Mexico, and he was banned for five years, along with the likes of Sal Maglie, Max Lanier, Ace Adams, etc. When that league folded, many of the jumpers went to Canada to play. When the five-year ban was lifted after three, he returned to the U. S.

All told, in 19 seasons, Adrian appeared in 753 games and pitched 3,062 innings, major and minor. He won a total of 235 games and lost only 170 (.580), with a 3.56 ERA. It was a long and effective career.

You had been a starter for years, but when I finally saw you pitch you were a reliever.

I think it was in '52 or '53, I think I was in 78 games. At one time, Tommy Heath was the manager and we was playin' in Minneapolis and I relieved in 20 games in a row and he said to me, "I want you to go out in the outfield and run about five or ten minutes." When I got back, he say, "I want you to take a shower and go sit down in the stands someplace where I can't see you because if you don't, you have to pitch today again." I say, "It don't matter." He said, "You been pitchin' 22 games in 20 days. That's good enough." So he gave me that game off because he said I'd pitched too much. Most of the time it was one or two innings, but I was throwin' every day. It never bothered me or anything.

You must have a heck of an arm. Early in your career you were pitching more than 250 innings every year.

You know how I build my arm? When I first came to the United States I was too wild. I signed with Joe Cambria. We went to play and they won't let me pitch because I was too wild. They want to bring me down here to Florida; I say, no, I go back to Cuba. That was in 1936. I was only about 19 years old.

So I went to Cuba and there's a scout — I don't remember his name — he told me to build some kinda thing behind the plate — lumber, you know — and put a hole in the middle — 12 inches around hole — and try to throw the ball in the hole in there. I did this for 60 days in Cuba. After 60 days my arm was gettin' tired, too, because I used to throw about 15 or 20 minutes a day. I don't throw hard, I just try to let the ball go on the front of my eyes, which was lookin' on the corner outside or the corner inside, which one I wanna throw to.

After two months my arm was real swollen so I think I better rest.So I rest for a week. After one week or two weeks, somethin' like that, my arm got all right again. I went to pitch for the team there and I throw real hard right in the middle of the plate. Everybody say, "Hey, man, how the heck do you throw harder!?" And after that I never got wild again.

Bill Taylor was my catcher [at Jacksonville in 1939]. I used to say, "Bill, you call the pitch you want to and tell me where you want it. Up, down low." That's what I used to do with him. We got along real good. He was smart behind plate. He never forgot the hitters. He'd talk a lot with the hitters, tellin' jokes. [Taylor was a schoolteacher who never played beyond the low minors.]

You pitched more than 3,000 innings. Did you ever have any arm trouble?

No, no. The only time I had arm trouble — I forget what year it was — we was playin' an exhibition game in Knoxville, Tennessee, and our team [Minneapolis] was gong to play Knoxville, which was a Class B team. The manager says, "Adrian, I want you to pitch for Knoxville," because Knoxville belongs to Minneapolis, to the organization. "I want you to pitch for Knoxville against our team. I want you to throw the ball hard to them to see how we're doin'." So I went to pitchin'—five innings, I can't remember — and Ray Dandridge, he used to play third base for us, hit a line drive to the mound and hit me in my shoulder — my left shoulder. You know how the catcher gets hit on the shoulder from a foul ball? He hit me right there. God almighty, I can't move my arm around; I can't do nothing with it for two or three days! That's the only time I had trouble with my arm. For two or three days, I can't do nothing. I can't even put on my overcoat; it was too heavy to put on.

Did Joe Cambria bring you to the U.S.?

Yeah. He's the one that give me a contract. In 1933, I think it was, he bring Bob Estalella. He was much older than me. And he bring some other Cuban guys, too — somebody named Morales or somethin' like that. And he bring [Alex] Carrasquel, the pitcher with Washington. Every year he used to go to Cuba. He bring Mike Guerra, he got [Camilo] Pascual, Zorro Versalles. All the Cubans [who] used to play for Washington, Cambria signed them. He was in Cuba from 1935 almost all year 'round until Castro take it over. *[laughs]* He had to run away from Castro, too. That's when he came up to United States.

[Joe Cambria, an Italian by birth, came to the U.S. as a boy and played minor league ball until he was injured. He owned several minor league clubs, then began a long scouting career for Washington and, after they moved, Minnesota. He signed more than 400 ballplayers to contracts, but they were not all Cubans. He scouted and signed Mickey Vernon, Early Wynn, and Eddie Yost, among others. He scouted a young Cuban pitcher named Fidel Castro, but decided he was not a prospect.]

How did you get with Panama City in the late 1930s?

When they give me my release — in 1936 I can't make the team because I'm wild — then I went to Cuba and do

Adrian Zabala (courtesy Adrian Zabala).

like I say. In 1937, a friend of mine, he was playin' with Panama City, Florida, and they need a pitcher so they call me to see if I wanna play there. It was Class D.

So I went there. I pitched in 1937 — the last month-and-a-half of 1937, something like that. In 1938, I pitched in Panama City again. So then I come down here to Jacksonville, Florida, in 1938 for one week and from then I come in '39, '40, '41, and in '42 they sold me to the New York Giants. I went to Jersey City, New Jersey, then.

You were having a great season in '42 when the Giants bought you.

I was pitchin' pretty good. The first year with the New York Giants I pitched about one month in '45. Between there I was in the army: '43 and half of '44, and in '45 I come back to Jersey City. I went about 15-4 or something like that and they take me to the big league.

Sal Maglie and myself and Danny Gardella, we all three went to the big league in 1945. That's when the war was over. And then I went back in '46 and they give me a contract for $4,000 a year and I told 'em I can't make a living in the big league that way. They don't want to give me no more money so I say, "Okay."

[Jorge] Pasquel was the main man from Mexico City. I think he got about 30 or 32 ballplayers. Maglie was the same way. They [the Giants] offered Maglie $5,000. Pasquel give me $15,000 and $3,000 bonus. Maglie got about $14,000-15,000, plus $10,000 bonus. Max Lanier, I think he got about $15,000, too. Ace Adams was a big relief pitcher, was a good one. He was makin' about $5,000; he got about three years for $40,000. They gave half the money before we went to Mexico. I did pretty good. *[laughs]* I was *tryin'* to do pretty good.

When the league folded, you guys weren't allowed to come back so you went to the Provincial League.

We went to Canada. Pasquel, he lost a lot of money. I wouldn't come back because they was gonna cut my salary, so in '48 and '49 I went to Sherbrooke, Quebec. Roland Gladu, Maglie, Max Lanier, a bunch of players from the colored league — it was good ball there.

We was suspended for five years but they take off my suspension and I come back to New York, but then I went to Leo Durocher and play with Leo Durocher. He want me to sign for $4,000, and I say, "I don't play for $4,000. I go home." He said, "Well, I give you the [major league] minimum — $5,000." I said, "I don't think I want it." We talked back and forth and he say, "If you make the team, I might get you more money." So I went ahead.

I pitched in the Polo Grounds and I win a game. I went to Cincinnati and I pitch and win a game with three days' rest, and then next day I relieved one inning with one day rest. Then with two days' [rest] I'm the starting pitcher against Cincinnati again. I expect more money, so then I went to him. He said, "I can't do nothing now. You'll have to wait for next year." I said, "You know, Leo, you lied to me." I don't think he liked it too much. *[laughs]* "There's nothing I can do," he say, and I got mad. When you get mad, you know, you say a lot of different things that later on you be sorry. You know what I mean.

Then I was pitching in Pittsburgh and the catcher give me the sign. They were hittin' me pretty good, so I say to the catcher, "Let's change the sign. It looks to me like they got the signs." They got about seven or eight hits. He came to get me out and I told him, "The best thing to do is send me to the minor leagues because I don't wanna play with you no more." So at the end of the season he send me to Minneapolis.

I was pitchin' pretty good ball in Minneapolis. The Chicago White Sox wanted to take me to the big league when [Paul] Richards went to manage, but Durocher don't let me go. "Leave him there," he say.

In the meantime, this other ballplayer, [George] Hausmann, he told me, "Zabala, you make a big mistake." I say, "Why?" He said, "You shouldn't talk in front of catcher — what you said about Leo Durocher — because you never come back to the big league." I said, "Why?" "Because you don't know Leo. Leo, he never let you come back. He's gonna keep you down there until you don't be able to pitch." And he did.

You had four very good years at Minneapolis. Each season your ERA was lower.

Yeah, I was pretty good there, but, you now, back there they pitched completely different from today. Today, you can't say nothing to the ballplayer because if you say something they've got the baseball association [union] to back them up. Back there where I was, you was independent.

Like when they send me to California; you know why they send me to California? Because I wrote a letter to Carl Hubbell, the [Giants] general manager. I told Carl Hubbell, "Listen, Hubbell, if you want me to play baseball send me someplace because I don't wanna play with Rosy Ryan." Rosy Ryan was the general manager for Minneapolis. One year, like I was telling you a while ago, I was in 78 games. I forget, I won 13 games, lost four, or something like that, plus I save about 25 or 26 — I don't remember how many. He [Ryan] said, "I can't give you a raise because you don't pitch complete games." Boy, I blew up.

Tommy Heath, he was the manager. I used to be in relief and then start games with Tommy Heath for two years—in 1950 and '51. He said to me one day, "Adrian, no matter where I be, if I'm in the big leagues or anyplace, you're gonna work for me because you never say 'no' to pitch." Every time he asked me, "You wanna pitch?" I went ahead and pitched. I did pretty good work for him.

The best relief pitchers we had at that time, they weren't so good. I was pretty lucky — saving a lot of games— and he was usin' me both ways: starting pitcher and relief pitcher.

When I went to San Francisco he was my manager over there, too. He was reasonable; he say, "Well, you pitch five, six days in a row, you don't do nothing today." The other guys were a little bit different. *[laughs]* Rosy Ryan, gee, I don't wanna know nothing about him!

You ended up playing back in Jacksonville.

I got married here in Jacksonville and my boy was born here in Jacksonville and my wife's brother lives here. My daughter, she was born in Minneapolis, Minnesota. That's why I've stayed here. I know a lot of people here in Jacksonville. By the time I quit playing baseball, I was getting old, you know — I was about 40 years old. I got a job here in the paper mill, a pretty good job. I retired in 1980. I played last in 1956. I coached here with Ben Geraghty and in 1957 I quit.

You pitched a shutout in 1949 with the Giants.

Cincinnati. I don't forget Cincinnati because Larry Jansen, he pitched the first game and he shut out Cincinnati and then Leo Durocher told me, "Zabala, you gonna pitch." So I pitched against [Ken] Raffensberger, left-handed pitcher, and I shut 'em out, too. I'll never forget, it was two shutout games.

What was your biggest thrill in baseball?

My real thrill was when I was a kid in Cuba; I was 15, 16 years old. My brother used to love baseball. He used to play baseball. I started to pitch amateur baseball. I was only about 140-150 pounds; I say I can't play baseball either. He said, "No, you gonna pitch." He was the manager of the team, too, so he make me a pitcher.

I went to Havana to pitch, to play amateur baseball, and I was a champion pitcher. My brother said, "The way you go, you're goin' to the big league." I say, "I don't go to no big league because I don't go to the United States." He says, "Oh, yeah, you go to the United States." I got a job workin' in Havana and he got mad at me. He said, "You gonna quit your job. You're not gonna work anymore; you're gonna play baseball. If you need money, I give it to you."

He owned two buses and he was workin' one night and he has a wreck and he got killed. After that, I wanna quit. I say, "I don't play ball." My other brother said, "Wait a minute. You gonna play baseball because your brother said he wants you to go and you told him you will. Now you not gonna back out."

I knew he was right so I say I gotta make the big league. That's what I was workin' for. When I got in the big league, the first game I pitch in

Adrian Zabala (courtesy Adrian Zabala).

the Polo Grounds I pitch in front of 55,000 people; I was nervous. Somebody was with me. I beat St. Louis, which was a hell of a good team. They
were the best team in the league. I got so happy but at the same time I was
sorry because my brother was not there.

You played a long time. Who was the best player you saw?

The best catcher I saw was [Ernie] Lombardi. I went to ask him, "Hey,
what kind of sign you using?" He say, "I don't use no signs." *[laughs]* "Just
throw what you want to." He was a big son of a gun. He didn't want no
signs and the glove he got look like a first base glove. I said, "Where the
heck you get that?" and he say, "Aw, shut up." You know, he talk like that
but he was a *real* nice man. He was wonderful—friendly, everything. Nothing bother him.

Maglie was a good guy—good friend, too. He was friendly. In the
game, all he wanted to do was win. Another guy, too—Johnny Mize. He
was really nice, too. I never hear nobody say nothing about him. He died
but I know him since 1936, the first year he went to Cuba. It was my first
year in professional ball and he went to Cuba with Mike Gonzalez, he was
coach for St. Louis [Cardinals]. I saw Johnny Mize—big son of a gun. I
say, "Gol-darn, he's a *big* man!" *[laughs]* You know, I weigh about 155
pounds. But he was a real nice man.

He was a hitter.

Oh yeah! No matter—lefthander, righthander—he hit it. He was a
great guy. Ace Adams was a pretty good guy, too. He was friendly. A lot
of the guys were good guys.

Did you enjoy your time in baseball?

Oh, yeah, I loved it. That's what I told you. When I finished, I used
to go down here to the high school and pitch to the guys. I pitched practice and messed around with them.

And my boy—he was doin' pretty good, but when he went to college—he get a scholarship—the first game he pitched in college he shut
out Florida State—no hit, no run. I was telling him the way to do, but
when he went off to college he got buddy-buddy with some other pitcher
there and he started pitchin' different ways. I told him two or three times,
I said, "You better quit doin' this. Do like I told you." He don't pay no
attention so finally he got a sore arm and then he went to sign with Cleveland, he don't wanna sign because he wanna get a master's degree. They
offered him $25,000 to play ball to sign him.

I told him, "If you get four years college, nobody can take that away from you. And $25,000, in three years you not have one penny. Nothing. If you get four years college, you get a place anywhere you want to." And then when he get five years, I say, "You much better now." So that's what he did.

About three of four years after he quit — he was married — he and his mother and myself, we were walkin' the beach, and he said to me, "Daddy, you know what? If I do like you told me, I make a big leaguer, but I never listen to you."

His youngest daughter go to college to learn to sing. She want to sing opera. She wants to be a big shot. *[laughs]* Jennifer Zabala — she went to England with the college — LSU, over in Baton Rouge. So far, she's been doin' real good. I hope she keep it goin'.

When did you learn English?

[laughs] I learn here. My wife try to teach me and she say I don't know how to speak English yet. We married almost 60 years and she say I haven't learned yet. *[laughs]*

Did you save souvenirs from your career?

Baseballs, but they're no good because I didn't take care of them. I got 'em in a trunk for the past 20 years. I got a picture of Maglie, Mel Ott, and myself. I used to have a uniform for the Giants, but I give it away. It say "Giants" on the front, but I wore it in Jersey City. I went to Cuba and some kid over there wanted it so I gave it to him.

Do you receive much fan mail?

I get a lot of letters all the time. The people want me to sign. I get 'em; every month I get some. I don't do like some guys, you don't have to give me some money. *[laughs]* They don't bother me. Some guys send three or four or five cards. I say, "What they do? They do business?" I don't like that. I just a country boy.

Adrian Zabala's major league debut was on August 11, 1945. The Giants had called him up from Jersey City the week before. At Jersey City, his 14 wins were second in the International League and his 3.21 ERA was sixth. Jersey City was not a good team that year. They were last in batting and next to last in pitching but finished, somehow, fifth, 24½ games out of first (Montreal) but only 7½ out of the cellar (Rochester).

Back to August 11, 1945. Adrian tossed a six-hitter against the reigning

World Champion St. Louis Cardinals, allowing only one third-inning run. It was the finale of a four-game series in which the Cardinals had taken the first three games.

ADRIAN ZABALA (Y RODRIGUEZ)

Born August 26, 1916, San Antonio de los Baños, Cuba
Ht. 5'11"   Wt. 165   Batted and Threw Left

Year	Team, Lg	G	IP	W	L	Pct	H	BB	SO	ERA
1945	NY, NL	11	43.1	2	4	.333	46	20	14	4.78
1949		15	41	2	3	.400	44	10	13	5.27
2 years		26	84.1	4	7	.364	90	30	27	5.02

JOE CLEARY

The Last Irishman (1945)

When Joe Cleary pitched in the second game of a Red Sox–Senators doubleheader on August 4, 1945, he became the first native-born Irishman to play in the major leagues since 1918 and no other has appeared since.

Unfortunately, it was an inauspicious debut for Joe and he was never given an encore, so he entered the record books as the man with the highest measurable ERA in history: 189.00.

Born in Cork in 1919, he came to the United States as a small boy with an athletic background of hurling (field hockey), soccer, and Irish football, none very popular around New York in the 1920s. When he was about ten, his father's sister gave him a complete baseball outfit: glove, bat, ball, and uniform. "And my mother had to drag 'em off me at night," he recalls.

His uncle took him to Yankees games in those days and his favorite player was Babe Ruth. "Baseball started and ended with Babe Ruth," he says. "I can still see one of his homers leaving the bat, a line drive to the right center field bleachers."

Cleary played the high-level semipro baseball that existed in those days. Grover Cleveland Alexander saw him pitch in the late '30s and told him, "You've got a hell of an arm there, son." Eventually, Joe turned pro and met with success along the way in the minor leagues but lost 1943 and '44 to World War II.

Back in baseball in 1945, he was assigned to Chattanooga, the top farm team of the Washington Senators, and took up where he left off. In early August, his record was 10-5, he was leading the team in wins, and he had been selected for the All-Star team when he was called up to Washington, at that time fighting for the AL pennant.

He joined the Senators (then called the Nationals) on August 4 in Washington, in time for the doubleheader with Boston. In the first game Washington pitching was iffy and manager Ossie Bluege had his new pitcher warming up in the bullpen off and on throughout the game, but the call never came.

In the second game, the Washington starter again wasn't sharp and Joe warmed up again several times. Finally, after nearly pitching the equivalent of a game in the bullpen, he was brought in, but it was not his day. The Red Sox batted around; the only out he recorded was a called third strike on pitcher Boo Ferris. Joe's pitching line read: 1/3 IP, 5 H, 7 R, 7 ER, 3 BB, 1 SO. And a wild pitch.

Bluege, evidently never having seen a pitcher have a bad day, hollered at Joe from the dugout to come out, not even showing the decency to go to the mound. When Joe got to the dugout, Bluege said, "Pitcher my fucking ass!" Joe, already frustrated, angry, and embarrassed, responded with, "Go fuck yourself!"

The two started for each other but some players broke it up before it really got underway. The next day, club owner Clark Griffith talked to Joe and told him that he couldn't play for Bluege. He was farmed out to Buffalo and never returned to the major leagues.

But today Joe has things in perspective. He says, "You know, in the neighborhood bars they kid me. I take an awful needlin' about that — that one appearance. The main thing I get kidded about is the earned run average; it's the highest in major league history, you know." *[laughs]* "But I always say to them, 'I was there.'"

And wouldn't we all love to be able to say that?

When did you come to the U.S.?

It was in the '20s. New Year's Day.

Had you heard of baseball before?

Nope. Never heard of it. All I was interested in then was playin' soccer and Gaelic hurling. It's an Irish game.

Joe Cleary with Chattanooga, Southern Association (courtesy Joe Cleary).

You were doing well in Chattanooga in 1945, leading the team in wins, and Washington called you up.

I was on the All-Star team. I had just come out of the Army a little before that and I didn't feel like pitching baseball that much; a lot of my friends had been killed. I had come out a year-and-a-half before that. My first year out I didn't even feel like playin'.

After I left Washington I went up to Buffalo—they were in last place—and I think in the last month I won four games. I did well with 'em. To get even with me, would you believe that they [Washington] sent me down to Class B at half my salary [in 1946]? Would you believe that?

How long were you with the Senators in '45?

Hang on to your hat. A week. They can do that now but they couldn't do things like that then. And there's this fight with the manager. You know, in those days you didn't do things like that. Now, of course, they fire the manager.

Let's talk about the Southern Association in 1945. While you were with Chattanooga, Harry Chozen of Mobile got a hit off of you in his league-record 49-game hitting streak.

He got a hit off me? He must have been good! *[laughs]* I never had luck with Mobile. That was a Dodger farm team. They also had [George] Shuba.

The whole league was a hitters' league that year. The league batting average was .282.

Well, they had that lively ball. Goldschmidt 97. I wanna tell you somethin'. You see balls bounce on this artificial turf now? When you go to deliver it you could almost hear it tickin' like it was goin' to explode. You just stick your bat out and the ball went a mile. It was a hitters' league.

Any league that had that ball was a hitters' league and yet, if I had a choice of goin' someplace I'd always pick that, where they had that 97 ball, for the simple reason that I had very small fingers for a pitcher. I was a small guy anyway [5'9", 150]. They had the stitches that were a little bit raised so I didn't have any trouble grabbin' it, so I used to like it. I played in, oh, four or five leagues with that ball in it.

I went on to pitch with American League balls or whatever and I just couldn't grab 'em. I had no excuse but the size of my fingers. The third baseman would get blisters from rubbin' up the ball. If I had bigger fingers, okay, but I just couldn't hold onto it; it was glossy.

How and when were you signed?

I signed in '41. In 1940, the last year I was playin' semipro baseball up in Connecticut, a fellow by the name of Joe Cambria saw me and he was a scout for Washington. This Cambria was one of the first ones to scout Latin players. He was scouting the team I played with because the name of the team was Danbury Cubans. He was actually their [Washington's] Caribbean scout. He signed me.

I think I pitched in two games at Class A Springfield — the Eastern League. When the season was over and I went to pick up my check, the secretary told me that I'd been sold to Washington but I wasn't to report until the following season.

So then I went to spring training with Washington in '41. I did well in spring training yet I was just a rookie. I thought they were gonna take me north with 'em but instead they said they were goin' to send me to Charlotte in the Piedmont League. I was just a kid; I was upset. No tantrums or anything, you know.

They said, "If you'd rather stay here with Orlando in the Florida State League, you can." So I figured I'd stay there and I pitched the whole year there. I think I won about 19 games and they have a short season.

Then the following season they sent me to Charlotte, which I think with about six weeks or two months to go in the season I won about 13. I knew I was gonna go in the Army. When I came out, I was with Chattanooga.

You played about ten years. Who was the best player you saw?

Of course, I played with a lot of the future big leaguers. A little left-handed pitcher played with Buffalo, went up to Detroit. This guy was my size; Billy Pierce was his name. Then, let's see, in '42 that Piedmont League was a *very* good league, a pitchers' league. They didn't have that 97 ball. I think they called it the Reach baseball. A whole bunch of guys from that league made the big leagues: Vic Wertz, Ted Gray. Every team in the league was affiliated with the major leagues.

Pierce was a nice kid, too. Bucky Harris wanted me to teach him how to throw my curveball, but, you know, lefthanders and righthanders have a different style of pitching. I could never teach him.

Was the curve your best pitch?

Yeah, but I threw hard, too. I don't think there was a league that I played the whole season in where I wasn't up there in strikeouts. I had a great curveball — downer, drop. But I couldn't teach Pierce; he was left-handed.

I had a great change of pace, but my pride would never let me throw it much. *[laughs]* But I threw very hard. In other words, they were loose, you know. They didn't dig in too much. At times I was conveniently wild. *[laughs]* You got a hit off me, look out. You went down the next time up. *[laughs]* And I mean knockdown pitches; I don't mean brushbacks. Now they throw a ball a little bit inside, they wanna fight. In my time, you went down! When that manager told you to stick one in this guy's ear, that's what you aimed at.

Is there one game that stands out?

Well, there's quite a few but I'll tell you the game I pitched in '47 or '8 against Orlando.

[In] '48 I'm with Gainesville. I pitched against Orlando, the Washington [farm] team. I struck the first two guys out; third guy I struck out. The ball got away from the catcher. He chased the ball, threw wild to first base. The right fielder fielded the ball so I went over to cover third. Right fielder throws it wild and the guy went on to score. I lost the game, 1-nothin'. I struck the next guy out.

The ball ended up right 'longside of [Joe] Tinker. 'Member Tinker to Evers to Chance? The field was named after him and at that time he was old; he had diabetes and they let him sit in a wheelchair in back of third base, where they figured no ball would ever come. I remember pickin' the ball up 'longside of him. He said, "You know, son, I've *never* seen anything like this in all the games I've seen." *[laughs]* Would you believe?

That stands out, and I pitched a doubleheader shutout one time, too. That was '41 when I was with Orlando against Daytona Beach — Cardinal farm. I think I gave two hits or something like that in the first game; in the second I gave two hits: a swingin' bunt and a bunt. Two shutouts.

I wanted to get even with [Daytona Beach]. At the beginning of the season they beat me. They scored 15 runs off me. They murdered me and the manager let me stay in because the general manager said let him take his beating. I vowed I was goin' to get even with them. The reason I pitched the second game was because it was toward the end of the season. You know, when you played in the minor leagues everybody wanted to go into the playoffs; it was extra money. The Shaughnessy playoffs— the first four teams are in it. And they were in fourth or fifth place and I knocked 'em out of the playoffs. I was gonna beat 'em to get even with 'em.

In '45, Montreal, they had a great team; they were leadin' the league by many games. They'd be a big league team now; they were great. I pitched against 'em up there. First of all, I had pitched against 'em in Buffalo and I threw nothin' but curveballs. My catcher looked like he had a grape between his fingers; he couldn't put down one finger. He was down with the curveball all the time.

Now I pitched against 'em up in Montreal the last week of the season and I was extra fast. I threw one curveball the whole game. I 'member Branch Rickey was there, come up to scout some kid that had just come out of the Marines and was burnin' up the league. I struck this kid out four times. They were all lookin' for the curveball but in the course of the game — in the bottom of the eighth or bottom of the ninth — they had a man on base and there was a routine fly ball to center field and the center fielder lost it and I lost the game, 2-to-nothin' or something like that. But I only gave two hits. They had a hell of a ballclub.

I figured I pitched so well I'd be hearing from Griffith, you know, to come to spring training. But I get a contract from Charlotte Hornets, Class B. I looked at it and I called the business manager down there, who I'd known. He was there in '42 — Phil Howser was his name — and he says, "Look, Joe, this is what they told me to offer you. Why don't you come down and we'll talk it over." So I went down. I told him I'm not playing for that. I says, "This is a dirty trick to get even with me."

The fill-in for Landis, Baseball Commissioner, was a fella by the name of O'Conner — Leslie O'Conner — and he wrote a letter. When he saw me gettin' only a week — one game — he figured there was a fix between Detroit and Washington to get me up to Buffalo to go to Detroit. Somehow or other he figured that and made me a free agent. About two or three teams called my house but Bucky Harris said to me — he told me what happened — he says, "You're goin' to be gettin' a lot of offers, Joe. Please, Detroit wants to talk to you. They'll better any other offer."

So I says okay and I waited and waited. Next thing you know I got a letter from O'Conner saying that Griffith protested his original decision to make me a free agent. He said he had sent me to play up in Buffalo because my mother was sick and he wanted me close to New York City. Would you believe that? He says I believe him and they'll have to recall you at the end of the year, that's all.

Calvin Griffith, that's Clark Griffith's son — nice guy — he called me up and he explained to me, "Joe, look. They're not goin' to recall you. You'll hear from 'em during the winter time." I said, "Okay, long as I get paid." Then they sent me a contract from Charlotte.

I told him [Howser], "Look, do what you want, Phil, but just as a matter of principle, I'm not gonna play for that kind of money after what I did last year." "Well," he said, "they told me to fight as long as I could with you but I'm not gonna fight anymore." He said, "If you won't play, you can have your free agency."

Joe Cleary, spring training, 1941, with Washington (courtesy Joe Cleary).

I signed with Jersey City; '46 I played with Jersey City. They had a lot of 'em — Bobby Thomson, etc.; they had a whole bunch of guys. I'm makin' double what they're makin' and I'm pitchin' batting practice. Would you believe that? The manager says to me, "Geez, Joe, I know you can win in this league," he said, "but Hubbell tells me who to pitch." Carl Hubbell was the farm director [for the Giants] then.

When they let me go, I said, "I'm going after the money." So I went down to Florida to Class D and I looked around and I signed with a team called Palatka in the Florida State League. I did well after that. I went to Gainesville in the same league, won a lotta games for them.

I was drafted by Atlanta; they were in the Southern Association. During the year a number of teams had approached the business manager — I know Pittsburgh did — and he said, "I can't sell Cleary. The people'd run me out of town." I said, "Don't let me get drafted." Atlanta had the fifth choice and wouldn't you know, he let Atlanta draft me. I was supposed to get half the purchase price. Now, he turned down three big league clubs and let me go to Atlanta. I got $500. *[laughs]* Draft price was a thousand. And they even took tax out of it.

I wouldn't go to Atlanta, so Earl Mann — he was the big man in Atlanta then — he called me. "How much did you make last year?" I told him; I said most of it was under the table. He says, "Oh, I can't pay you that!"

So now I'm disgusted with bein' pushed around. I said, "Look. You can't pay me, you can't pay me." So he says, "Will you play someplace I send you if they'll give you the money?" I said, "Yes." So I went to Anniston, Alabama, Class C, and when the season was half over I won four games and lost 11 and I was picked for the All-Star team. *[laughs]* The players and the managers picked it.

Augusta bought me I guess for a dollar-eighty. I played with them for a while, then there was a big deal goin' on between Yankees and White Sox. The Yankees wanted a second baseman at Charleston — that's a White Sox farm — but Charleston wouldn't trade unless I went to pitch with them.

So I went home and, believe it or not, I went out to Minnesota, a town called Owatonna. There were eight teams in the league; it was an amateur league supposedly. The big leagues I think had set this league up, calling it an amateur league. At that time, the Big 10 was very good in baseball. They probably still are. Another thing — part of bonuses in those days, instead of a bonus they sent a guy through college, the big club did. So to get more experience, they put 'em in this summer league, this amateur league. I'm supposed to be an amateur now, right? A thousand a week I made. Would you believe? Tax free. I made big money.

I was gettin' up there then. It was about ten years of gettin' pushed around but for those days I always made good money. I went to work in Wall Street and after that my wife and I bought two bars so I ran them for 20 years.

Did you save souvenirs?

No. Something interesting, though. I get letters—couple a week— most of 'em want a picture, you know, and I never had a picture in a Washington uniform. So I was lookin' through a drawer a number of years ago and I see a picture of me and I recognized it. It was Orlando and my uniform says "Nationals." That's what Washington was called then. I said, "Oh, my God!" I said, "They must have given me a hand-me-down uniform." It was spring training in Orlando with Washington.

But I never kept much. I've got a ball here from the league I was tellin' you about where I was 4-and-11. The ball's got autographs but you can't even see the writin'. Willis Hudlin was the manager of the All-Stars; he was an old Cleveland pitcher.

So that's it: the short and unhappy baseball life of Joe Cleary.

Before Joe Cleary played in the American League in 1945, there had been 39 other players of Irish birth in the major leagues.

IRISH-BORN MAJOR LEAGUERS

Debut Year	Name
1871	Ed Duffy
	Tom Foley
	(These first two played only in the National Association)
	Jimmy Hallinan
	Andy Leonard
	Fergie Malone
1874	Tommy Bond
1876	John McGuiness
1879	Curry Foley
	Pat McManus
1881	Tony Mullane
1882	Barney McLaughlin
	Frank McLaughlin
	(These two were brothers)
1883	Mike Hines
1884	Tony Cusick
	John Horan
	Ted Sullivan
	Mike Scanlon
	Mike Walsh
	(Scanlon and Walsh were non-playing managers)
1885	Joe Mack (McNamara)
	(Not listed in *Baseball Encyclopedia*)
	John Tener
1887	John Fields
	Cyclone Ryan
1888	Sam Nichol
1889	Bill Collins
	Jack Doyle

1890	Pete Daniels
	Patsy Donovan
	Tom Dowse
	Charles McCullough
1893	Con Lucid
	Denny O'Neil
	(First name Dennis or Daniel)
1901	Mike O'Neill
1902	Jack O'Neill
	(These two were brothers, as well as brothers of Steve O'Neill and Jim O'Neill)
1904	Jimmy Archer
	(Played through 1918)
	Tom Needham
1906	Irish McIlveen
1908	Paddy O'Connor
	(Played through 1918)
1912	Jimmy Walsh
1916	Johnny O'Connor
	(Not listed in *Baseball Encyclopedia*)
1945	**Joe Cleary**

JOSEPH CHRISTOPHER CLEARY

Born December 3, 1918, Cork, Ireland
Ht. 5'9"   Wt. 145   Batted and Threw Right

Year	Team, Lg.	G	IP	W	L	Pct	H	BB	SO	ERA
1945	Was., AL	1	0.1	0	0	—	5	3	1	189.00

LOU KRETLOW

100 MPH? (1946–1956)

Lou Kretlow pitched in the major leagues for ten years even though he didn't begin his professional career until he had reached an age — 23 — at which a young player might not even be signed today.

World War II was responsible for the delay. Lou left the University of Oklahoma in 1942 and spent the next three years in the military service. When he got out in late '45 the Tigers gave him a $35,000 bonus to sign. By today's standards that doesn't sound like much, but put it in perspective. That's nearly 20 times what the average worker made in a year back then; that translates to several hundred thousand dollars today.

The return on the investment for the Tigers looked as if it would be quick. Lou began 1946, his first pro season, with Williamsport [Eastern League] and progressed through Buffalo [International League] to Detroit by the end of the season, where he hurled a complete game victory in his only appearance for the big club.

An arm injury in 1947 set him back, but in '48 he rejoined the team and remained in the majors through 1956.

After he retired from baseball, he became a golf pro. He once qualified for the U. S. Open and in 1961 he scored a 427-yard hole-in-one to establish a new record. In 1962 he set a course record at Tascosso

Country Club in Amarillo, Texas: 61 with ten birdies, an eagle, and a
bogie.

*At the end of 1946, after only a partial season in the minors, you made a start
for the Tigers. Older sources credit you with seven innings, but newer ones
say it was a nine-inning complete game.*

I think I won, 6-3, and pitched nine innings against the St. Louis
Browns.

*You went back to Buffalo in '47 and did not have a good year. What hap-
pened?*

I hurt my arm. Pulled a muscle. They sent me home in about June.

*In '48 you came back in great shape and rejoined Detroit at the end of the
year. You won 21 at Williamsport and two at Detroit: 23 wins for the season,*

My arm was fine. I won 21 ballgames for a fifth-place club and also I
set a new strikeout record in the Eastern League. The old books say 219,
but I actually had about 230; they had me short on that thing, too.

In 1952, you pitched two consecutive two-hitters for the White Sox.

I shut out the Yankees and I shut out Boston. I pitched some pretty
good games. In St. Louis one year I pitched three ballgames, I allowed one
run in 27 innings, and I never won a game. Marlin Stuart came in —
[Marty] Marion [the manager] took me out for a pinch-hitter all three
times — and pitched one inning in each game and won all three games. He
took me out in the last of the eighth, last of the tenth, and last of the ninth
for a pinch-hitter.

Playing for the Browns was pretty frustrating.

That's it. I played for the Browns and I went over to Chicago and it
was a seventh-place club. We finally came up. I pitched 'em into first place
in '52 a couple-three times. I didn't win but four games with a 2.96 earned
run average.

I started but I did quite a bit of relieving, too. They said I had the
best arm in baseball; they said I threw about a hundred miles an hour. I
don't know how hard I threw, but I know my name comes up every once
in a while after all these years. Guys talk about how hard I threw, and my
ball was alive.

Every time there was a trade, they wanted me. I was traded for Gerry

Priddy when I went to St. Louis and I was traded back for Virgil Trucks and Bobby Elliott in '53. There was money involved, too.

You never had the good fortune to play for a good team. The Tigers were going downhill when you joined them, the Browns were always down, and the White Sox weren't much when they acquired you.

I had lots of potential and pitched a lot of good games that don't show. I'd get beat 2-to-1 and 1-to-nothing and stuff like this, so when there was a trade teams would want to get me. I know one year I won one game for St. Louis and it stopped a 21-game losing streak.

Does one game stand out as your best?

The night I hurt my arm in '56 with Kansas City, I actually had a no-hitter against Baltimore with two outs in the eighth inning, although they'd been credited with one little hit — a little pop fly that [Gus] Zernial had misjudged. I think if I'd have gone ahead and finished, they'd have reversed it and I'd have had a no-hitter. I was really quick that night. I hurt my arm and that kind of forced me to quit.

In 1956, I pitched Opening Day. I opened the season for Baltimore in Washington and I got beat. The next day we had some guys that really didn't want to pitch so I told Paul — I thought a lot of Paul Richards — I'd pitch any time he wanted me to. I told him, "My arm feels pretty good so if you need me today ..." and I was in the ballgame in the second or third inning and pitched three or four innings. That's two days in a row.

I was 0-and-4 before I could turn around and my arm got kind of dead on me. He said, "We need to send you out and let you rest a little bit," so I went to Seattle [PCL]. On the way out there, my car broke down in Cut Bank, Montana, and I was there a week. And what I needed was rest.

I went to Seattle and I pitched four straight shutouts, I won 12 straight ballgames, I pitched 'em to a pennant. We were fifth when I got there. I finished 14-and-3 and was voted the outstanding pitcher in the Pacific Coast League that year. I went down there at the end of June.

That earned you the trip to Kansas City. That's where you hurt your arm.

I had just beaten the Yankees and I'd beaten Boston and I was pitching good and I hurt my arm. I hurt it like Dizzy Dean; underneath it hemorrhaged and the blood clotted and I was out for about a month. I came back and started against Washington and rehurt it. Then, at the end of the year, I came back and beat Baltimore, 5-1 or 5-2 or something, and my arm was fine.

I went to spring training the next year and I couldn't even throw. What I should have done, I should have thrown all winter and I'd have been all right, I think. Finally, at the end of spring training, they sent me to Seattle. This guy wanted me out there but I told him I couldn't throw. I won a few ballgames; I could put a little on, take a little off.

I was eventually sold to Little Rock and I just didn't want to go to a bus league and play, so I quit. I started playing golf then and turned professional about a year after that.

Who was the best hitter you saw and who was the toughest on you?

The greatest hitter I ever pitched to was Ted Williams. No doubt about it. I've got a big picture of him and

Lou Kretlow, 1950.

he says on this picture, "To Lou, one of the nicest fellows I've ever met and as good a fastball as I've ever looked at." He couldn't follow my fastball real well and I had pretty good luck against him, but he was the greatest hitter. [Joe] DiMaggio and [Mickey] Mantle were two great hitters, too.

The guys that hit me were the guys like Yogi Berra. He was real quick with the bat. He had to be pretty quick to hit me. A guy like Bobby Avila or somebody who just met the ball a little bit like that was the guy that gave me a little bit more trouble. Nobody really ever dominated me. Mickey used to say my ball would jump about a foot. I didn't realize I threw that hard until I hear these guys talk about it.

You played for several managers. Who stood out?

Paul Richards was the greatest manager I ever played for, the smartest baseball man. He could take a mediocre guy and make a good ballplayer out of him. He had a knack.

Steve O'Neill was the first guy that was my [major league] manager, but when you come up and you're young you don't really know that much; you don't know if a guy's a good manager or a bad manager. Down the line, after you've played for eight or ten years, then you realize who can manage and who can't.

[Lou] Boudreau was a good manager and the other guys were good managers or they wouldn't be in the major leagues, but Paul was outstanding. He was the smartest man in baseball, I thought.

I went to the World Series in '45 after I got out of the service and he hit a couple of doubles that day and they [Detroit] won the World Series. Dizzy Trout was pitching [for Detroit] and he [Richards] called for a forkball with 3-and-2 on the hitter and the bases loaded or two men on. Diz threw it and they struck the guy out. Paul used to tell that story.

He took weak ballclubs and made good ballclubs out of 'em. If you played for him you had to respect him and had to like him.

We [Baltimore] traded off Don Larsen and [Bob] Turley and [Billy] Hunter to the Yankees and one player was supposed to be named later and that was me, but Richards didn't want to let me go. I was a holdout and he told me to hold out. He said, "If they take you, I'm gonna give you a $40,000 a year contract." *[laughs]* And he kept me.

Paul always liked me. I pitched some great games for him. I would have pitched him into first place there in '53 [in Chicago]. I got beat a ballgame. I had two outs in the ninth inning, and I had a 3-and-2 on Eddie Yost. I threw a curveball right down the middle of the plate and the umpire called it a ball.

Gil Coan came up and I said to myself, "I'm not gonna let him pull the ball. They'll have to get two basehits to beat me." He hit a ball to left field for a basehit and Don Lenhardt let it go between his legs and they beat me in 12 innings, 2-to-1. They beat us four straight and Richards and them talked about it a lot of times, how that one pitch to Yost cost the ballclub half a million dollars.

Yost was a good ballplayer. His reputation helped him out a lot. [Ed] Hurley was umpiring and he thought it was gonna be a fastball.

[For those unfamiliar with Ed Yost's reputation, his nickname was "The Walking Man." He had one of the best eyes in baseball history and usually got the benefit of the doubt on borderline pitches.]

Did you save souvenirs from your career?

Yeah. I have a lot of balls. I got a ball signed by [President] Eisenhower when I pitched Opening Day in '55. The night I hurt my arm in Kansas City, the old-timers had a game and I've got a signed ball by Gehringer, Cobb, Dickey, Foxx, Hubbell, Lyons, Frisch, Schalk, Cochrane, Speaker, Grove, Vance, and Paul Waner.

Do you receive much fan mail now?

Yes, probably 30 or 40 a month. I sign and send 'em back. Baseball's great and they're our fans, they're the ones who've paid their money.

Your chief claim to fame is your hole-in-one.

I made the world's longest hole-in-one in 1961: 427 yards. I'm in the Guinness book and Ripley both. I used to win all the driving contests. I hit the ball a very long way at that time. I still hit it pretty good for my age. I was a club pro—I'm not now—and I'd go to tournaments. I'm in property and oil now. I've been pretty fortunate.

Would you go back and be a ballplayer again?

Oh, sure.

I have no regrets. I just regret that I never won as many games as I should have, with the potential I had. When I got to be a good pitcher I hurt my arm, but I pitched some good games.

Yeah, I'd go back.

The St. Louis Browns were a hand-to-mouth operation in the final years of their existence. One of the main requirements of any trade they made was a large amount of cash coming to them so expenses—player salaries, for instance—could be met.

From the end of the 1947 season until the move to Baltimore after the '53 season, the Browns made 79 deals at the major league level. Forty-one of them involved cash (more than $1.5 million) coming to them, while only 24 involved cash (less than $300,000) going the other way. It was the only way the team could stay afloat.

Lou Kretlow was involved three times in bringing money to the Browns:

December 14, 1949: The Tigers sent Lou and $100,000 to St. Louis for Gerry Priddy.

July 5, 1950: The Browns sold Lou to the White Sox, amount not disclosed.

June 13, 1953: The White Sox traded Lou and $75,000 back to the Browns for Virgil Trucks and Bob Elliott.

Louis Henry Kretlow

Born June 27, 1921, Apache, OK
Ht. 6'2"   Wt. 185   Batted and Threw Right

Year	Team, Lg	G	IP	W	L	Pct	H	BB	SO	ERA
1946	Detroit, AL	1	9	1	0	1.000	7	2	4	3.00
1948		5	23.1	2	1	.667	21	11	9	4.63
1949		25	76	3	2	.600	85	69	40	6.16
1950	StL-Chi, AL	20	35.2	0	2	.000	42	45	24	7.07
1951	Chicago, AL	26	137	6	9	.400	129	74	89	4.20
1952		19	79	4	4	.500	52	56	63	2.96
1953	Chi-StL, AL	31	101.2	1	5	.167	105	82	52	4.78
1954	Balt, AL	32	166.2	6	11	.353	169	82	82	4.37
1955		15	38.1	0	4	.000	50	27	26	8.22
1956	K. C., AL	25	118.2	4	9	.308	121	74	61	5.31
10 years		199	785.1	27	47	.365	781	522	450	4.87

FRANK BAUMHOLTZ

A Good Man in a Pinch (1947–1957)

A lot of great athletes have tried their hands at more than one professional sport. Rarely have any excelled at more than one, however.

Jim Thorpe, Red Badgro, and Ernie Nevers are football Hall of Famers but were marginal major league baseball players. Bo Jackson was almost a star in both sports, but Deion Sanders was/is only an okay baseball player.

Gene Conley was a good pitcher for several years and is one of the few ever to have both a win (1955) and a loss (1954) in All-Star competition, but he was only an NBA backup. Steve Hamilton's better sport was also baseball. And there are others: Chuck Connors, Ron Reed, Dick Groat, Bill Sharman (he never played in a big league game but he was on the Dodgers in late 1951), etc.

Frankie Baumholtz was easily one of the best two-sport stars. He was an All-Star in both seasons he played professional basketball and as a baseball player he had a ten-year batting average of .290, despite not appearing in a major league game until he was 28 years old. In 1952, he batted .325, second in the NL.

Although the most home runs Frank ever hit in a season was five, for two years he was an integral part of one of the game's most powerful outfields. In 1953 and '54, he spent a great deal of time between Ralph Kiner and Hank Sauer and as a result is an important part of one of Joe

Garagiola's better stories. Frank tells it in the following pages.

A little-known fact about Frank — one that even he didn't know — is that he was one of baseball's best pinch-hitters. In both '55 and '56 he led the NL in pinch hits and in 153 pinch at bats in his ten years he had 47 hits for a .307 average. That's the third best in the game's history for players with at least 150 at bats as a pinch-hitter. He is the *only* lefthanded batter to have better than a .300 average in the pinch!

You were a rarity in your day, although it's not uncommon now — you finished college before you began your professional athletic career. Did you play both baseball and basketball in college?

Yes, both of them. At Ohio University.

You played one year of pro ball after college, then you entered the Navy. Did you enlist?

Yes, I did. Before graduation exercises I was sighed by the Cincinnati Reds by Frank Lane. They sent me to Riverside, California, with the Riverside Reds [California League]. After about six weeks or so, the league folded up and I was sent to Ogden, Utah, in the Pioneer League and I finished the season there. In those days, the minor league season ended on Labor Day.

I got on a Greyhound bus and came to Cleveland, where my college sweetheart lived. From here I got on another bus and went down to Midvale, Ohio, where I was born and raised, and told my mom and dad that I was enlisting in the Navy. I enlisted to get my one-year conscription out of the way. *[laughs]*

During the period I was playing ball that summer, the services were building up and I'd gotten a few letters from a Commander Cook at Great Lakes Naval Station, talking about the qualities of Great Lakes Naval Training Station, etc., and what they were going to do. While I was there, I played on both the basketball team and the baseball team. When I enlisted, I got up to Great Lakes at the end of September and they'd already started their basketball practice so I got right into that. In the spring, the baseball season began.

In the meantime, one of the officers told me to apply for an ensign's commission, which I did. About two-thirds of the way through the baseball season I was sent to submarine training school but I didn't get into that.

I stayed at Great Lakes until my commission came through, then they sent me to Treasure Island out on the West Coast. Remember the old cowboy movie star, Johnny Mack Brown? He was the commander of the destroyer where I learned the mechanics of being an officer.

Then I got my orders to report to Brooklyn Navy Yards. I was assigned to a ship because we were in the war full-scale now.

I spent almost five years in the service. I was in the North Atlantic and the Mediterranean and I was in the Pacific, so I didn't get to play ball after that first year at Great Lakes.

When you came out, you evidently hadn't lost too much because you started playing professionally in both sports.

I was in Cleveland when the war ended and I found out I had more than enough points to get out.

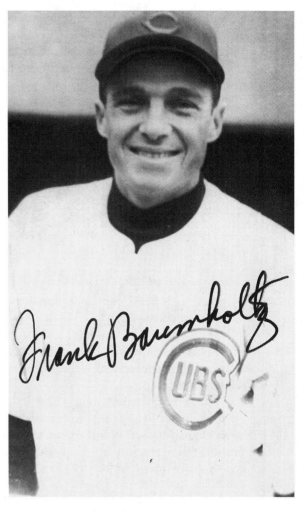

Frank Baumholtz, 1952 (courtesy Frank Baumholtz).

After the second bomb was dropped, they wanted me to take a group of ships to Japan but I found out I had an overabundance of points to get out, so I decided I'd get out of the service.

After I got home I got a call from Youngstown, Ohio; it was the basketball coach of the Youngstown Bears, who were in the old National Pro League. It had teams like Oshkosh and Sheboygan, Ft. Wayne and Indianapolis, Cleveland and Youngstown. I think Syracuse and Rochester were in there, too.

So I played basketball with the Youngstown Bears that winter and during the winter I wrote a letter to Warren Giles, who was the general manager of the Reds. I asked him what my status was in regards to the Cincinnati Reds. He said I was the property of the Reds and I was to report to spring training. *[laughs]* That was near the end of February in 1946.

I played four-fifths of the basketball season and I went to spring training. I stayed with them until about the middle of May and then was sent to Columbia, South Carolina, of the Sally League. I played there rest of the year. [.343, *162 H, *43 2B.]

Then I played basketball with the Cleveland Rebels in the first year of the NBA, which was called the Basketball Association of America then.

You were named to the all-league team.

Yeah, the All-Ten team or whatever you call it. I was named to the All-Ten team in the old National Pro League, too.

Why did you finally choose baseball over basketball?

[laughs] When I came up to the Reds in '47, I felt I was going to be there on a regular basis.

During the latter part of the summer, the guy who owned the Cleveland Rebels sold the franchise to Providence, Rhode Island. After being away from home for so long — the War and sports — I got to feeling maybe things had to change.

I had a fairly decent year in '47 [with the Reds], so Warren Giles called me in the office before the season ended and gave me a check and asked me not to play basketball that winter. I looked at the check and said, "Well, you just talked me into not playing." *[laughs]* So after not playing basketball that winter I decided to stay with baseball as long as I could.

You had an awfully good rookie year and an awfully good second year. What happened in your third season?

A lot of things happened. Managerial changes, conflict of personalities. Everything didn't go well, even when Hank Sauer and I were sent over to the Cubs in the middle of the year for Peanuts Lowrey and Harry Walker. I went over to the Cubs and for some reason I wasn't in [Frank] Frisch's plans; he was the manager then. Consequently, I was left on the outside looking in. *[laughs]*

Do you think your age was a problem? You were not a young rookie.

No. I was four years in college and spent almost five years in the war, so you're talking about nine years. I was, what, 27?

The Cubs sent you to Los Angeles in the Pacific Coast League and you had a fantastic season out there. [*.379, *53 2B, 126 R, *254 H.]

He [Frisch] still didn't want to bring me back from all that I heard from friends of mine, but the next year [1950] he couldn't keep me off the team.

You had a solid year and then in '51 you almost won the batting title. You and Stan Musial were close nearly all season.

The greatest thing I remember about that is what a super guy Musial is.

The funny thing about that year — I became the only major league ballplayer that ever batted against Stan Musial. He threw one pitch and I took one swing — righthanded!

The Cardinals and us were both out of the race that year and we played the last game of the season in St. Louis. None of us knew that Eddie Stanky had worked up a deal with the press that Musial was going to pitch to me. I was the leadoff hitter for the Cubs.

Harvey Haddix was announced as their pitcher and Musial was playing center field and Solly Hemus was their third baseman. When it was time to play ball, Stanky came out of the dugout and called time and brought in Musial to warm up. Phil Cavaretta was my manager and he came out to the plate to talk to me. He said, "It looks like Musial is going to pitch to you." I said, "I'm going to bat righthanded if he does." *[laughs]* He said, "Did you ever bat righthanded?" "No, I never swung the bat righthanded in my life." He said, "If you don't bat righthanded, you don't have a gut in your body!"

Well, I did. He threw one pitch and I hit the blazes out of the ball! *[laughs]* I hit a low line drive that hit Hemus on the right shin and rolled down in the left field corner. I ended up on second base and they flashed the error on the board.

Then Stanky came out and had Musial go back to center field and brought Haddix in to pitch.

At the end of the inning he [Musial] called the press box and said, "If I ever saw a basehit in my life, that was it." But he had three hits that day, so it didn't make any difference; I could never have beaten him — or really wanted to— in a batting race. He was a super ballplayer and a super guy.

That's what I remember about '52 and then I had a good year the year after that.

You played between Ralph Kiner and Hank Sauer for a couple of years there in Chicago.

Frank Baumholtz, 1956.

That wasn't really that bad. [Joe] Garagiola would bring that up about once a month when he was announcing; it kept my name alive throughout all the years. Other guys picked it up — Ernie Johnson and some others.

Garagiola said something like, "I'd look out there in left field and see Kiner practicing his batting stance and then I'd look over in right field and there's big Hank Sauer swishing around a big chaw of tobacco with his arms folded and I'd look out in center field and there's Frankie Baumholtz taking oxygen." *[laughs]*

Those guys weren't great fielders but I don't think they were quite as bad as Joe leads us to believe.

I don't know what kind of a fielder Kiner was. When he came over to the Cubs he already had bad legs. He couldn't sleep well at night because his legs or something was bothering him. But he could hit! They couldn't put him in right field, so they put Sauer there. Sauer was actually a very good *left* fielder.

It turned out to be a good thing for me; it brought me a lot of publicity after I got out of baseball. And I enjoy every bit of it. *[laughs]*

You were an outstanding pinch-hitter. You had a .307 career pinch hitting average and you led the NL in pinch hits twice.

I did?

Yes. In 1955 you had 15 with the Cubs and in '56 with the Phillies you had 14.

I'll be darned. I didn't realize that. *[laughs]* Thanks for telling me.

Other than the at bat against Musial, what was your biggest thrill?

I used to say it was my first big league game, batting against Howie Pollet. I had two hits off of him.

But then one day it dawned on me what my greatest thrills in my career were: I played in the era where I felt the greatest major league ballplayers played or would ever play. The middle '40s through the middle '50s, overall, they were the best. Every team had talent galore.

Who was the one best hitter you ever saw?

I used to like to watch Ted Williams. I think, as a hitter, Williams was the greatest.

I think Musial, from my playing against him, was a great, great hitter. Right at the top. But in those days there were super ballplayers. Willie

Mays. Joe DiMaggio. I think Joe DiMaggio was the greatest all-around player.

For a five-year period, the greatest player I played against — I'm, not saying he was the greatest home run hitter or the greatest hitter — but the greatest *player*, who could do the most things to hurt you, was Jackie Robinson. For a five-year period.

Ernie Banks is a tremendous guy and is a good friend of mine; he was a terrific ballplayer. Henry Aaron was great. Roberto Clemente was great. It's hard to single out any one player. So many guys from the years I played are in the Hall of Fame and more will be.

Who was the best pitcher you saw?

It's the same situation as before. You take all those teams, my God! Johnny Sain, Warren Spahn, Robin Roberts, Curt Simmons, [Sal] Maglie, [Larry] Jansen.

I didn't get to face [Ewell] Blackwell much. I played right field when he pitched that no-hitter and I was in right when he had eight and two-thirds innings into the second no-hitter. Being a big, tall guy, with his delivery, it almost made it look like the ball was coming from between the third baseman and the shortstop. When I went to the Cubs I batted against Blackie but he had already hurt his arm. He had already lost it.

Oh, there were some great, great pitchers in those days.

Was there a pitcher who was particularly difficult for you?

The one pitcher that I'd say overall was tough — in regards to getting basehits — was Robin Roberts. I used to hit the ball hard off of him, but most of the time it was *at* somebody.

Was there a pitcher who was particularly easy for you?

It's funny, but when your timing is right and everything is going well, even the tough ones are easy. But when you're struggling a little bit, even the ones that shouldn't *ever* get you out get you out.

Baseball is funny; when you're going good and you see the ball well, you can hit anybody. When you're not, anybody can get you out. All you have to do is lose a little bit of timing. It's a matter of concentration.

What was your first big league salary?

$4,000. *[laughs]* I made more money in my first year in professional basketball.

One of the things I'm proudest of in my sports career is that I'm the first major league player that played major league basketball at the same time. [Gene] Conley played a little, [Dick] Groat played one year, [Dick] Ricketts played a little — but they were all after me. Then [Ron] Reed was a long time after that. [Steve] Hamilton was much later.

Most of the guys who played both sports were real good in one and only average in the other, but you were a .300 hitter in one and an All-Star in the other.

I was very pleased. I always thought I was a basketball player who became a baseball player.

Basketball has changed. The basketball *itself* changed. The baseball has never changed, but the basketball has become much smaller and a more perfect sphere. The big changes that came about were the youngsters coming up — the kids who played in the alleys and on the dirt and all that. Especially in the bigger cities where the only place they could go to do anything was the basketball courts.

As the years went by, the more affluent whites gave way to the eager and fast-growing blacks, who turned out to be better basketball players. Not only can they run, they can shoot, they can jump. That's what happened. The court stayed the same — you know, the size. But the basketball became different and the players became different.

What about changes in baseball?

The changes have helped the modern-day player. I was an up-the-middle hitter and if they had the synthetic turf in my day, I tell you, I'd have probably hit 20-30 points higher.

Even the bats have changed. In my day, practically every bat you saw was a Louisville Slugger. Some of these bats they use out there now I've never heard of. One thing I hope never happens in the big leagues: I hope aluminum bats never come in.

All these things have made it easier for the average player to play. Maybe it's the dilution, too. When I played there were only eight teams in each league, so you had a total of about 400 players. Now there's more teams and they're talking about increasing it. When you start adding that many teams, your talent kind of dwindles.

Did you save souvenirs from your career?

When my wife was alive she used to have a lot of things. I still have some memorabilia around, but not much. As my son grew and the kids discovered his dad was a major league baseball player, they had him scrounge around and he cleaned my wife's cedar chest out of all kinds of what today would be sensational memorabilia.

When I first got to the big leagues, there was a little kid in New York who was always there and greeted us and we signed autographs for him. Every time I went to New York I spent a little time with him. His name is Bob Keidanz and, wouldn't you know, he was at the first major league alumni reunion — a grown man in his 40s and still getting autographs. He looks the same as he did when he was an eight-year-old kid. *[laughs]*

Do you receive much fan mail?

Oh, yeah. I'm surprised; I get seven and eight letters every week. Some are autograph requests, some want me to write something to them, a lot of different things. I've never turned down a request. Never.

People have asked me what I might have done differently in my big league career. Well, if I'd have been smart, I'd have kept all those letters and put them in book form. It would have been fantastic! You wouldn't believe some of the things they write. And you can tell right off the bat if they're sincere; you can't miss that.

If you went back to Ohio University, would you do every thing the same?

I think so. I tell you what, I wouldn't trade my college career at Ohio University or my major league baseball career for anything in the world. I have very close ties with Ohio University. I was on the Board of Trustees for nine years; I'm on the Foundation Board of Trustees now. I'm closely affiliated with the whole athletic department and the School of Health and Human Services. Athens [Ohio] is like my second home.

And I loved playing major league baseball. Yes, I'd do it all again.

The following table lists the Top Five career pinch-hitting batting averages (minimum 150 pinch-hit at bats).

Player	B	PHAB	PH	PHBA	Career BA	Led*
Tommy Davis	R	197	63	.320	.294	0
Frenchy Bordagaray	R	173	54	.312	.283	1
Frank Baumholtz	L	153	47	.307	.290	2
Red Schoendienst	S	185	56	.303	.289	1
Bob Fothergill	R	253	76	.300	.326	1

*Number of years led league in pinch hits.

FRANK CONRAD BAUMHOLTZ

Born October 7, 1918, Midvale, OH
Died December 14, 1997, Winter Springs, FL
Ht. 5'10½"   Wt. 175   Batted and Threw Left

Year	Team, Lg	G	AB	R	H	2B	3B	HR	RBI	BA
1947	Cin., NL	151	643	96	182	32	9	5	45	.283
1948		128	415	57	123	19	5	4	30	.296
1949	Cin.-Chi., NL	85	245	27	56	9	5	2	23	.229
1951	Chicago, NL	146	560	62	159	28	10	2	50	.284
1952		103	409	59	133	17	4	4	35	.325
1953		133	520	75	159	36	7	3	25	.306
1954		90	303	38	90	12	6	4	28	.297
1955		105	280	23	81	12	5	1	27	.289
1956	Phil., NL	76	100	13	27	0	0	0	9	.270
1957		2	2	0	0	0	0	0	0	.000
10 years		1019	3477	450	1010	165	51	25	272	.290

CHUCK DIERING

Team MVP (1947–1956)

Gary Pettis was a very fast center fielder who excelled on defense. Back in the late 1980s, the Texas Rangers signed him to a three-year, $2.7 million contract, even though his batting average had settled in around the .230–.240 mark.

Chuck Diering played from the late 1940s through the mid '50s, time when stealing bases was not encouraged and before the days of the Gold Glove awards. There are many, however, who will tell you that he had few peers when it came to chasing down long flies and that he was right up there in speed and base-running ability. Maybe he wouldn't steal as many bases as Pettis, but he would strike out far less often and hit for a higher average.

Chuck was born in 1923. Maybe if he had been born in, say, 1963, he, too, would have been a high-priced free agent.

Today he's retired and has no regrets from his career or any other aspect of his life. And, maybe best of all, he avidly collected memorabilia during his playing days.

You signed with your hometown Cardinals in 1941 when you were 18. Those weren't bonus days. Did you receive anything to sign?

Nothing. They sent me to Hamilton, Ontario. My dad and I drove up there and they didn't need an outfielder up there so they sent me down to Daytona Beach, Florida [Class D Florida State League]. That was a real drive; it took me a week to play some ball. I played down in Daytona for a couple of months.

In '42 you went to Albany in the Georgia-Florida League and had a heck of a year.

I was signed to a Class B contract in spring training, but then they sent me to Albany, Class D. Yeah, I had a good year down there. [.305, league-leading 102 runs]

When I went to the service from Albany they sold my contract to Rochester, Triple-A, so I was on the Rochester roster when I was in the service.

Chuck Diering, 1952 (courtesy Chuck Diering).

Did you play ball in the service?

Oh, yeah. I was in the medical corps. I went to Fort Sill for training and then they shipped us over. We landed in Australia and we were going to be in on the Leyte invasion, but we shipped directly to Coral Sea and then they sent us back to Australia and we set up there.

We stayed there for a year and then, as they moved forward, they moved us into Leyte and set up our camp there until the war was over. As the war escalated up north, we were the last stop on sending the boys back home from our hospital. We maintained some amusement for them; we played ballgames for them.

Were there any other professional players where you were?

Not in our outfit, but toward the end of the war we went up to Manila and we played a series against the Manila Dodgers, which consisted of Kirby Higbe, Joe Garagiola, and guys like that. We beat 'em and became champs of the South Pacific. We won three out of five games and the place was packed! It was like the World Series. It was great!

You went to Rochester in '46 when you got out of service.

There were 80 guys on the roster and you had to beat a lot of guys out to get down to the 22 or 25 they kept. I made the club. I had a good year. I was fast, a good outfielder, good arm, but an average hitter — you know, around .255-.265. [Chuck produced double figures in doubles (22), triples (13), home runs (10), and stolen bases (19).]

It wasn't a running game then. With your speed, would you have been more of a runner today?

I don't know. I can't answer that. I guess it would depend on the team. The only time we really stole was when we needed them — to advance the tying run or the winning run or something like that.

In '47, your rookie year with the Cardinals, you were mainly a defensive replacement. Who did you go in for?

Terry Moore. He was on the end of his career and he was having a lot of trouble with his knees. All I did, more or less, was be there in case he broke down and to learn the ropes and play defense for him toward the end of a game. I pinch ran a bit. I got some good experience.

I had a fantastic spring training. It was one of those deals where I was great and in those days a rookie would just often replace the fringe guys and I was better than them.

The Cardinals always had good teams in those days.

And they had a lot of good ballplayers in their organization.

I was talking with Roy Sievers the other day and we were saying that the kids today don't really have the incentive because they don't have one-year contracts. The Cardinals at that time had 600 people under contract, I think 36 farm clubs. If you didn't do it, there were enough guys downstairs. You had to work to stay, not have it given to you; there were enough guys downstairs to take your job.

In '49, you were the regular center fielder between a couple of pretty good ballplayers.

Yeah, Musial and Slaughter.

You came close to a pennant that year, but just missed.

We were two-and-a-half games in the lead with ten to go. It was one of those things where nothing went right in those ten days. We sent pitchers ahead to give 'em their rest because we were traveling by train, but it just didn't work out.

One example: We were in Pittsburgh winning the ballgame. They get the bases loaded, one out, the ball was hit to Marty [Marion]. Marty scoops it up, throws it to Red [Schoendienst], ball hits him on the finger of the throwing hand, he drops it, no double play. Next guy comes up — Tom Saffell — hits the foul pole for a grand slam home run. That's the way things happened. It just wasn't supposed to be.

On the last day, if we won and Brooklyn lost we're in. If we both won, then they were in. I was center that day in Wrigley Field and people were getting the ballgame on the radio and they'd give me the scores before they got up on the board. I'd run in and tell the bench. Brooklyn won something like 14-to-12. We clobbered the Cubs, 12-4 or something.

We were close other times when I was with 'em, but that was the closest.

You went to the Giants a couple of years later.

That was a sad experience for me. After being with the Giants for a while, I just didn't care for it. Leo [Durocher] was a man who was in a league of his own and he had his guys like Willie Mays and [Henry] Thompson and Monte Irvin and I don't think the guy spoke ten words to me the time I was there. I was really glad to go.

Henry Thompson and I were playing center field and he told me one day that Leo said I was going to play from here on out. But Leo didn't tell me; Henry told me. So I started that day and along toward the end of the game — I think Murry Dickson was pitching — in come a guy to pinch-hit for me. It was discouraging. I was glad to leave.

I went back down to Minneapolis and finished the year out there. That was in '52 and in '53 I played a full year there and had a great year. I almost led the league in hitting. [.322, 116 runs, 39 doubles, 10 triples, 12 home runs, 74 RBI.]

That attracted the Orioles to you.

Yes. The Browns moved to Baltimore and they drafted me.

That was the return of major league baseball to Baltimore. A lot of people thought the Orioles were going to be a real good team because of some changes, but it was not a good team. How were you guys received that first year?

Great! It was fantastic! They gave away television sets to the player of the week. You were honored with many things. The people were really nice to us. They gave a Most Popular Player award, which was a Cadillac; Bob Turley won it. And at the end of the year they picked the Most Valuable Player on the team. And it was me. That was the greatest honor that I've ever had and it surprised me because there were stars like Vern Stephens, Bob Turley, Don Larsen, Eddie Waitkus—a lot of big name ballplayers. I sat in the dugout to see who was going to get the award and they called my name. I went out there and I didn't know what to say. I've got pictures they took of me and a nice trophy.

You saved many a run for them out there in center field.

Yeah, I had a good year defensively and not a bad year hitting. I was a regular there a couple of years. And then in '56 they were trying to build and they were signing a lot of bonus kids and that was a phase-out thing for me. I actually stayed one more year than I probably would have. I was 33 then.

In '55 Harry Brecheen was our pitching coach and Willy Miranda was playing shortstop for us and he was having all kinds of trouble. I always worked out in the infield and Brecheen told Paul Richards, "Hey, let Chuck play short." So he came up and asked me if I wanted to play and I said, "Heck, it makes no difference to me."

So I went out and played. I played short and then they put me on third. I started 30-some ballgames at third base, never made an error. I always had good hands.

I was kept over in '56 because I was versatile. I could do a little of everything. But then I made my first error against Al Kaline. He hit a ball that almost went through me and then somebody else got a basehit to right and he [Kaline] came into third base. I caught the throw and tagged him and he slid into me very hard and knocked glove, ball, and all. Two errors in one game on the same man.

The hardest part of the switch [from the outfield] was throwing. I always threw overhand from the outfield so the ball would take off; put some backspin on it so it would jump when it came into the infield. But in the infield I had to bring my arm down to the side because if I threw overhand the ball constantly would be hitting the grandstands. That was the biggest adjustment for me.

When I was playing short one time, a double-play ball was hit to the second baseman. I went over to second, caught the ball, and forgot to touch the base! But it was an automatic double play and the umpire told me later, "Chuck, next time tag the base. You'll make us both look bad if you miss it."

Where did you go after 1956?

I was sent up to Montreal. I finished out the year there in '56. I didn't like the team; it was the Brooklyn Dodgers organization.

The Cardinals again in '57 were looking for a center fielder and I called up Frank Lane and asked him if he needed a center fielder. He said yeah, so I asked if I could have a shot in the spring. He said, "Chuck, I know you're a heck of a defensive ballplayer, but we need somebody who can drive in runs." I said, "I understand; just give me a crack at it."

Well, they signed me to a nice contract and sent me to Omaha under Johnny Keane. I joined them in Indianapolis and I didn't play too good. I guess Keane sent a report that I wouldn't be good enough to get back into the majors so they sold me to Montreal and I finished up there and I ended up having a good year. I hit .285.

I asked them, "What are you going to do with me because I have to make plans? I'm at that stage of life." They said they were going to keep me. Well, they didn't; they sold me to Louisville. Louisville sent me a contract for $1,000. I told them that wasn't right and asked them what was the best they could do. I never heard from them so I just retired.

What did you do when you retired?

I went into the automobile business and I stayed in that for 23 years. I closed that out in 1980 and then I went to work for a customized van company for four years, then in 1986 I retired.

In the summertime it's fine. I play golf about three times a week and in the wintertime I bowl, but it's boring. I saw Stan Musial the other day; he autographed some bats for me. He's having the same thing. He said, "This retirement life isn't any fun."

Who were the best players you saw?

Stan Musial was one of the greatest all-around baseball players. In fact, that whole Cardinal club was good; I enjoyed it so doggone much. And, of course, I saw Willie Mays with the Giants.

Ted Williams, Mickey Mantle, Yogi Berra. Blackwell of Cincinnati. Brooklyn, there was [Jackie] Robinson, Pee Wee Reese, Duke Snider, Carl Furillo, [Roy] Campanella, Newcombe — you could go over the whole eight teams in both leagues. There were so many great players.

Which pitcher was the toughest on you?

Ewell Blackwell. He was the toughest pitcher, period. Don Newcombe was tough. I'd have to have the rosters in front of me to remember them all. Blackwell and Newcombe were the toughest, though — both big, tall guys.

Does a game stand out?

Well, batting-wise, I remember up in Brooklyn I hit two home runs once; '49, I guess.

Defensive — that would be hard. I had a lot of good ones defensively. I guess the best one I'm known for — it's been written up a few times — was up in Baltimore when I made a catch against New York. The ball was hit out in right-center field. Don Lenhardt was playing right field and the ball was hit way over his head and I went back behind him and caught the ball. They said it was 450 feet or something. Paul Richards made a statement in the paper the next day, "We had to send a taxi cab to bring him back to the ballpark."

But I had a lot of good defensive games. Against Brooklyn one day I was all over the ballpark. Another game in Brooklyn I didn't get maybe the credit I should have. I went in the outfield defensively in right field. They were up in the ninth inning and Carl Furillo hit a line drive into right field and I picked the ball up and threw the guy out at home, which would have been the winning run. The next inning when we came up [Whitey] Kurowksi hit a home run and we won the ballgame.

Most of the stories were about Kurowski and a reporter asked me why I didn't get any write-ups; if it wasn't for me he wouldn't have come up. I said, "That's the way it goes. The people like offense."

But the two home runs — that was my best offensively. I don't remember the pitcher's name; they must have buried him so deep in Class D after giving up two home runs to Chuck Diering.

What do you consider the major change that's taken place in baseball since you began playing in 1941?

I think it's the ballparks that's made the game change so much. I think the grass fields make better games for the spectators.

We played against concrete walls, so you had to play the game differently in going to get the ball. Today they're all padded and soft. I broke my arm in Sportsman's Park, ran into the wall going after the ball. Bases loaded, fly ball hit my way out there and I could see where I was going to catch it, but the wind carried it a little. I caught the ball, but I only had one more step and I crashed into the wall and I broke my arm.

In my day you had to learn to play ricochets off the walls. You had a lot of angles and you had to learn the caroms in the different parks. Today the ball hits the wall and it dies right there.

Your grass infields you had to play differently. Back then with a man on first and a basehit the man would try to go to third. Today it gets out there so fast they don't try to go to third. With a grass field a guy had to be good at judging the speed of the ball.

You don't see as many plays at the plate anymore because the guys are playing so deep to prevent the ball from getting between them. Close plays in general you don't see as much for the same reason. A lot of the excitement is gone.

And in the infield, the hop is altogether different. Ozzie [Smith] did a good job and he'd probably do it on natural grass as well. But now the ball zips right through. This lessens the excitement, too.

Did you save souvenirs along the way?

I did. I collected, at the end of my career, 40 bats from players. They're downstairs. These give me something as a memento. I took two of 'em over the other day to have Musial autograph 'em. He said, "Boy, that feels good to get that old bat in my hands!"

And I've got some pictures and a few baseball cards left. I was never fortunate enough to get a uniform, but I've got a hat and a pair of socks from the Giants and I've got three of my gloves left. I guess I have about 15 of my bats left. But I've got three kids and a few years ago I told 'em I was dividing it all up between them.

I've got baseballs autographed from every team. I've got new balls still in their wrappers, balls from every league. I did collect stuff. I was a real collector.

Books, programs, articles, even things from banquets—I've got a thing from Sam Breadon's memorial dinner and a red pencil with gold letters, "Sam Breadon's Testimonial Dinner." That stuff there is probably pretty good collector's stuff; I doubt if there's any of that around.

My son said a fellow at a card show offered $250 for Musial's bat, so I figure I've got, in bats down there, $7-8,000 if I wanted to sell, but what good will it do me to sell 'em? I'd just spend the money; this way I've got the bats.

Chuck Diering (courtesy Chuck Diering).

Do you receive fan mail?

Oh, yeah, I still do, but not a lot. Two or three a week.

Do you honor autograph requests?

Oh, yeah. I mail every one back to 'em. People send baseball cards. Some of these guys today are pretty stinko. Like Roy [Sievers], he likes to collect baseballs autographed by Hall of Famers and he's sent three of 'em out to a couple of guys and they never even sent 'em back. And we played against these guys! A lot of guys just won't reply.

If you were 18 again, would you do it all again?

Oh, definitely! That's all I lived for at that time. I graduated from high school on a Friday; Saturday I was leaving to go play baseball. Never even went to my high school graduation. I was so wrapped up in baseball, that's all I had on my mind.

I've been lucky. I've been able to do everything in life I've ever wanted to do. Baseball was number one and I've always loved automobiles and when I was playing ball I'd go visit the dealers and do P.R. and stuff like that. And then when I got out of baseball I got in the car business.

Heck, I've got a nice family, a nice home. I've accomplished everything in my life.

Maybe I could have done things differently in the business world and been able to afford a home in the south — Phoenix or Florida — which I can't. These are the only things maybe I wished I had more money to do.

My kids are all grown into good citizens; none of 'em smoke, no dope or stuff like that. I'm proud of 'em.

Remember Ted Savage? He's in St. Louis now, works for the Cardinals, and once in a while I get to see him. And he told me, "You were my idol." That's nice to hear things like that.

I'm proud of my profession. I brag about my baseball time; it makes me feel good. I'm proud I was a ballplayer. Guys I played with, we like to have our names clean. We're proud of the years we played in and we kind of get disgusted with what's going on now — the attitude they've got now.

Do you see anything wrong with a kid having a ballplayer as a role model? Guys today don't seem to want to be looked up to.

They're leaving so many other bad images, not only baseball but football and basketball, too. The dope situation leaves a bad taste and they're so free and easy with their money. Drinking, womanizing, carrying guns. How can anyone picture these guys as heroes anymore?

In my day these things were taboo. Oh, I guess it was done, but it's all in the open now. There's nothing secret anymore. The players are heroes, but some of these heroes are leaving bad tastes in people's mouths.

I had a few heroes: Pop Haines, Bill Hallahan. I enjoyed them. Maybe they went out and had a few beers; I didn't know about it. What a guy does away from the ballpark is his business. But there's no privacy today. Today there's overexposure.

❖ ❖ ❖

CHARLES EDWARD ALLEN DIERING

Born February 5, 1923, St. Louis, MO
Ht. 5'10"   Wt. 165   Batted and Threw Right

Year	Team, Lg	G	AB	R	H	2B	3B	HR	RBI	BA
1947	St. L., NL	105	74	22	16	3	1	2	11	.216
1948		7	7	2	0	0	0	0	0	.000
1949		131	369	60	97	21	8	3	38	.263
1950		89	204	34	51	12	0	3	18	.250
1951		64	85	9	22	5	1	0	8	.259
1952	NY, NL	41	23	2	4	1	1	0	2	.174
1954	Balt., AL	128	418	35	108	14	1	2	29	.258
1955		137	371	38	95	16	2	3	31	.256
1956		50	97	15	18	4	0	1	4	.186
9 years		752	1648	217	411	76	14	14	141	.249

CLIFF CHAMBERS

Pirates' Ace (1948–1953)

On September 20, 1907, Nick Maddox tossed a no-hitter for the Pittsburgh Pirates. He defeated Brooklyn, 2-to-1. It was the first time in Pirates' history that a no-hitter had been pitched by a member of the team, although it had been on the receiving end three times previously (plus four more times when the city was in the American Association in the 1880s).

Forty-four years were to pass and the Bucs were to be no-hit twice more before another of their own would throw another one. On May 6, 1951, Cliff Chambers climbed out of a sick bed and hurled a 3-zip no-hitter in Boston. (It was the only major league start and only major league decision for Braves' starter and loser George Estock.) Chambers, a southpaw, became the first lefty to author a no-hitter in seven years. Cincinnati's Clyde Shoun had no-hit the Braves on May 15, 1944.

The no-hitter was Cliff's last win as a Pirate. He hurt his arm in the game but, even so, on June 15, 1951, the Cardinals traded five players to acquire him and Wally Westlake. Going to Pittsburgh were Joe Garagiola, Howie Pollet, Bill Howerton, Dick Cole, and Ted Wilks.

The trade paid off for St. Louis; Cliff, sore arm and all, went 11-6 the rest of the way as the Cardinals finished in third place. His win total was second only to Gerry Staley among Redbird hurlers.

A broken wrist in 1952 effectively ended Cliff's playing days, but he left behind a National League career during which few lefties approached him.

❖ ❖ ❖

Did you serve in World War II?

When the war broke out I signed a contract with the Los Angeles Angels [PCL], which was a Wrigley organization. I went down and played in the Texas League in Tulsa, and then I went back to college [Washington State] and from there went into the Air Force for three years.

When I got out of there, there was a whole mass of ballplayers to work through and I went to spring training with Los Angeles and there were five jobs and I got one of 'em. I stayed at L.A. and they sold me to the Cubs in '46 and in '47 they sent me back to L.A. They wanted to win a pennant and we won one. I had a great year [*24-9, *175 K).

Then the next year I stayed with Chicago and they tore that ballclub up. They had a lot of rookies and it was a lousy ballclub. I won two and lost nine. They traded me [to Pittsburgh] for Frank Gustine — Clyde McCullough and me. They had to have a third baseman; they tried to put [Andy] Pafko at third and he wouldn't go. He couldn't handle it. They had more lefthanders than they wanted and I wound up at Pittsburgh and that's where I really centered in.

That was a great trade for both you and the Pirates.

I think so.

Outside of Warren Spahn, you were one of the top two or three lefthanders in the league at that time.

I would say so, yes.

You led Pittsburgh in wins the two full years you were there.

Then Branch Rickey traded me to St. Louis in 1951. At St. Louis before I broke my wrist, I was getting two wins for every loss. You know, for 34 starts that's 20 wins. The next year I was four-and-two or something like that and I was hit in the wrist — broke my wrist.

The next year when I went to spring training it was very obvious they weren't gonna use me, so I put in the year and then I said, "Well, the hell with it. I'll quit."

They traded me out to the best manager in baseball: Lefty O'Doul, who was then managing San Diego [PCL] and I just put in time there and

Cliff Chambers, 1949.

quit. He said, "I'm gonna send you back to the big leagues," but I said I didn't want to go.

When you were with Pittsburgh it was a terrible team. Your winning percentage was well above that of the team both years.

It wasn't a good team. [I was] 13-and-7 the first year with Pittsburgh and the next year I pitched a lot. I didn't pitch much until about June that first year I was with 'em and the next year I won 12 and lost 15 pitching regularly and we finished last.

The next year I pitched a no-hitter and I got a sore arm and even with the sore arm they traded me to St. Louis, which was a third-place ballclub, and I won two for every one I lost. I didn't become a great pitcher overnight; it was because I had a better ballclub, that's all.

It was a terrible ballclub at Pittsburgh. [Second baseman] Danny Murtaugh was done; he couldn't get the ball. We didn't have anybody to play first base, we didn't have anybody at third base. [Ralph] Kiner couldn't field the ball if his life depended on it. Wally Westlake was *not* a center fielder. Gus Bell was a pretty good ballplayer but he wasn't a good defensive ballplayer. We had nobody to play first base; Jack Phillips was there and the best we had was Johnny Hopp. We didn't have anything. [Catcher] Clyde McCullough was a .240 hitter.

Talk about your no-hitter.

I was sick. I'd pitched a ballgame and beat Brooklyn in their ballpark. As a lefthander, I thought that was a pretty good job 'cause a lot of managers wouldn't even *start* a lefthander against that club, let alone start him in Brooklyn. I had just beat them and I got the flu and I stayed in bed while they finished that series. They went over and played the Giants and I still didn't even go to the ballpark.

We took the train and went up there [to Boston] and we played a doubleheader on Sunday. I went in and laid down on the rubbing table the first ballgame 'cause I didn't feel good.

[Coach] Bill Posedel took over temporarily as the manager 'cause the manager [Bill Meyer] was left in New York. He said, "Can you give us four or five innings? We don't have anybody to pitch." Half the club was sick.

I said, "I'll do my best," and I went out and cranked up and pitched a no-hitter. I felt terrible at the end and I got a sore arm from it. I don't know whether it was from the flu or what it was, but I had trouble in the shoulder after that. It finally took about three or four months and it worked out.

They ran a film clip of the last out on CNN on the anniversary of the no-hitter [May 6, 1992]. I never saw it myself; I was getting phone calls from all over hell, asking me if I'd seen it. I was out shoveling manure; I didn't even know it was on. *[laughs]*

After I broke my wrist, my fastball wouldn't hop. I guess I had at least a 95 mile per hour fastball or better, and it was live. Nobody could pull me. There wasn't a hitter in the big leagues could pull me if they knew what was coming and I threw it right down the middle.

I developed better control. The guy who taught me control was a relief pitcher named Hugh Casey, pitched for Brooklyn and came over to Pittsburgh. He straightened out my footwork and once I got my footwork straightened out I began to get control. After I broke my wrist I came up with a slider and stuff like that, but I had to pitch differently.

How was Bill Posedel as a pitching coach?

He was a wonderful coach. I knew him in the Coast League when he was playing with Seattle. He finally wound up his career as a pitching coach at Oakland when they had the great teams.

Bill Meyer was the manager and my normal catcher was Clyde McCullough, but the guy who caught me in the no-hitter was Eddie FirtzGerald, who came out of the Coast League. He caught at Sacramento. He was a very good catcher.

You were a good hitter.

Yeah. I could have went pro as a hitter. In fact, if the war hadn't come along, the Yankees and Red Sox were both after me as a hitter. They said, "We'll use you as an outfielder or first baseman *first*, and if you don't hit, then you can pitch."

I am in the Athletic Hall of Fame at Washington State University mainly on my hitting. I hit .440 my sophomore year and my junior year I hit .375. I could hit all right; I think my [major league] lifetime was about .223 or something. [It was .235.] For a pitcher, that's not too bad.

I hit .289 one year and nobody paid any attention to it. *[laughs]* Pitchers don't get any batting practice and when you don't get any batting practice they throw the ball right by you.

You hit three home runs.

[laughs] The one I liked best was the one I hit off of a knuckleballer named Willie Ramsdell and, of all places, I hit it to left field. It was like hitting a butterfly. *[laughs]* If he'd have thrown the ball harder he'd probably have thrown it right by me. Hitting is the fun part of the game.

[The late Willard Ramsdell's chief claim to fame, if you can call it that,

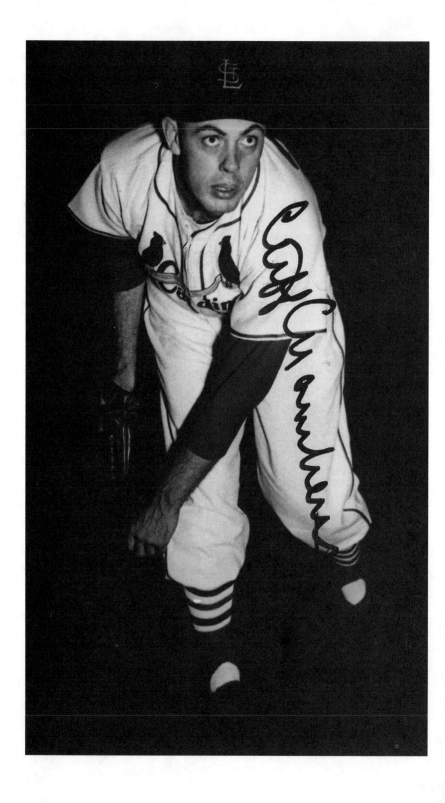

came in 1952 against the Dodgers. Brooklyn pitcher Carl Erskine pitched a no-hitter against Ramsdell and the Cubs. A walk to Ramsdell was all that prevented Erskine from tossing a perfect game.]

Other than the no-hitter, is there a game that stands out?

Yeah, there is, but it was in the Coast League. The Coast League was kind of a world apart. It was the only minor league with no salary limit. A lot of guys that just couldn't quite cut it in the big leagues, they played in the Coast League. It was *not* a farm set-up to develop players to go to the big leagues. The weather was good, the towns were good.

I was with L.A. [in 1947] and we wound up, in that good year I had, at a dead heat with San Francisco. I'd pitched nine innings on Saturday night and we finished the season on Sunday with a dead heat.

We were in Sacramento and San Francisco was down in San Diego, so we met in L.A. the next day — Monday — one game, sudden death. My ballplayers wanted me to pitch and I did, on one day's rest. The game went eight innings, nothing-to-nothing, and in the bottom of the eighth inning a kid named Clarence Maddern hit a home run with the bases loaded and another guy hit a home run and I shut 'em out, five-to-nothing.

I pitched a *hard* nine innings on Saturday against Sacramento — they were always a tough ballclub for me — and then came back and pitched on one day's rest. I thought that was pretty good when all the money was on the line. We won the pennant and then won the playoffs [defeating Oakland].

Who was the best hitter or player you saw?

[laughs] Of course, the best I faced or played with was [Stan] Musial. The best defensive ballplayer I've seen, against or with, was Red Schoendienst. I think he was the most underrated of anybody I've ever seen. He could go to his left and make the double play and I've never seen anybody do that. He did it consistently. And he was a good, solid .290 switch hitter. *Good* ballplayer.

Musial was kind of a streak hitter and maybe [Ted] Williams was a better hitter overall, but he was in the other league. I only got to see him in spring training and I didn't get to see much of [Joe] DiMaggio. [Ted] Kluszewski was a good hitter, but he didn't give me any problems. [Johnny] Mize was a good hitter, but he didn't give me any problems, either. They were both lefthanded.

Opposite: Cliff Chambers, 1951.

Who was the toughest on you?

Musial would hit his average. Regardless. He stood so far away from the plate it didn't make any difference whether you were right- or left-handed anyway.

There were only 400 ballplayers then — there's 700 now — and when I went out to pitch, a mediocre lefthander [batter] didn't get to play. The lefthanders I faced were the very, very best. It would be like Earl Torgeson in Boston and Enos Slaughter and Musial in St. Louis and Kluszewski and [Johnny] Wyrostek in Cincinnati and I always worked those clubs because there were two lefthanders in the lineup.

The Brooklyn club, my God; the only lefthanded hitter they had was Duke Snider. He was no push. *[laughs]* They had a lot of big righthanded hitters. I learned how to pitch against them and the guy that really helped me a lot — taught me — was Johnny Schmitz. When you got a hard-swinging club like that you have to just throw a lot of off-speed stuff and they didn't do well with that. *[laughs]* He [Schmitz] threw that big, slow curveball.

The guy that really put you in stitches was a kid named Stu Miller. It was the funniest thing you ever saw in your life. He had a great change. It was something in his motion; you'd swing ahead of him in a pepper game. *[laughs]*

Who was the best pitcher?

Probably Spahn or [Robin] Roberts. I beat Spahn a few times and, of course, he beat me.

I never had good luck against Philadelphia. I don't ever remember beating Roberts. I beat [Curt] Simmons. Simmons was probably as good as Roberts but he cut his toe off in a lawn mower and he never was as good after that. He had *great* stuff! Geez, he had great stuff. But Roberts had what I call a double-breaking fastball and I never saw anybody do that. He was a *super* guy, a super pitcher.

Do you still receive fan mail?

I get about four letters a week: bubble gum cards and photos and stuff. I sign. I've got nothing better to do. I'm retired. I really appreciate it. I usually write a little something extra. If they like the game and they're that interested in it and they want to do that, that's fine with me.

Did you save souvenirs from your playing days?

I gave most of my autographed balls away but I've still got five left. I've got a couple of my own gloves. I've got some eight-millimeter movies but other than that I don't have much.

Any regrets from your career?

Like anybody, if I could do it over again I would think I would try to be a different kind of guy and I would be able to take the game a little more in stride. What set me off in terribly bad straits was World War II. I'd say that cost me four to five years of big league time.

I have a physical condition which is inherited called Stork Leg and I couldn't get up on my toes and run after I was 30 years old. I was always a slow runner anyway and I began to get back problems, so I don't know if I could've went to 38 or 39. I guess all things considered, I maybe shouldn't have thrown my career away when I did. O'Doul said, "I'm gonna send you back to the big leagues," and I said, "No, I don't wanna go."

I guess a lot of it was money. If you're only gonna make 15-, 18-, 20,000 a year, what the hell. If I hadn't had a college degree, I would have probably fought it right down to the last. But I had a degree and I figured if I was smart enough to get a degree I was smart enough to make a living doing something. I think that was one of the reasons that I quit. Not many guys that played in the big leagues [then] had a college degree.

Back then with a degree you could make as much out of baseball. It's a different story today.

[laughs] It's a different ballgame today. The only other guy I knew was Danny Litwhiler. He and I were the only two I knew that had degrees. A lot of ballplayers never finished high school and they really fought just to stay in the game 'cause that's all they knew.

How else has the game changed?

Look at the averages. You've got guys hitting .220, .230. When I played, Billy Cox on the Brooklyn Dodgers was the worst hitter on the club hitting .270. And the worst one on the Cardinals was Marty Marion hitting .265. That's the *worst* hitter on the club.

And they expected pitchers to go nine innings. My job was to hold 'em to three runs and pitch nine innings. I'd pitch every third day if they were only gonna pitch me six innings like today. *[laughs]*

You said you're retired now. What are you up to?

We have 160 acres in the back country, right next to a wilderness area. We have a house up there and I spend about five-six months a year up there. We go up there and we hunt and we horseback. We ride almost every day.

We have elk on the place and deer running around. We're completely surrounded by national forest. For a hundred miles east there's no roads. No TV, no telephone. Water out of the creek. *[laughs]*

When my daughters were growing up I had horses for them and then we got out of it for a while. We decided to go back and I got into Arabs. I had a half–Arab and they were so superior that's what I got when I went back into horses. I've got a Morgan that's ten years old; I use him to pack and ride — all-purpose horse. But my Arabs — they're just something else. They have a distinct personality and you have to treat 'em different. When you have to feed 'em twice a day and you're around 'em all the time you learn to really appreciate that. They're like big dogs.

They're not really a beginner's horse and a lot of horse trainers don't like 'em because you can't get after 'em too hard. You gotta make 'em think it's their idea and you work with a lot of praise and they really dote on that praise business. It goes a long way with these guys.

Mine are good in the mountains and we ride in some very, very tricky stuff — one slip and you're dead. They're strong and they don't eat very much and they're tough and they'll take you on those tough trails where you're looking over the toe of the boot 2,000 feet down. *[laughs]* Too many people get Arabs because they think it's like owning a BMW; they're not in it for the horse.

Both Cliff Chambers and I are of the opinion that he was in the top handful of lefthanded pitchers in the NL when he was sound. The following three tables show the four top NL lefthanded hurlers in the 1949-51 period ranked by Total Wins (Table 1), Percent of Team's Wins (Table 2), and W-L Percent Above Team's W-L Percent (Table 3).

Table 1		Table 2		Table 3	
Total Wins		*Percent of Team's Wins*		*W-L Percent Above Team's W-L*	
Warren Spahn	64	Spahn	27.4	**Chambers**	22.5
Preacher Roe	56	Raffensberger	24.5	Roe	22.2
Ken Raffensberger	48	Roe	19.8	Spahn	16.0
Cliff Chambers	39	**Chambers**	19.4	Raffensberger	11.8

CLIFFORD DAY CHAMBERS

Born January 10, 1922, Portland, OR
Ht. 6'3"   Wt. 208   Batted and Threw Left

Year	Team, Lg	G	IP	W	L	Pct	H	BB	SO	ERA
1948	Chi., NL	29	103.2	2	9	.182	100	48	51	4.43
1949	Pit., NL	34	177.1	13	7	.650	186	58	93	3.96
1950		37	249.1	12	15	.444	262	92	93	4.30
1951	Pit-StL, NL	31	189	14	12	.538	184	87	64	4.38
1952	St. L., NL	26	98.1	4	4	.500	110	33	47	4.12
1953		32	79.2	3	5	.333	82	43	26	4.86
6 years		189	897.1	48	53	.475	924	361	374	4.29

CLINT CONATSER

Spahn, Sain, and a Whole Bunch of Others (1948–1949)

> There are words that are hard to say,
> words that will tear your heart, ruin your day.
> And the hardest words to say for any man
> are these: "My wife is a Red Sox fan."
>
> —

It's not really her fault, though. She was born near Boston into a large family of Red Sox fans. A victim of circumstance. One of her sisters now lives in Connecticut, right outside of New York City, and the reason she and her husband have cable TV is so they can see Red Sox games. Another sister gave me a Red Sox cap for my birthday one year. I have since forgiven her. My wife wants me to wear it. No way.

The family seems normal in other respects.

It's only the Red Sox I don't like, however, although I'm not real sure I could ever live in Boston. But as a boy I had a fondness for the Braves—the *Boston* Braves. Earl Torgeson, Willard Marshall, Sid Gordon, Sibby Sisti, Ebba St. Claire—I liked these guys. They weren't Tigers and the team wasn't the Tigers, but I liked them nonetheless.

(Life holds many mysteries. One of the greatest is why the city of Boston would embrace so fondly the Red Sox and reject so soundly the Braves.)

I visited the Hall of Fame several years ago (all baseball fans should) and to show my wife (we'd only been married a year or so then) that I didn't have total disdain for baseball in her city, I purchased a Boston Braves replica cap.

I expected her to be pleased when I showed it to her. "What's the 'B' for?" she asked.

"Boston," I replied. "The Boston Braves."

"What in the world are the Boston Braves?"

It took me a few seconds to realize that she was serious. She had never heard of the Boston Braves! But I thought about it. I'm old enough (sad but true) to remember Boston as a two-team city, but there is more than a decade between my wife's age and mine. As far as she knew, Boston never had more to offer than the Red Sox. (This is only one of the problems with having a child bride.) I began to feel my age.

My normal attire as I work on my equine patients consists of jeans, sweatshirt when it's cold or polo shirt when it's not, canvas shoes (socks in sweatshirt weather), and Tigers cap. It's a fashion statement heeded by few. Horse work is usually dirty and frequently sweaty, so I go through three or four caps a year.

Several years ago my Tigers cap of the moment was particularly gross and I hadn't taken the time to purchase a replacement. The Keeneland November sale of Thoroughbred breeding stock was underway and I needed to attend to either buy something or sell something (I don't recall which now) and as I started out the door my wife stopped me.

"You're not wearing that disgusting hat to Keeneland," she pronounced.

I examined it and had to agree with her. It looked as if it had been in a stall overnight with a nervous horse. She offered me the Red Sox cap. I went back in and got the Braves cap.

At the sale, where people were spending money on horses as if they were signing free-agent southpaws, I noticed another person with a Braves— a *Boston* Braves—cap. I had never seen anyone else wearing one.

"Nice cap," I said.

He stopped and looked at me — at my cap. "Where in the world did you get that?" he asked.

I told him. "Where did you get yours?"

"I played for 'em."

His name was Clint Conatser. As a rookie in 1948, he played on the

Braves' first pennant-winner since 1914.

Clint is in the Thoroughbred business today and has been for more than 30 years now. He and another ex–Brave (Milwaukee), Joe Adcock, had a lot of dealings. Clint kept horses with Joe at his Louisiana farm. In fact, Clint was there at Keeneland that day with Joe.

Clint has a lot of great horse stories and great baseball stories. We'll limit this to his baseball reminiscences, in deference to the readership.

You got a World Series ring as a rookie in 1948. That was the Braves' first pennant since 1914.

Right. The Miracle Braves.

There were four rookies who made big contributions to the team; Vern Bickford, Bobby Hogue, Alvin Dark, and you.

Those other three really contributed tremendously. Bickford and Hogue didn't get any credit.

Neither did Nellie Potter. Without Nellie Potter, who just died recently, we don't win. They brought him over from the American League and he was a screwball pitcher and the [opposing] manager was going by the book — they'd put up those lefthanded hitters against him and that screwball. He got us out of jam after jam.

But Bickford and Hogue — they made a tremendous contribution. You know, they talk about Spahn and Sain and two days of rain. Spahn only won 15 games, Sain won 24. We'd have been in a lot of trouble if that's all we had. We won 91 games that year.

Of course, Alvin Dark was an outstanding athlete.

It was one of those teams where everybody contributed. We should have won the World Series. You know, I pinch-hit [in Game 6] with the bases loaded and hit a screaming shot to left-center field and Thurman Tucker made a *great* play — hit the fence — or we win the Series 'cause they've got nobody to come back with the next day. [Clint's fly scored a run.]

Lou Boudreau took [Larry] Doby out of there, put Tucker in for defense. He could *really* run. He looked like Joe E. Brown, by the way. He made a hell of a play. Next guy up, [Phil] Masi, who also just died, doubled in a run.

A lot of guys don't give [Bill] Voiselle any credit just because he got bombed in the sixth game. But he won 13 ballgames. And [Red] Barrett won some games. He was one of those kind of pitchers where they'd hit line drive after line drive but always right at somebody. Somebody'd make a great play in the outfield and they'd go back to the bench and somebody'd say, "Red, aren't you going to tell him what a great play it was?" and he'd say, "That's what he's supposed to do," *[laughs]* And Bob Elliott had a good year.

Even with the four rookies, the Braves were the oldest team in the major leagues that year.

Is that right? I thought Cleveland was older than us. [The Braves averaged about 3 months older that the Indians.]

The Braves were a predominately righthanded hitting team.

I don't think a lefthander beat us more than once or twice all year. I hit .323 against lefthanded pitching I've been told. They pinch-hit me 20-some-odd times, but I think I hit over .300 in games I started. They've got me down in the book at .277; it was really .282.

We played a lot of low-run ballgames. We didn't have a lot of big innings. We had pitching and we played in tight ballgames.

Back to Bickford. His contribution was tremendous. Did you know he spent four years in a Class-D league?

So did Johnny Sain. Johnny was a good friend of mine. He told me that he was a five-inning pitcher before the war and when he got on an Army team they only had one pitcher and he had to learn to pace himself so he'd just aim and throw the first ball right down the middle. *[laughs]*

I saw Spahnie out here a few years ago. He started out, I think, as a first baseman. He said, "Clint, I never thought I'd get in the Hall of Fame. I never thought I'd win all those games. I was just a first baseman when I started." *[laughs]* He was with the Braves when Casey Stengel managed there before the war. When he was with the Mets he said, "I'm the only player who ever played for Casey Stengel both before and after he was a genius."

I think the greatest practical joke ever played on the sportswriters in New York was when [Dan] Topping hired Casey. Something was wrong with his brain. He'd be talking and cut the sentence off and go to another subject completely, then come back to another subject and you'd sit there and say, "What'd he say?" It's *really* funny; he wasn't trying to do it. He could never remember [Joe] DiMaggio's name; he called him "that big guy in center field." *[laughs]*

But anybody could've managed those teams he had. He was a good manager—don't get me wrong—but I think the best quote I ever heard was when he came to the Mets after all those great Yankee teams he had.

Clint Conatser, spring training, 1947, with Detroit (courtesy Clint Conatser).

They asked him, "Casey, how come you're not winning games over here like you did with the Yankees?" He said, "These players won't execute my plays." *[laughs]* He got to believing it himself!

In the Series in '48, the Braves both outhit (.250 to .199) and outpitched (2.60 ERA to 2.72) the Indians. And both teams scored the same amount of runs.

I'll be darned.

One thing I remember: in Cleveland they had the grass real long. [Gene] Bearden was a sinkerball pitcher, and so was Lemon. I was only up four times and I hit three balls right on the nose, but I couldn't get it past [Ken] Keltner at third base. They had about two inches of grass. [Clint, a righthanded batter, was platooned with Marv Rickert, a lefthanded batter.]

And they had no speed—their team. They had the bases all dug up and the dirt was real soft. You've got to give Boudreau a lot of credit.

The greatest exhibition I ever saw was when they [Cleveland] had that playoff game in Boston [against the Red Sox]. You know, they tied at the end of the season. Boudreau managed the team and drove in about five or six runs, hit two home runs, sucked up everything at shortstop. That's the best exhibition I ever saw in a crucial game. He didn't look like an athlete. I guess he was a great basketball player, too.

Let's talk about some of your teammates. Alvin Dark: Hall of Fame?

I only saw him those two years [1948 and '49]. A lot of it is where you play. If Pee Wee Reese is in the Hall of Fame, Alvin Dark should be in the Hall of Fame. You take him [Reese] out of Brooklyn and he was a pretty good ballplayer but he wasn't a great ballplayer. But he was in Ebbets Field — a great park to hit in — and he was a sort of take-charge guy.

My idea of the Hall of Fame was always guys like Cobb and Waner and Speaker and those guys, but I think the thing's been diluted, don't you? Guys hit home runs but can't run or throw.

You were one of the first ballplayers to go in for body-building

That's right. I was the guy who got Ralph Kiner started body-building. I had quit playing ball; I had played three years in the lower minor leagues and I wasn't getting anywhere, so I decided to get some education and I was going to [Oakland] City College and the war broke out so I enlisted. I weighed about 155 then. I got with a friend of mine — a writer — and we started pumping iron. We worked out in a gym down in Oakland where Dillinger had his gym next door. This guy let us work out for nothing and we would teach the guys that would come in.

So, anyway, I went from 155 to 185. I didn't just lift weights, I did body-building.

So I started playing again. I went to the Texas League in '46 and finished second in the league in home runs. I hit some real big shots. I broke my back in July and then I came back and hit five home runs in the playoffs and Dixie Series.

I was born and raised in Watts, but we called it southwest L.A.— in fact, right in back of Bobby Doerr. He lived on the next street. I went home that winter and I see this big, tall guy come up the street and this husky guy next to him. He said, "Are you Clint? I'm Ralph Kiner, this is Bobby Brown. I was talking to Dan Crowley and he said that you were body-building and how much it helped your power and your arm and your athletic ability and everything. He said he couldn't believe it was the same ballplayer. Do you think it'll make you muscle-bound?"

I said, "I don't think so but I don't think you should take a chance. I think you should just work on your arms and maybe your calves, your legs."

He went home that winter — he lived in Alhambra — and built a gym down in the garage and pumped iron all winter. I didn't know it 'til lately, but he only hit 23 home runs the year before. He wound up hitting 51 in '47. *[laughs]*

He told me, "I studied the great home run hitters and they're all strong. I'm not strong. If they throw me high or change up on me, I can't jerk it out of the ballpark. Jimmie Foxx, they used to fool him and he'd still hit it out. I realized I need to get strong in my hands and arms to be a great home run hitter."

Bobby Brown was a very tense individual. If I knew as much about it then as I know now, I'd have given him flexibility exercises. That's what he needed more than strengthening.

I had pitchers try to rehabilitate their arms. I did it just on my own because it had strengthened my arm so much. I got a guy named Bob Chesnes — hurt his arm. He was with Hollywood and I took him to this gym in Oakland. But he didn't follow through.

Today they're rehabilitating torn muscles and strained ligaments.

Another teammate: Earl Torgeson.

Torgy died, too. We lost four in 1990: Torgy, Masi, Potter, and Barrett.

[Braves manager Billy] Southworth had great hopes for him. He thought he was going to be a great ballplayer. He wore those thick glasses; that may have had something to do with it. Maybe his vision wasn't good enough.

I just saw him the one year. In '48 he had just a fair year. In '49 he separated his shoulder going into second base and missed almost the whole year. He went to take out the second baseman and he rolled and he popped his collarbone out. And he got cancer quite a long time ago. Maybe that was part of it. Who knows?

I roomed with him for a while. He was a good guy — a character. He was funny. *[laughs]* Marched to his own drummer.

Tommy Holmes.

I saw Tommy at the end of his career. Tommy was a singles hitter and he hit the ball to left field. He could lay the bat on the ball. Good hitter, not a strong hitter but a *good* hitter.

I didn't see him in those good years he had. He told me in '45, the year he hit 28 home runs, for the first time in history the wind blew to right field in Braves Field all year long. *[laughs]* He says, "I'm not a home run hitter, but the wind blew out all year long." It was hard to hit 'em out of Braves Field. It was right on the Charles River there and it was real damp and the ball didn't carry there at all. He just laid the bat on the ball. He had very fast hands; he was a champion speed bag puncher when he was a kid.

I roomed with him for a while, too. *Good* guy. Really a nice man — good habits, honest, trustworthy. He was an example. He's working with kids now in New York.

[Tommy Holmes' 1945 season: .352, *.577 SA, *224 hits, *47 2B, *28 HR, 125 R, 117 RBI, 70 BB, only 9 SO in 636 AB.]

Bob Elliott — it was also the end of his career when you saw him.

Yeah, Bob was just winding up then. It was very sad. He put all his dough into a saloon in San Diego with a friend of his and he lost everything. He died young.

His daughters were sitting at the same table as I was at our banquet in Boston when Perrini had us back there. It was sort of touching and sad. The one daughter said, "What was my dad like? I never got to know him." She was only two or three years old when he died.

I told her he was a fine man. I said, "I never heard him ever say anything bad about anybody." And I didn't. He was a professional; he went out and did his job. He was a very cheerful guy — always smiling.

He was *tough* to get out.

Warren Spahn — you saw him early. He had 15 wins in 1948; was he a great pitcher then or just a good one?

He was an outstanding pitcher. He didn't win that many that year, but I think Southworth got the hook out on him too quick too many times. He was so smooth. He'd work the hitters in and out; he'd put a little spin on it here and a little spin on it there. He was just like a musician. So smooth.

What was Johnny Sain's earned run average that year?

2.60. Harry Brecheen [Cardinals] led the league with 2.24.

I'll tell you something about Harry Brecheen that Tommy Holmes told me. Tommy didn't hit against lefthanded pitching [late in his career] and he said, "Clint, I've studied this guy for years. Contrary to what everybody thinks, he gets you out on his fastball so whatever you do when you get up there, if he throws you the screwball outside," which he did and it was always a ball, 'he'll get you leaning in an inch and he'll bust you right in on the hands with a fastball. So you straighten up after every pitch and look for the fastball in on you." And I wore him out. *[laughs]* I did what Tommy told me to do.

Batters today run when someone brings one in on them.

I don't see many guys hitting on top of the plate; they're all way back in the box. Your better hitters really should be right there and *dare* 'em to throw 'em inside. You take so much away from the pitcher when you stand on the plate.

I think that the stars of yesterday would be stars of today. I think overall the players are faster, bigger, better coached, have more ability *but* they don't have the one thing and that is the will to give 100 percent every day. The incentives aren't there. It's just money. Before, the incentive was back to the minor leagues—somebody would take your job. There were too many guys waiting to take your place on a Triple-A team.

Here's a couple of salary stories for you.

I roomed with Jeff Heath, also. Jeff broke his leg three days before the season ended. He didn't want to play; he was afraid he'd hurt himself. He broke his tibia sliding into home. He was down in pain and we ran out there and Campy said, "I didn't block him! I let him through!" He really hurt! Morphine didn't even work [to ease the pain]. That got Marv Rickert into the Series; he was put on the roster.

Heath was accused of being the leader of the Cry-Baby Revolt in Cleveland [in 1940] when Oscar Vitt and [Cy] Slapnicka were there. Here's what happened.

Roy Weatherly went up to him and said, "Jeff, you're a star here; you're established on the club. We got some real gripes and they won't listen to us. Will you take this letter up to the office?"

Jeff's a real easy-going guy. He says, "Sure."

So he takes it up to the office and they have a big meeting in the clubhouse. They say, "All right, you guys have some complaints. Let's have it out."

Not a soul stepped out. They dumped it right on Jeff.

When he first came to the big leagues, his salary was [$]3500. He hit .325, as I remember him telling me [it was actually .343] and they raised him to 6500. The next year he hit .305 or something [.292] and they cut him back to 3500 again. *[laughs]*

And I'll give you one more salary story — about Johnny Sain. He wins 24 games [in 1948], wins a game in the World Series, should have been the Most Valuable Player in either league. His contribution was outstanding. Beats [Bob] Feller [in the Series] one-to-nothing when Feller allows two hits. He was really something.

He holds out the next year. This guy's entitled to a big raise in salary. I don't know what he's making at the time, but we get the papers down in Bradenton and the papers are saying John wants $45,000.

You've got to understand. In those days Duffy Lewis [Braves' traveling secretary] had a $50,000 a year fund and all he did was wine and dine the sportswriters. They wrote what he *wanted* them to write. That was prevalent in the big leagues then. That was Duffy Lewis's job — whatever they wanted, they got. But they were also on the side of the club. They only made about 125 bucks a week.

There are 23 sportswriters in Boston; all those little hamlets have a newspaper. They're really getting on John. "Who does he think he is?" "He thinks he's bigger than baseball." "No man is worth $45,000." "He'll bankrupt the ballclub." It went on and on and on and on.

Finally, after about three or four weeks, John shows up in spring training and he signs. I wasn't one of the beer-drinking boys, and Sain didn't drink or Spahn or Stanky or Dark, so I got to know them very well. John and I are walking around at night, going to get a milkshake or something. I said, "John, I hope you got the 45,000 'cause you're worth it."

"Clint," he says, "I wish I was making 25,000."

They screwed the ballplayers. They had the reserve clause; they *screwed* us.

Let's talk about you. When did you originally sign?

I signed in 1938. I signed a contract for 1939 for $100 bonus and $75 a month with Springfield in the Middle Atlantic League. That was a Cleveland farm club.

The scout was named Johnny Angel. He went around to the public playgrounds and he signed guys that were not playing on the Detroit Juniors and the Yankee Juniors — the great big guys. So here he signed for practically nothing myself, Bob Lemon, and Cliff Mapes. *[laughs]* He got us early.

All three of us changed position. I started out as a second baseman because of Bobby Doerr and I ended up an outfielder. Lemon started out as a shortstop and ended up as a pitcher. And Mapes started out as a catcher and ended up as an outfielder.

I moved around to three different Class D leagues and finally at Johnstown, Pennsylvania, I found I could play a little bit. Then the next year I had a pretty good year but tore my ankle up. The history of my career is as a tissue-paper ballplayer. I got hurt a lot. I was born with weak ankles and I busted them up every year. That's why I quit when I was 30 — it was so painful. I was only playing at about 50 percent of my ability.

After three years [in the minors] I figured I wasn't getting anywhere; I was still in a Class C league. I hit .255 my third year. So I went to City College and I was going there when the war broke out. I became a free agent because I had gone on the Voluntary Retired list with Cleveland.

I came out of the service and I'm working out over at the playground. Bobby Doerr and George McDonald and Bryan Stephens and a lot of guys saw me and I looked like a different ballplayer, so they told a scout — Dan Crowley — about me and I got a $3,000 bonus to sign with Detroit.

I went to spring training with Detroit in '47, then they assigned me to Buffalo. I was only at Buffalo a month and they sent me out to Seattle. I hit .305 and I was drafted by Boston. In '48 I played with the Braves.

Then I was with Boston part of '49 and came out to Hollywood. I was with the Hollywood Stars for two years, then I played half of '51 with Portland and quit — went back on the Voluntary Retired list.

I hit good against Brooklyn and they bought me in that [Sam] Jethroe deal. I understand they gave $100,000 for me when I was 28. In the latter part of '49, when Jeff Heath came on the active list, they optioned me to Milwaukee; I was the only guy on the team who had three options left.

I was working on a boys' ranch in Texas, so I said, "To hell with it," and I quit. Branch Rickey comes down there and talks me into playing and I said I wanted to play near my home so they sent me to Hollywood. The Pacific Coast League was good — had a lot of good ballplayers. There's nothing in the minors to compare with it today.

I wasn't playing up to capacity then; I was getting broken down. I'd given it my best shot in the big leagues — I really did. 125 percent. I could hit the ball, and I could run and I could throw, but I wasn't an outstanding ballplayer.

Do you remember Joe Brovia? You and he were at Portland together.

A good hitter. They'd hit the ball to the outfield and he'd say, "You got it, Clint!" *[laughs]* I had Eric Tipton in left and Joe Brovia in right and neither one of 'em could run. "You got it!" they'd yell.

[Joe Brovia played many years in the PCL and hit everywhere he played, but fielding and foot speed were problems. Cincinnati bought him from Oakland late in 1955 when he was 33 and he finished the season with the Reds. He never played in the field, but in 21 games as a pinch-hitter he went 2-for-18 and drove in four runs. The next season he was back on the Coast.]

Tod Davis.

Out in the Coast League, shortstop at Hollywood? What a *great* prospect he was that first year at Hollywood! There was just no way you could stop him from being an outstanding major league ballplayer. I don't know what happened.

He started out young at Hollywood — 17 or 18. Later he went to Oakland. A big shortstop — good-looking guy — he just flattened out but he had all the tools. All-American boy — he looked the part, like a quarterback or a gunfighter. *[laughs]*

[Tod Davis—Thomas Oscar Davis—was a huge shortstop for his time: 6'2", 200 pounds. He appeared in 42 games for the Philadelphia Athletics in 1949 and '51 and compiled a .233 major league average.]

Emmett Ashford. [Ashford was the first black major league umpire; he worked in the PCL for years before being called up.]

He was a good umpire and he was colorful. He was funny. I was all for him. A guy like [Ron] Luciano made me throw up, but a guy like Ashford was enjoyable to watch. He was great! Nobody ever accused him of not being a good umpire. They accused him of being a showboat, but I never heard anyone say he *wasn't* a good umpire.

I've heard from ballplayers that the showboating wasn't intentional; it was just his nature. He was exuberant in everything he did.

Yeah, right. It was probably natural for him. I don't know who he could have copied; he was an original.

He was the first black major league umpire and it's my opinion that he belongs in the Hall of Fame. When you consider what he had to put up with and as good a job as he did, he has to be there.

I would think so. I would have to say so, too. Who knows how tough it was, what he went through? That's the loneliest job in the world anyway, being an umpire, and then to be black and have to move around like he did and the ridicule he took from a lot of people. Every league he went through, he was the only black [umpire] for years.

He kept his nose clean, he was pleasant and cheerful and they'd get on him and he'd just grin back at 'em. He was really a good example for young blacks. I never heard anyone make a racial slur toward Ashford. But other than Dixie Walker in Brooklyn [with Jackie Robinson], that wasn't much of a problem.

Before the war, blacks couldn't even play American Legion baseball. There was a kid I played American Legion ball with and they weren't going to let him play until he proved he was born in Algeria and he was an Algerian Jew. He was just dark-skinned.

You've also got to remember, it was a different time and the cultures were so far apart. The cultures are coming closer together now, but they were *really* far apart and neither one trusted the other. They were afraid of each other. I always said it wasn't skin color, it was culture more than anything, and fear. There were so many other races.

Being born and raised in Watts, that was really a polyglot. Everything was there. There wasn't a race that wasn't represented there — Japanese and Chinese and Jews. In fact, poor Jews. There was a synagogue down the street in a house; they were so poor they couldn't afford a temple. And we had blacks. We had one guy who went to junior high school. We couldn't understand how he couldn't run. We said, "Miles, you've got to run! You're colored!" But he just couldn't run. He was the best-natured guy.

And of course there was prejudice. There's nothing wrong with being proud of what you are, as long as you aren't bigoted and go hurt somebody and deprive them. That's wrong.

Nobody ever took more of a beating than the Irish did in New York. My grandfather used to tell me stories about it — "No micks or dogs allowed." An Irish cop was the worst paying job in New York and a scrub woman was next. Fortunately, they moved out of it politically, which is what the Negroes are doing now. They'll come out and in about 200 years from now we'll all look like Sicilians. It's coming – that's Nature's way. Integration.

Who was the best player you saw in the time you played?

Players will all tell you that [Joe] DiMaggio was the greatest, but if you said I had the first pick to go start a ballclub, I'd take Jackie Robinson. I'd have to take him. And I'd take DiMaggio next; he was so graceful.

But the kind of ballclub I'd have would be a scrappy ballclub. Fast. He [Robinson] could beat you so many different ways. He was a very unpleasant guy to be around. Warren Spahn and I were walking down the street one time, walking to the train station in Boston. He's [Robinson] with [Roy] Campanella and Campy says, "Hey, fellas!" — happy and friendly. Robinson wouldn't even look at us. But he probably had a reason. He had a lot of things happen to him all through school.

He was a *bright* guy and what a *great* athlete. Probably him and Jim Thorpe had to be the world's greatest all-around athletes.

He was kind of old when he got up there. He was probably 20 pounds heavier than he should have been when he got there. When he played out here at UCLA he was thin.

Who was the best pitcher you ever saw?

Boy, that's tough. That I played against or saw?

Either one.

I'd have to say Sandy Koufax. I've never seen anything like that in my life. You talk about somebody unhittable! When he had his curveball, just forget it.

I only saw Feller when he was a curveball pitcher, in the '48 Series, but I'm sure he was just as tough. I remember Bobby Doerr told me when he had the good fastball and the curveball, just protect yourself.

I have to say, in my era, it would be very, very difficult to say who would be the best pitcher that I saw. When you're talking about a pitcher, do you mean who had the greatest stuff or who was the smartest or was toughest in a jam — all those kind of things.

For raw talent, I'd have to take Koufax.

Who was the toughest on you?

There were two guys and they both threw the same: Hank Borowy and Sad Sam Jones. I couldn't pick the ball up from them; they had that herky-jerky motion. I hit against Jones in the Coast League. I could *not* time him. And Borowy was the same way.

[Rex] Barney threw about a hundred miles per hour, but the ball was just straight as a string. And he'd throw the ball down the middle a lot, too, so if you swung in the middle he was gonna hit your bat.

Was there one game in your career — majors or minors — that stands out in your memory?

There was a doubleheader in Philadelphia, actually not too long before I went to the minors. I got 8-for-10 in the doubleheader and knocked all the runs in in one game and I won the game in the second game. And a month later I was in the minors. *[laughs]* I think I hit two home runs and a third one hit the foul pole and in that ballpark [Shibe Park], if it hit the foul pole it was in play so I got a triple out of that. I never hit the ball so pure as I did that day. And it was against righthanded pitching and I didn't play against righthanders very often.

Do you remember the pitchers?

I remember Schoolboy Rowe was one of 'em. He threw sliders a lot. I can't remember the others. Maybe Robin Roberts was in there; I'm not sure.

I hit three home runs in a playoff game against San Antonio; that was a big thrill. Sig Jacucki was pitching, a knuckleball pitcher. I beat him in the last half of the ninth inning; that put us [Dallas] in the Dixie Series.

That was minor leagues, though, but it was still thrilling. [Dallas swept Atlanta, 4-0, in the Dixie Series.]

There's one more. I've got the write-up, I've got the box score. We [Boston] had about a six or seven game lead and Brooklyn was back about fourth or fifth the early part of the year. And all of a sudden here they came! They made a big move and they were within one-and-a-half or two games of us. We were playing them and we were behind in the eighth inning, 3-to-1 or 4-to-1, and the bases were loaded and they bring in [Erv] Palica. I hit a home run into the left field bleachers. Put us ahead, took the wind out of their sails, and we were never headed after that. Of course, it was me but I thought that was the most important hit of the year because we had really been playing badly and that picked us up.

Palica was a righthander.

Fastball pitcher; he had good stuff. It was a ball, low and outside, and I hit it to left-center over [Duke] Snider's head. They didn't like to pitch inside to a righthanded hitter there.

I had some good days against them [the Dodgers], so they bought me — paid $100,000 for me the next year. *[laughs]*

Talking about home runs, you know Joe Adcock hit four [in one game] and just missed the fifth one — hit the top of the fence [for a double]. He said, "That's the damnedest day I ever had. Do you know how many times I swung the bat? Five times. I made five swings and hit four home runs and the fifth one should have been a home run." That was against Brooklyn — '54, I think. He's got that plaque up there on his wall with the four silver half baseballs.

He could hit it. He got hurt a lot; he broke a lot of things. He could have had a better career, but he was like me; he did things hard and got busted up.

Did you save souvenirs?

I've got scrapbooks, but, no, I didn't save much. I've got my World Series uniform, I've got that bat they send you — that black bat — and a few little trinkets. The batboy at Boston, Tommy Ferguson — he's now a scout for Philadelphia — he's got a garage full of stuff.

I didn't know my uniform was worth anything. I used to lend it to people for Halloween. It's worth some dough; there's only one like it.

Do you get much fan mail?

Yeah, generally autograph requests from kids, once in a while from an adult. They've got some postcards with my picture on it; you know, we didn't have the baseball cards when I was there. They usually write a nice little letter with the request.

I can understand the players selling their autographs; they're worth some dough. It isn't the kids, but it's the promoters that make the money off the autographs. They're giving away something that some guy's selling so I can understand it, but not when you're making three million bucks a year. *[laughs]*

Have you ever done a card show?

We went back there [to Boston] for a reunion. The grandson of Perrini paid all our ways back there and put us up real nice. We did that one [show] in Boston is all. They had just the remaining Braves. Other than that, I've never done one. They had a good turnout for us there. A lot of people remembered us.

Boston U plays where Braves Field used to be. Half of Braves Field is still there. The first base side stands are still there and the original offices are behind the stands. We had a dedication ceremony to dedicate the new athletic facility there and they put up a plaque.

What are your feelings toward card shows?

I think it's a good way for an old-timer to pick up 12-15 hundred dollars and get a trip somewhere, especially if the old guy isn't making any money.

A lot of guys from your day and before aren't getting a baseball pension.

That's right. And even some of those that *are* getting a pension are not getting much.

Remember Clint Courtney? His widow's getting $150 a month in pension. All that money laying there all these years. He died years ago and that poor woman was driving a school bus trying to raise three or four kids. That's not right with all that money there. They've revised it a little bit now but they haven't done it where it needs to be done.

We've got a ballplayers association out here, the APBA. Chuck Stevens runs it. It's done more good than any of 'em. Jimmie Foxx was dead broke in Phoenix, Arizona, living in a room in his brother's home. Chuck was sending him $300 a month.

What about the organization that Early Wynn headed? Is that doing any good?

I don't know too much about it. If it wasn't for Early, these guys wouldn't have revised the pension plan. He's the guiding light for it.

That's like when we split up the World Series money. I was so disappointed. "Let's not give this guy anything because he's not a good guy," and "this guy's a good guy; let's give his some." As a rookie I got up and said, "I've got only one vote, but what you're doing is wrong."

They gave Johnny Beazley a full share and Al Lyons a half-share and they were both there and contributed the same — both there a half a year. I said, "That's not right." Al Lyons was from out here and a friend of mine. They said, "Well, we wanted to help Johnny; this is his last year." And they passed it over real quick and went on.

And guys that had been with the club a couple of weeks— I said, "Why don't we send a hundred or so. It would mean so much to them to get part of a World Series check, whether it's $100 or $50." Do you know what they said? "Fuck 'em!" And I'm sure it prevails today. The more they get, the more selfish they are.

What did you do after you left baseball?

When I was 14 years old, my dad made me learn a trade. He said, "What are you going to do when you get big?"

I said, "I want to be a ballplayer."

"What if you aren't?"

I was going to John C. Frémont High School in L.A., which is a vocational school. Bobby Doerr went there, and Mickey Owen and a bunch of guys. Gene Mauch. They had a big shop class, so I took four hours a day of sheet metal. I carried eight classes a day for two years and I learned something about the sheet metal business.

In the meantime, my dad was superintendent for a water heater company and he got let go. A new company bought it and he had to start over again. Because he was in an allied industry he had applied for a heating license. He went up to Big Sur and put in floor furnaces and water heaters.

When I quit [playing] in '52, I opened up an air conditioning branch using his license and just through baseball I was probably the largest [air conditioning contractor] in the number of housing units I did. For about three years.

I'll tell you how that came about. The guy that built the city of Lakewood is a guy named Mark Boyer, and his brother, Lou Boyer. They were great baseball fans. They were building bigger houses and needed heating and air conditioning and I went to call on Mark.

He was a gambler. He used to sit up back of third base at Hollywood and he said, "How come I ever bet on you guys? You struck out."

[When I went to see him] we just started talking and he said, "Oh, gosh, I've got to run."

Clint Conatser, 1948 (courtesy Clint Conatser).

So I go back to the office and my dad says, "How'd you do?"

And I said, "Terrible. He was in a hurry and he couldn't even talk to me, so it looks like I blew it, Dad."

A week later when the mail came, there was the largest contract ever let for a housing tract: 3800 houses.

I had a few ballplayers work for me. Jim Baxes was married to my sister and he worked for me. And there were others. I had about 45 guys there.

He [Boyer] was building about 65 houses a day and I had no dough to finance anything like that, but he was paying me without me paying my bills. He became a great friend of mine and his son became a great friend of mine. I just got lucky, that's all. We made enough money for my dad to retire at a very early age and I raised my family right.

How did you get hooked up with Joe Adcock?

I had acquired one [race] horse and [Angels' coach] Jack Paepke told me I should meet Joe, who was with the Angels then. He said he was always carrying around horse books all the time.

We've had a lot of fun [with horses]—kept our heads above water. *[laughs]* Joe's had great success. He's the best I've ever seen in matching up mares and stallions. Some guys have a certain instinct.

Like Billy Southworth. He had an instinct for managing. Things worked for him that didn't work for anybody else. In fact, Tommy Holmes told me that when I first joined the club. He said, "You watch this guy. You're going to see some things you won't believe." And I did!

He'd take a .150 hitter off the bench and the guy'd hit one off his ear. He did that with Bobby Sturgeon. Billy would perch on top of that batting cage and watch the hitters as they took their cuts, looking for something. You know, he was a hell of a ballplayer himself.

Things worked for him, consistently. There's a Hall of Famer in my book. Look at his record. [Thirteen years as a manager, .597 winning percentage, four NL titles, two World Championships.]

❖ ❖ ❖

CLINTON ASTOR CONATSER

Born July 24, 1921, Los Angeles, CA
Ht. 5'11"   Wt. 182   Batted and Threw Right

Year	Team, Lg.	G	AB	R	H	2B	3B	HR	RBI	BA
1948	Boston, NL	90	224	30	62	9	3	3	23	.277
1949		53	152	10	40	6	0	3	16	.263
2 years		143	376	40	102	15	3	6	39	.271

World Series

1948	Boston, NL	2	4	0	0	0	0	0	1	.000

WAYNE TERWILLIGER

40 Years to the Top (1949–1960)

It took Wayne Terwilliger 40 years to get into a World Series. When the surprising 1987 Minnesota Twins went from last in 1986 to World Champions, Twig was their first base coach. And when the equally surprising 1991 Twins also went all the way, he was still there.

He began his professional baseball career way back in 1948, when he signed with the Chicago Cubs. He was 23 years old, a little late to be signing his first contract, but he had good reasons for his delayed start.

First, he served in the Marine Corps in World War II and saw a whole lot of action: he was at Saipan, Tinian, and Iwo Jima. Then he attended Western Michigan University for a while, eventually earning his degree in the off-seasons after beginning his baseball career. Although he's been employed in baseball ever since that first contract with the Cubs, he did make use of his college degree. He taught school during the winters for a couple of years when he was a minor league manager.

Wayne is in his seventies now and has spent his life in baseball. As he says "How lucky can you be?"

❖ ❖ ❖

You had a very short stay in the minor leagues.

Yeah. I signed my contract [with the Cubs] with the stipulation that I would go to spring training with the Triple-A club the following year [1949]. That was in the contract. I didn't get any [bonus] money, but because I was a little older I wanted to get a shot at Triple-A.

You spent most of 1949 with Los Angeles in the Pacific Coast League.

Most of the year. I came up with the Cubs at the end of the season.

After you joined the Cubs that year, you had a streak of eight consecutive hits, which is the third longest ever in the National League. Do you remember that?

Oh, sure. Are you kidding? I remember one of the basehits went right through Ted Kluszewski and they called it a basehit. I hit it good, but it went right through him. I think he led the league in fielding that year. They probably gave him a break on the call. I remember I struck out the ninth time at bat, when I had a chance to get the ninth hit.

After being the Cubs' regular second baseman in 1950, you were traded to Brooklyn in 1951. What did you think of the trade?

I was kind of shocked, really, 'cause I didn't think I'd be leaving the Cubs that soon. It was kind of a surprise to me. I was hoping to stay with the Cubs 'cause I liked Wrigley Field and I liked the idea of day ball and the whole thing, but I realized I was going from a last-place club to a first-place club at the time. But, then again, I also knew that Jackie Robinson was playing second base, so it was kind of a half-and-half job.

You had a little punch with the Cubs.

I hit ten home runs that one year [1950]. They told me the next year that they wanted me to lead off.

Back then, there wasn't really a hitting instructor. I remember one guy telling me that I should go to right field more. Well, that was it. I couldn't hit to right field and I didn't have any idea how to go about it. I didn't do much the following year; I was all screwed up. As my career went along, I got a little better. I finally became a pretty good hitter at the time I quit. *[laughs]*

You had some speed.

Not so fast; I was quick. I got good jumps and I knew how to run.

Back then, stolen bases were not stressed at all. Would you be a base stealer if you were playing today?

I would be up there at 15, 20. I don't believe I'd have stolen a lot of 'em. I could steal probably 20 bases a year, that is if I could have gotten on. *[laughs]*

How did the Senators get you?

Brooklyn optioned me to St. Paul and playing part-time there I had a pretty good year with the bat. I hit .312 and Washington picked me up, bought me from Brooklyn.

You became their regular second baseman and had a very good year.

I had a good year the first year with them — '53. The second year was kind of a strange year. I was a regular in '53 and I expected to be a starter in '54 and it was one of those years that nobody said anything to me and all of a sudden there was a new bunch in spring training. It's a long, sad story, but it was a lousy year in total. I'm trying to forget that one. It was a frustrating year but I got a break and went to the Giants after that.

You spent '55 and part of '56 with the Giants, then in '59 you were with Kansas City. What happened in between?

I was optioned out to Minneapolis in '56 and played here in '56 and '57 and then traded to the Detroit organization and went to Charleston in '58 and then Kansas City drafted me.

I did pretty well [in '59]. I didn't start to play regular until late in the season and I hit pretty good. It was getting around to the tail-end of things. The next year I didn't get a chance to play much and the Yankees bought me and I went to Richmond and finished out my career there.

When did you begin managing in the minor leagues?

I got a shot at Richmond. The business manager asked me if I'd be interested in managing if I didn't play anymore and I said, yes, I would be, so the next year I managed Greensboro in the Carolina League. That was the start of my managing career.

You came back to the majors as a coach with the Senators.

In spring training [1969], Ted Williams gave me the job.

You managed or coached for more than 30 years. You must have enjoyed it.

[laughs] You bet! I still get a big thrill out of winning ballgames, being on a club that wins.

Wayne Terwilliger with Brooklyn, 1951.

Did you ever have any major league managerial aspirations?

At one time I did. I managed two years at Triple-A and we didn't win enough. I was with the Washington organization and I was probably the same age as a lot of my players. I had Hector Lopez and Gene Freese; I had some old-timers. We did all right and we had a good time but we didn't win many ballgames. You've got to be successful at the Triple-A level, I think, to get a shot at the major leagues.

I really enjoyed managing in the minor leagues, especially in the lower minors, 'cause I think I was as good at working with young kids as anybody. I still do, in fact.

You spent time in both leagues. Who was the best ballplayer you saw?

No question: Willie Mays. All-around. Of course, Ted Williams was the greatest hitter I ever saw. He might have been the greatest hitter ever.

I played with Willie Mays with the Giants, not for very long, but he could do it all and do it all well. He had great instincts; he was just an *outstanding* ballplayer in every phase of the game.

Best pitcher?

That's tough. There were so damn many of 'em. I guess the guy that I remember threw the ball hardest for me when I played would be Allie Reynolds of the Yankees. There was one particular game I remember that his ball got on me so fast, and I was a pretty good fastball hitter. I couldn't get around on it.

Clem Labine had the best curveball I ever saw. I faced [Bob] Feller when he was at the end of his career and I faced [Sandy] Koufax in spring training. No question, he had to be one of the all-timers.

You played and coached for many managers.

I played for Frankie Frisch [Cubs]. He was a lot of fun. He had a bad ballclub, but it was fun playing for him.

I played for Charlie Dressen [Brooklyn]. He's dead now, but I didn't like him and he didn't like me. He didn't know how to handle the guys on the bench. He put that great nine out there every day; my grandmother could've managed those guys.

Bucky Harris [Washington] was older when I played for him. Great guy, but I don't remember him doing much except sitting on the bench back in the corner.

I played for [Leo] Durocher [Giants} and he just came off 1954 when he won it all and I played there in '55 and we were in third place — and stayed there — and I think he kind of lost interest. He was a guy that let you play and I appreciated him for that.

In Kansas City I don't even remember who managed. He couldn't have impressed me too much.

Coaching — I was impressed with Don Zimmer [Rangers]. Maybe that's a surprise, but I coached for him a couple of years and I liked him. I felt good; when he said bet the house on today's game, I felt like we were gonna win that game no matter what. More times than not he was right. I thought he did a good job.

The guy we got here is about as sound as anybody can be at managing. [Tom] Kelly. He really is. He doesn't miss a trick. I've been very impressed. He just knows the game. When the bell rings and you cross the lines, you're ready to play.

Ted Williams [Washington] was underrated. He handled pitching better than a lot of people gave him credit for. I coached third base for him; he said, "I don't know that part of the game. I know that little game between the pitcher and the hitter." And he did. He let me do what I wanted to do at third. I thought he did a great job with what pitching we had there.

I don't have one guy that stands out. I was with Kelly for years and I think he's one hell of a manager and probably will be a great one before he's done.

Is there one game or event that stands out as your biggest thrill?

I never was on a winning ballclub in the major leagues as a player. I was there at Brooklyn in 1951 when [Bobby] Thomson hit the home run, but I was a bench man then. It was a shock to lose a game like we lost it, but it wasn't anything that knocked me for a loop or anything.

I didn't have a lot of big games myself. My biggest thrill probably was coaching for Ted Williams the first year. Managing in the minor leagues it seemed like forever and then getting the shot with Ted. So coaching for Ted Williams — especially 1969, the first year — was probably about as big a thrill as I've ever had in baseball, outside of maybe being on two World Champion teams here.

Did you save souvenirs along the way?

No, I don't have any souvenirs. I've got a few pictures is all. I've got a picture when I was with the Dodgers. I got a basehit against the Cardinals in Ebbets Field to win a ballgame in the ninth inning and they got a picture of me coming off the field — the game's over — and Jackie Robinson and Pee Wee Reese are extending their hands to shake my hand. I've

Wayne Terwilliger (aloft) with Minneapolis Millers, American Association, 1956).

got that picture; there's two pretty good ballplayers in there — Robinson and Reese. That's one of my favorite pictures.

Do you get many autograph requests?

Yeah. I might get half a dozen letters a week probably. Being in the Series helps; they see your picture and hear your name, but I've been getting 'em right along ever since I've been coaching. The card collectors now, they know everything.

Are they from people who remember you as a player or from younger fans who only know you as a coach?

I think some of it is remembering me from my playing days, but I think a lot of it is just looking in the book and seeing my name down there and they say, "Let's see if we can get this guy." *[laughs]* I think that's a whole lot of it.

Gail Harris, a fellow you played with, said his autograph requests increased about six-fold after he was interviewed.

Let me tell you a story about Gail Harris. Remember Bud Daley, left-handed pitcher with a crippled right arm? I think he was born that way. I played with Gail when we were both at Minneapolis and Bud Daley, a pitcher with Indianapolis, struck him out. Harris came back to the bench and he couldn't stand it, he got so mad. He got up in front of the dugout and he was yelling at Daley, "You crooked-armed S.O.B.! You'll never strike me out again!" *[laughs]* I'll never forget that.

Do you have any regrets from your playing days?

I sure do. I should have been a better hitter. Toward the end of my career I began to realize what it took to hit. I just wish that I had somebody to work with somewhere along my career 'cause I should have been a much better hitter. That's my biggest regret.

I ended up as one hell of a fielder the last few years of my career. I could do it all out there and probably made the double play better than anybody who ever made it. I had a couple of old-timers tell me that.

But I had a .240 lifetime batting average and I should have been a much better hitter than that.

But otherwise, how lucky can you be? Two World Championship teams when you're in your sixties; you can't hardly beat that.

Would you go back and do it all again?

Oh, sure! Are you kidding? Of course!

How lucky can you be? How many guys would like to be in baseball their whole life? That's what I've been and I got a chance to do just about everything. No question I'd do it over again — in a hurry!

What does the future hold?

I'm gonna stick around. As long as I can throw batting practice, I think I've got a shot to stick around here. The coaches throw batting practice nowadays and so far my arm's hung in there pretty good. I work out all winter long. I'll start in after Christmas and go down to the university's field house and start throwing and get my arm in shape and go from there.

I'm very thankful that I've been healthy and as long as the club keeps winning I'll be okay. They don't fire coaches too often when you win. If they play good, I've got a shot to stick around for a couple more years.

Since 1900, major league batters have knocked out eight or more consecutive hits on more than 60 occasions but only four rookies have done it.

Rookie, Team	Year	Cons. Hits
Babe Herman, BrkN	1926	9
Ted Williams, BosA	1939	9
Glenn Wright, PitN	1924	8
Wayne Terwilliger, ChiN	1949	8

WILLARD WAYNE "TWIG" TERWILLIGER

Born June 27, 1925, Clare, MI
Ht. 5'11"   WT. 165   Batted and Threw Right

Year	Team, Lg	G	AB	R	H	2B	3B	HR	RBI	BA
1949	Chicago, NL	36	112	11	25	2	1	2	10	.223
1950		133	480	63	116	22	3	10	32	.242
1951	Chi-Brk, NL	87	242	37	55	7	0	0	14	.227
1953	Was., AL	134	464	62	117	24	4	4	46	.252
1954		106	337	42	70	10	1	3	24	.208
1955	NY, NL	80	257	29	66	16	1	1	18	.257
1956		14	18	0	4	1	0	0	0	.222
1959	KC, AL	74	180	27	48	11	0	2	18	.267
1960		2	1	0	0	0	0	0	0	.000
9 years		666	2091	271	501	93	10	22	162	.240

Bibliography

Charlton, James, ed. *The Baseball Chronology*. New York: Macmillan, 1991.
Johnson, Lloyd, and Brenda Ward. *Who's Who in Baseball History*. New York: Barnes and Noble, 1994.
Kelley, Brent. *The Early All-Stars*. Jefferson, NC: McFarland, 1997.
Marazzi, Rick, and Len Fiorito. *Aaron to Zuverink*. New York: Avon, 1982.
Marshall, William. *Baseball's Pivotal Era: 1945–1951*. Lexington: University Press of Kentucky, 1999.
Reichler, Joe; revised by Ken Samelson. *The Great All-Time Baseball Record Book*. New York: Macmillan, 1993.
Shatzkin, Mike, ed. *The Ballplayers*. New York: William Morrow, 1990.
Smalling, Jack. *The Baseball Autograph Collector's Handbook*, number 10. Durham, NC: Baseball America, 1999.
Thorn, John, and Pete Palmer. *Total Baseball*, 4th ed. New York: Viking, 1995.
Wolff, Rick, ed. *The Baseball Encyclopedia*, 9th ed. New York: Macmillan, 1993.

Index

Page numbers in *italics* include a photograph.

1/04
3/05